CRY OF THE FISH EAGLE

**Experiences in Malawi from
initiation to deportation
with an interlude in
Morocco**

By

Wilfred J Plumbe

Dudu Nsomba Publications

Glasgow

1997

DUDU NSOMBA PUBLICATIONS LTD

4 Gailes Park, Bothwell. Glasgow G71 8TS Scotland
Tel. 01698854290
Fax. 01698854472
E-mail 106671.3551@compuserve.com
Copyright 1998 Wilfred J Plumbe.   ISBN 09522233-9-2
Copyright 1998 Dudu Nsomba Publications Ltd.

Autobiography/Sociology/Post-colonial History/Malawi/African.

British Library Cataloguing in Publication Data:
A catalogue record of this book is available from the British Library.

Library of Congress Cataloguing in Data:
A catalogue record for this book has been requested.

Also by Dudu Nsomba Publications:

The Second Harvest by John Lwanda ISBN 09522233-1-7

Cry of the fish Eagle by Wilfred Plumbe ISBN 09522233-9-2

Black Thoughts from the Diaspora by John Lwanda ISBN 09522233-2-5

Kamuzu Banda of Malawi by John Lwanda ISBN 09522233-0-9

Living my destiny (an autobiographical medical and historical narrative) by Austin C Mkandawire ISBN 095222233 -3-3

Promises, Power Politics and Poverty: the democratic transition in Malawi 1961 to 1999 by John Lwanda ISBN 09522233-4-1

Forthcoming:

The Rhino's Lament by Hastings Mabvuto

Kamtengo and other recycled Stories by Elizabeth Pililani

Publishing Editor: John Lwanda
Printed by Antony Rowe Ltd, Chippenham, Wiltshire. England

CONTENTS

Acknowledgements

Thanks are due to William Blackwood & Sons Ltd for the text of 'Moroccan Journey' which appeared in *Blackwood's Magazine* in 1969.
Thanks are due to the University of Malawi for excerpts from reports on the university libraries.
Thanks are due to the late Fred Johnson and the late Grace Snowden, to Jeffrey Stickley and to Malawian friends for kindly providing the photographs.
I am grateful to my son Antony for drawing the maps.

W J. Plumbe

Illustrations
(not in the order listed)

Maps

DRAMATIS PERSONAE

ABISI CHIVELI, a gardener
AGIGA, a fisherman, Senga Bay
AGNEW, Sir FULQUE MELVILLE GERALD NOEL, Assistant Registrar, University of Malawi
AGNEW, Lady SWANZIE, Professor of Geography, University of Malawi; formerly Principal of the Royal Ballet School, London, and Head of the Geography Department, University College of Fort Hare
AISA, JUSTIN, a leper
AKA MSENI, a beach labourer
ALI, a cook fond of beer
ALLEN, A RICHARD, Principal, Domasi Teacher Training College
ALLEN, B JOAN, wife of Richard, a retired librarian
ALUMI, WELLINGTON, a schoolboy, Nkhata Bay
AMBALI, OSWIN, a very tall assistant librarian, National Archives of Malawi
AMEDEKEY, EY, University Librarian, University of Ghana
BAKER, COLIN, Principal, Institute of Public Administration, Mpemba
BANDA, ALEKE K, Minister of Finance, Minister of Information & Tourism, Minister of Development & Planning; Secretary of the Nyasaland National Congress at age 15. In 1994 became a Vice-President of United Democratic Front and Minister of Finance
BANDA, John R, first Malawian Registrar, University of Malawi; after imprisonment in Malawi he became Registrar, University of Swaziland and moved several times among countries of southern Africa
BANDA, Ngwazi HASTINGS KAMUZU, Life President of Malawi
BARTLETT, MANSER WILLIAM, settled in Malawi at Sekwere
BENNION, MJ, Principal, Institute of Public Administration, Mpemba
BHARUCHA, Salima merchant who built a bungalow at Senga Bay
BIJL, Dr, ACM, much esteemed medical practitioner in Limbe
BINNS, BLODWEN, visiting Professor of Botany, University of Malawi
BLACKMUN, BARBARA, photographer, part-time lecturer in Art appreciation
BLACKWOOD, MICHAEL, MP, Solicitor, Blantyre, who kept record of land conveyances
BROOMFIELD, SPENCER 'KACHALOLA', one-time elephant poacher, prospector for gold, hunter, farmer, father of 36 children in Feira district
BVUMBWE, Chief, settled in Thyolo 1893, died 1925; succeeded by his son
CARVER, JOHN CN, Assistant Registrar, University of Malawi
CHIBAMBO, QABANISO YESAYA, Minister for the Northern Region, Minister of Health
CHIBAMBO, SUSAN, daughter-in-law of QYC, a secretary
CHIBISA, Chief at Chikwawa, southern Malawi
CHINDAMBO, JAMES, a builder's mate
CHINTAMBO, Grace Snowden's invaluable cook and chauffeur
CHITIKA, KENNETH, enthusiastic listener to ear-battering 'pop' music,

architectural draughtsman
CHIWELE, MUSA, trader in animal skins and artifacts
CLARK, RICHARD MARTIN, tanner and shoemaker who built the first Christian church in Malawi
DALAMKWANDA, Headman, Dalamkwanda's village, Senga Bay
DERESSA, ATO SOLOMON, Broadcasting Corporation of Ethiopia
DOWNS, HOWARD J, auctioneer of Limbe
DUNN, GEORGE, administrator, Malawi Railways
DUNN, VERA, wife of George
FIDDES, MARGARET, Chair of House Committee, Newlands Homes for Elderly Europeans Association, secretary of Council of Women, Blantyre
FIDDES, WILLIAM, Limbe resident
FREEMAN, IVAN CH, first Registrar, University of Malawi
FREWER, LOUIS, Keeper of Rhodes House Library, Oxford
GREENWOOD, JOHN BERTRAM, VSO and acting Librarian, Malawi Polytechnic, pre-1967
GUPTA, DB, an economist, later deported
HABTE, AKLILU, President, Haile Sellassie I University, Addis Ababa
HABTE, Lady, wife of President Habte
HAMISI, JAMES NDICI, refugee from Mozambique, a gardener
HAYDON, Sir WALTER 'ROBIN', British High Commissioner, Malawi
HAZELDINE, GORDON DAVID, Sub-librarian, University of Malawi; later he became Librarian of the Technical Institute in Bandung
HOWSE, FOSTER, Assistant librarian, Malawi Polytechnic
HYNDE, RS, Church of Scotland missionary who was general manager of Blantyre & East Africa Company and served on Blantyre Town Council
JARVIS, JENNIE, Assistant librarian, Malawi Polytechnic
JEFFREYS, JEFF, Photographer used by Cecilia Kadzamira
JOHNSON, ALBERT FREDERICK, first Director, Malawi National Library Service; died in England 2 February 1996
JOHNSON, IRENE, wife of Fred
JOHNSTON, JEAN FRASER, retired Librarian of Edgehill Teacher Training College, Ormskirk; temporary cataloguer
JUMBE I, former slave-dealing chief at Nkhota-Kota
KABAZALI, ARNOLD, library messenger, later a policeman
KACISA, STAMFORD, library messenger
KADZAMIRA, CECILIA T, niece of JZU Tembo, once a nurse, later Dr Banda's official hostess and 'Mama Cecilia, Mother of the Nation'
KALK, JOHN, endocrinologist, working at Baragwanath Hospital, S. Africa
KALK, MARGARET, Professor (and later Emeritus Professor) of Zoology, University of Malawi
KALK, WILLIE, husband of Margaret, supervisor at Blantyre Sawmills, formerly secretary of trade unions in S. Africa
KAMANGA, JOHN, manager of Nkhata Bay government rest house
KAMANJA, McNIGHT, assistant, Lake Chilwa Research Project, killed in road

accident

KAMPONDE, JAMES, house painter, Blantyre

KANANJI, AUFI, 4' 11" tall, expert cook (for Yarrs and several British High Commissioners)

KANDAWIRE, Mr, energetic District Officer, Nkhota-Kota

KANDULU ('CANDLE') CHINTAMBO, son of Grace Snowden's cook Chintambo, an expert boat builder and carpenter at Grand Beach Hotel

KAUNDA, BERLINGS, Curator of the Museum of Malawi, Limbe; now Senior lecturer, Fine Arts, Chancellor College

KAUNDA, KENNETH, President of Zambia

KHURANA, MM, High Commissioner for India

KRISHNAMURTY, BS, Senior lecturer in History, University of Zambia

KULUUNDU, Bisi, paramount chief, descendant of Chief Mwase, sister of President Banda

KUMWENDA, BENSON R, traditional policeman of Phoka and Kaziwiziwi

LAMBA, ISAAC, associate Professor of History, Chancellor College

LARBY, PATRICIA M, College Librarian, Malawi Polytechnic

LEISTEN, JOHN A, Professor (later Emeritus Professor) of Chemistry, University of Malawi; now living in Australia

LEISTEN, JUNE, wife of John; now living in Australia

LOVEDAY, ANTHONY J, University Librarian, University of Zambia

LUCKHAM, ELIZABETH, editor with Rev. J.A. Mein of 'General Directory 1970-71' published by Council of Social Service

LWANGA, TUCKER, University Librarian, Makerere University, Uganda

MABOMBA, RODRICK SAMSON, National Librarian, Malawi National Library Service, author of many papers about Malawi libraries

MAKOMULA, SAINID, thatcher of buildings, Senga Bay

MALENGA, Chief of Nkhota-Kota, grandson of the Jumbe to whom Dr Livingstone gave an umbrella and a plate

MALENGA, MUSA, second son of chief Malenga

MALENGA, SEFU, youngest son of chief Malenga

MAMFWE, BARTON, a fisherman

MASANJIKA, RAPHAEL, detained by government 1974 and 1976-8, now College Librarian, College of Medicine, University of Malawi

MATEYA, HENDERSON, cook and cottage caretaker

MATORA, MEMBER, mechanical genius

MAXWELL, IAN CM, Secretary, Inter-University Council for Higher Education Overseas

MAYCOCK, Canon EDWARD, missionary, pastor to students

MERRY, DOROTHY THORA, former teacher of English in Secondary Schools, including Ashton-in-Makerfield, Liverpool, Buckingham, Hackney and Battersea

MERRY, ELEANOR JEANETTE, formerly General Superintendent of the Queen's Institute of District Nursing

MICHAEL, IAN, first Vice-Chancellor, University of Malawi

MKWATE, ELLATON, joined staff at age 15, became head bookbinder, University of Malawi; later he operated a lucrative bar beside road leading to Army Air Wing, Zomba; now runs a taxi business

MKWINDA, mat-maker of Ntimbasonja village

MNTHALI, FELIX WJ, Provost, University of Malawi; after being imprisoned in Malawi he became Professor of English, University of Botswana

MORGAN, PETER, Chemist, Lake Chilwa Research Project, University of Malawi

MOSES, SIMON, former Young Pioneer, expert tree climber, became gardener

MPHUNDI, BESTON, formerly acting University Librarian, University of Malawi; later with British Council

MSISKA, AUGUSTINE WC, ex-detainee in government detention camp, now College Librarian, Chancellor College

MSONTHI, JOHN D 'KAKA', Minister of Transport & Communications, Leader of the House, Malawi Parliament

MNTHAMBALA, AUGUSTINE, allegedly once engaged to Cecilia Kadzamira

MUGHOGHO, SK, associate Professor of Crop Production, Bunda College of Agriculture

MUWALO, ALBERT ANDREW NQUMAYO, Secretary General of Malawi Congress Party, Minister of State; convicted of treason and hanged in Zomba Central Prison 1977

MVAA, MARTIN, University Librarian, University of Dar es Salam

MWANZA, N PETER, First Malawian Principal, Chancellor College; after imprisonment in Malawi he joined UN Environmental Programme, Nairobi; now Head of UNEP in Africa, Addis Ababa

MYAMBO, KATHY, a psychologist

NACHITECHI, wife of Simon Moses

NADANASABAPATHY, VISUALINGHAM, University Librarian, Murdoch University, Australia

NAJIRA, DICK D, Librarian, National Archives of Malawi. He died 8 May 1996

NAMATE, GM, a maintenance officer, Chancellor College

NAMPONYA, CLEMENCE R, formerly College Librarian, Bunda College of Agriculture; later Documentation/Information Officer at Southern Africa Centre for Co-operative Agricultural Research, Botswana. Later he became Librarian, University of Fort Hare, and then deputy Librarian University of Eastern Cape, South Africa

NDEGWA, JOHN, University Librarian, University of Nairobi

NDEMBO, ASMANI, firewood merchant, Senga Bay

N'DIAYE, AMADOU ALAIN, Assistant librarian, Universite de Dakar, Senegal

NGWIRA, MARGARET, College Librarian, Bunda College of Agriculture, and then to a senior post in the University of Namibia at Windhoek

NGWIRA, TIMOTHY, associate Professor of Animal Science, Bunda College of Agriculture, then head of the College of Agriculture, University of Namibia

NIGHTINGALE, BRUCE, British Council Representative, Blantyre

NKUTI, MDALAMDOKA, Headman, Mdalamdoka's village, Senga Bay

NYIRENDA, LONELY, schoolboy, Nkhata Bay

NYOKA, PAUL, game guard, Nkhota-Kota

OPENIYI, OLUSEGUN, catalogue assistant, Chancellor College Library

PACHAI, BRIDGLAL, Professor of History, University of Malawi

PACHAI, LEELA, wife of Bridglal

PANKHURST, RICHARD, Director of the Institute of Ethiopian Studies, Addis Ababa

PANKHURST, RITA, University Librarian, Haile Sellassie I University, Addis Ababa

PARTRIDGE, RUTH, allegedly the wealthiest widow in Limbe, even in Malawi; she died 16 October 1973

PEACOCKE, Mrs, Rippling Streams Guest Cottages, Vumba, Zimbabwe

PEARSON, JAMES DOUGLAS, Library adviser to Inter-University Council

PINNEY, TC, Professor of Agriculture and Principal, Bunda College of Agriculture

PRIDEAUX, RM, Principal, Malawi Polytechnic

RABEKA, MILLION, a trustworthy cook and a source of interesting information

RAWLINGS, KENNETH, former College Librarian, Soche Hill College

ROBINSON, MARGARET W, Sub-librarian, Malawi Polytechnic

ROSEVEARE, Sir MARTIN P, designer of ration books World War I, Principal, Soche Hill College

ROUSSET DE PINA, JEAN, Bibliothecaire en Chef, Universite de Dakar, Senegal

ROWE, ERNEST, chief technician, Chancellor College

RYE, GEOFFREY P, second Director of Malawi National Library Service

SABATINA, FRANCA, elderly Italian signora of Limbe

SANUDI, DOUGLAS, electrician, son-in-law of Kandulu Chintambo

SCHOFFELEERS, Rev. JM, Catechetical Training Centre, Phalombe

SHABA, GODWIN B, Assistant librarian, Malawi Polytechnic; later in Central Services, University of Malawi Library

SHUMBA, MUPA, Lecturer in English, Chancellor College; after imprisonment with other Northern staff he joined Phwezi private secondary school and is now Head of English

SMART, JAMESU, hard-working gardener, confronter of leopards

SMITH, ETTY, daughter of missionaries, fluent Chichewa speaker

SNOWDEN, GRACE HILDA, widow of former Chief Engineer of Imperial Tobacco Company; died 27 July 1980, aged 94

SPICER, EILEEN, poultry farmer of Lirangwe

SPICER, GEOFFREY, farmer, dealer in maize, Lirangwe

STANSFIELD, WALTER HYDE, owner of Grand Beach Hotel, Salima, died at Senga Bay 17 August 1991, 12 days before what would have been his 100th birthday

STEPHEN, EZEKIEL, gardener, seller of woven grass hats and mats

STICKLEY, JEFFREY O, Bookbinding Officer, University of Malawi

STICKLEY, MARION, wife of Jeffrey

SUDI, TOM PETER, servant of Livingstone

SURTEE, ISHMAEL K, Speaker in Parliament; died 13 September 1982

SUSI, DAVID, servant of Livingstone

TAMBALA, AHMADI, young brother of Chief Malenga

TANDAZA, HESTON, farmer and market gardener at Senga Bay
TANGRI, ROGER, Research associate in Sociology, Chancellor College
TEMBO, JZU, Governor & Chairman Reserve Bank of Malawi, Chairman Malawi Book Service, Chairman of Council University of Malawi, later Chairman of the Press Corporation and Minister of State in the Office of the President & Cabinet
THOM, JOSEPH, messenger, Chancellor College Library
THOMAS, Mr, Forestry Officer, Chelinda, Nyika Plateau
THOMPSON, STEPHEN, VSO, Assistant librarian, Malawi Polytechnic
TRETARIS, Mrs, an elderly widow of Port Herald
UTTING, JEG, Dean & Professor of Economics, University of Malawi
VAN ZANTEN, ELLEN, Assistant librarian, Soche Hill College
VARLEY, DOUGLAS HAROLD, formerly Librarian, University College of Rhodesia & Nyasaland, later University Librarian of University of Liverpool
WAFI LAHOUSSEIN, friendly factotum, Hotel de l'Oued Issil, Marrakesh
WARREN, ELIZABETH, wife of Frank
WARREN, FRANK, Finance Officer, University of Malawi
WAZIKILI, AISA, aged cook, ex-askari World War I, younger brother of Chief Malenga, speaker of 12 languages
WELLINGTON, MATTHEW, schoolboy, Nkhata Bay
WIENS, ANNA, Assistant librarian, Soche Hill College
WILLIAMS, G, Principal, Malawi Polytechnic
WINTLE, CLIFF, settler, Limbe resident
WOODS, BW, first principal, Bunda College of Agriculture
WOODS, MOIRA, VSO, Assistant librarian, Chancellor College; deported 5 December 1972
YARR, ANN, wife of Brian, Chief cataloguer, University of Malawi library
YARR, BRIAN, Chief cataloguer, University of Malawi library

* * * * * * * * *

Our Kamuzu, who art in Blantyre
Hallowed be thy name,
Thy Kingdom come;
Thy will be done;
Lead us not into the Federation
But deliver us from the Imperialists,
As in Ghana, for thine is the Country,
The power and the glory
For ever and ever...

--A prayer taught to children in some
Malawian schools in 1959
before his Excellency Ngwazi Dr
Hastings Kamuzu Banda became
Minister of Natural Resources
and subsequently Prime Minister,
President and Life President.

MALAWI

WHAT I SHALL TRY to describe in this book are events at a young university where an assortment of expatriates rooted themselves in a small 'backward' African country; I shall try to evoke what we experienced on personal travels; and I shall record a few bizarre events in the beautiful land which brought us together, absorbed us, and finally spewed some of us out again as part of the prevailing powerful 'wind of change'.

The book is mainly about people: not so much the President and other persons important in public life but very much about village headmen, peasant farmers, artisans, craftsmen, lake fishermen, casual labourers, local policemen, Young Pioneers, colonial old ladies, undergraduates, schoolboys, and the poorest of the poor.

It is also about human friendship, courage, kindness, mutual trust, jealousy, fear of the unknown, the painful struggle towards a 'better life' and the sharpening of young minds that alone can shape the future they desire.

A brief interlude in Morocco is included, mainly because it provides contrasting images and alternatives we may ponder if we will.

Bvumbwe is ten miles out of Blantyre on the road that leads to Thyolo. Formerly it was a district covered by forest but all the lesser trees were cut down long ago and it is now an area where small scale agriculture and an important agricultural experiment station thrive.

Our first home in Malawi was at Bvumbwe. It was a small pleasant bungalow that belonged to a district commissioner who had retired and gone elsewhere; the university rented it from him. It was set among shady trees a hundred yards off the tarmac road from which it was hidden, and it stood - in perfect peace, it seemed - in two acres of lawn and fertile garden on the edge of a dark forest that sloped away into a valley in the direction of Mulanje mountain.

I settled into this bungalow on 6 February 1966 and took on Smart as gardener and Ali as cook the same day. Smart was tall, intelligent and strong; Ali was thin, knobbly and obsequious but he was a well experienced 'house-boy'. My wife Gladys arrived nine months later, after our son Antony had become a student at University College, London, and we - and the servants - stayed in Bvumbwe until November 1967 when the district commissioner made up his mind he would never return and notified the University he wished to sell the house.

In February 1966 the garden had been neglected for several months but a stroll of inspection revealed an abundance of fruit trees: mango, paw-paw, avocado, guava, banana, citrus, mulberry and almond. A few coffee bushes were heavy with green and red berries like cherries. A granadilla vine clung to a wall of the house. A few strawberries withered on unwatered ridges, and six hundred spiky pineapple plants languished in straight rows, plantation style, perhaps as protection against thieves, between the bungalow and the tree-lined lane that led to the dark forest.

I realized at once that we - and that meant mainly Smart - would be able to grow enough tropical fruit and vegetables, including as well 'temperate' cauliflowers, broccoli, lettuces, leeks, peas, beans, onions, radishes, parsnips, carrots and potatoes, for all our own needs and still have some to spare for friends.

Already the garden was full of flowers.

'Bvumbwe' I learned, derived from Chief Bvumbwe of the Ngoni tribe who came to Thyolo in 1893, following a raid into the Shire Highlands by his people nine years earlier. The first Bvumbwe died in 1925 and, as the tribe is patrilinear, his son became the next chief after him.

We lived side by side with some of the original fauna as well as the local inhabitants. *Vumbwe* is the Chichewa word for 'wild cat' which also has local significance.

Soon after I moved into the bungalow leopard cubs were seen playing at night on the main road. And one evening after dusk, when Smart was in the small thatched toilet surrounded by tall bushes, near the servants' quarters, he suddenly realized, in the light of his candle, that a pair of yellow eyes was watching him in the open doorway. Next morning he led me to look at a patch of mud and dead leaves where the spoor was unmistakably that of an adult leopard - not *Vumbwe* but *'Nyalugwe*.

Another visitor to the kitchen garden was a beautiful little antelope which the local people called a *gwape*. When we saw it we sent it leaping back into the edge of the forest as, otherwise, we should never have achieved any lettuce or french beans, most of which, anyhow, it ate at the crack of dawn or in the last few minutes of daylight in the evening.

In extent Malawi is 560 miles from north to south and 50-100 miles from east to west; it has an area about three-quarters that of England, one quarter that of California and about the same as that of Portugal, and its lakes cover more than 9,000 square miles.

It is wholly tropical, being part of Africa's Great Rift Valley, and its geographical neighbours are Zambia, Tanzania and Mozambique. Its most remarkable physical feature is Lake Malawi, 365 miles long, 15-50 miles wide, 2,200 feet deep, lying between high mountains in the north and among hills, high plateaux and undulating country to the south. The lake is fed by dozens of rivers, including the Livulezi, Linthipe, Lilongwe, Lifuliza, Dwangwa, Limpasa, Rukufu, Bumba, Lufira, Lupingo and Ruhuhu; its only outlet is the Shire river that carries its surplus water south to the Zambezi and eventually to the Indian Ocean.

The mountains of Malawi are mostly rugged and rise to heights that vary from 3,000 feet to nearly 10,000 feet. It is difficult not to be rhapsodic about its landscape and lakescape.

As for the people, there are now over eleven million of them and they belong to more than thirty different tribes, having diverse origins; and nine-tenths of them live in traditional villages of thatched huts away from towns. Some major tribes are the Chewa, Mang'anja, Ngoni, Nguru, Nkhonde, Tumbuka and Yao. These are easily recognisable if you live and work among them.

If the jaw bone of a single hominid found in 1993 by palaeontologists is sufficient evidence, examples of the precursors of man lived in north-west Malawi 2.5 million years ago. It is certain that settlements of some sort existed 100,000 years ago.

The discovery of rock paintings and pottery indicates that settlements existed along the lakeshore and in the river valleys hundreds and perhaps thousands of years before the migration of Maravi clans from what is now Shaba province of Zaire about 1,200 AD. It is likely that the Akafula lived simultaneously in the forests right up to 1,670 AD when the last of them were exterminated by the Maravi south of Senga Bay.

Over the centuries other major movements of people into Malawi included the Tumbuka and Ngonde from the north, the Phoka, Nkhamenga and Henga from the north and west, the Ngoni from the south, the Yao from the east. The Maravi 'Empire' stretched from the Zambezi River to the Dwangwa River, westward to the Luangwa, and eastward to the Indian Ocean.

It is perhaps significant that the Akafula people have also been called the 'Abatwa' which is the name of a tribe in the Lake Bangweulu area of Zambia, some of whose members were said by early western travellers to have webbed feet. Paintings on a rock in a mountain shelter twelve miles south of Dedza are attributed to them. To-day a people called 'Abatwa', short in stature, live in Rwanda in the Great Rift Valley 1,500 miles to the north of Malawi.

The Amaravi themselves, from whom the name 'Malawi' is derived (1), may have come remotely from Cameroon in West Africa; what is certain is that for over 600 years they became the ascendant people over a wide area of central Africa.

David Livingstone's efforts in the 1850s and 1860s to terminate the slave trade led to the establishment of Christian missions from 1861 onwards and to colonization by the British from 1891 onwards.

Malawi was designated the Shire (2) Highlands Protectorate in 1889; it was administered by the British as the Nyasaland Districts Protectorate (1891-1893) and subsequently the British Central African Protectorate (1893-1907) and the Nyasaland Protectorate (1907-1953); it was then incorporated into the Federation of Rhodesia and Nyasaland (1953-1963); but Nyasaland attained self-government on 1 February 1963 and it became the independent state of Malawi on 6 July 1964 and the Republic of Malawi on 6 July 1966.

The University of Malawi was founded in 1964 by the University of Malawi (Provisional Council) Act. Many people believe that it was the brain-child solely of Dr Banda but although its creation had his strong support and it is often referred to as the President's 'dream in Gwelo gaol', the idea for it was probably shared by Dunduzu Chisiza and Masauko Henry Chipembere, Banda's fellow prisoners in the gaol; steps to create it were actually started in the Ministry of Education of which the permanent secretary was I.C.H. Freeman, and 'it was only given definite shape by the International Survey Team who visited Malawi in 1963 and 1964, under the sponsorship of the American Council on Education, the US Agency for International Development, and the British Inter-University Council for Higher Education Overseas'. (*The Times*, Blantyre, Malawi, 5 October 1965).

Dr Banda (3) became Chancellor of the new University; John D Msonthi, MP, BA (Hons), BEd, Minister of Education, became the first Chairman of its Provisional Council; Ian Michael, BA, PhD, who had been Professor of Education at the University of Khartoum, was appointed Vice-Chancellor; ICH Freeman, CMG, TD, MA, DipEd, was appointed Registrar; Henry G. Hall, FCWA, FCommA, was appointed Finance Officer, and I became University Librarian.

The first students were admitted to temporary accommodation in September 1965 and the ceremonial opening of the University took place on 6 October 1965. Two sparrowhawks, regarded as a good omen, dived appropriately over the assembled crowd as soon as the open air ceremony began - and the same thing happened the following year at the first congregation of the University by which time some people, at least, had become doubtful about the beneficence of the government of Malawi and the significance of the birds of prey.

The intention was to create a degree college, initially in the buildings of a new secondary school at Chichiri (between Blantyre and Limbe) made available for that purpose and, as quickly as possible, to integrate all the country's facilities for post-secondary education 'under one umbrella' as a single institution.

The institutions to be integrated were:

Chancellor College, Chichiri (opened 1965 and given its name 1966).

The Malawi Polytechnic, Blantyre (started in 1964).

Soche Hill College (producing teachers for secondary schools, started in 1962).

The Institute for Public Administration, Mpemba (started in 1962).

Bunda College of Agriculture (opened 1966 in buildings of Dedza Secondary. School; permanent buildings were under construction at Bunda in 1965).

It was expected that university buildings would be built on a permanent site at Zomba and that the degree courses would move there in September 1968.

In 1966 when we were searching for senior expatriate staff likely to be suitable for our university library I sent them a personal 'blurb' as follows:

Four of the five parts of the University are in the Shire Highlands, about 3,600 feet above sea level, which gives us cool nights. In two years time it is expected we shall move to a slightly higher site, 40 miles away, at Zomba, near to Zomba mountain which rises to nearly 7,000 feet.

Blantyre and Limbe are small modern towns, about four miles apart. The streets are clean. The electricity supply seems to be reliable; the telephone works; one can drink water straight from the tap.

Health services are reasonably good. There are large general hospitals in Blantyre and Zomba and a small one - more like a dispensary - in Limbe. Various Missions maintain private hospitals, some of which provide dental service. There are also doctors in private practice. In Blantyre and Limbe the chemists' shops stock daraprim, sulphaguanadine and all the usual pills and dopes.

The local shops, small but well stocked, are owned mainly by Indians. There are supermarkets in Blantyre and Limbe. The cost of living to relatively low. Vegetables and fruits are available in great variety. Poultry, meat and freshwater fish are cheap if bought in the markets - chickens 3/6 and 4/6, ducks 7/-, eggs 2/6 a dozen. In the supermarkets mutton, beef and pork are 3/6 to 5/- a pound, fresh farm milk 10d a bottled pint, fresh cream 3/6 a half pint. Limosin brandy is 29/6 a bottle, French and Portuguese wines 31/6 a demi-john (7 bottles). A wide range of soft drinks is available.

There are three cinemas in the Blantyre/Limbe area, eight clubs, eleven restaurants (several of them night-clubs, others no more than snack bars), four hotels, several swimming baths at the clubs and one at the University.

It is possible to play golf, tennis, soccer, cricket, and to go dancing, yachting, crag climbing, or hoping to photograph elephant, lion, buffalo and antelopes in the game reserves. Fishing is available in the lakes and rivers.

Intellectually the country is not yet too lively although there is a museum, a so-called public library, an art club, a cultural centre, amateur dramatics societies and the usual activities provided by the British Council and the United States Information Service. A real public library service, to cover the whole country, is due to begin on 1. 1. 68.

Such Malawian graduates as exist have all had their university education overseas.

There are several mosques, a Sikh temple and churches of 38 Christian denominations in the Southern Province alone.

In this area the roads are tarmacked; up-country they are mostly laterite or gravel; some of them fairly good all-season roads, others atrocious. (4)

The University provides houses, flats or bungalows for rental and most of the staff in this area live in and around Blantyre and Limbe, not on campuses. Most of us have large gardens. The university accommodation is equipped with hard furniture, an electric stove, a refrigerator, mattresses and mosquito nets (which few people use) and an 'emergency kit' - crockery and cutlery - is supplied to newcomers for a few weeks if they need it. New arrivals may borrow enough money from the University to enable them to buy a car, and if they live more than four miles from the University a commuting allowance is granted.

The University of Malawi started with many administrative difficulties, weaknesses, uncertainties, and invisible handicaps (5) - some people said quite bluntly there was too great a willingness for liberal and long-winded discussion and too little decision-making. It was prevailed upon to adopt Malawi civil service practices far too closely and, if it wished to remain in existence, it soon had to accept 'guidance' stemming from Dr Banda.

By the end of 1972 eleven members of its senior staff had been deported from the country and soon afterwards the contracts of others (including the vice-chancellor and the principal of Malawi Polytechnic) were not renewed.

But some of its senior staff were naturally thick-skinned or learned how to become so: they had courage, integrity, determination, patience, and the ability to innovate and adapt. At the beginning, in December 1965, the vice-chancellor described the situation with his characteristic honesty and optimism:

In spite of its poverty Malawi offers a challenging and unusual opportunity for the formation of a university. While we fully accept traditional academic values and hope to win recognition as a member of the world-wide community of universities we are also free to evolve our own structure. We hope that from the beginning all staff, both academic and administrative, will have a common interest in, and appropriate opportunity for, helping to shape the University and its academic policy: to evolve an institution which, while in structure and curriculum it draws especially on the experience of Africa, Britain and North America, will seek above all to interpret and to meet the needs of Malawi. (6)

Heads of the various colleges were JEG Utting, MA, Dean and Professor of Economics, Chancellor College; Sir Martin Roseveare, MA, Principal of Soche Hill College; HM Prideaux, MA, Principal of Malawi Polytechnic; MJ Bennion, BA, Principal of the Institute of Public Administration; and (later) BW Woods, BSc, Principal of Bunda College of Agriculture.

Not all expatriates - or Malawians - stayed beyond a first three year contract. As one of the American professors remarked in Senate:

Any one who stays here more than two years is committing academic suicide.

But some of the best staff did stay on. Blodwen Binns, MSc, PhD, FLS, visiting Professor of Botany, stayed until she was 70; Swanzie Agnew, MA, Professor of Geography, stayed till after the death of Sir Fulque Agnew her husband - she was devoted to the country and only the political situation that developed caused her to resign; and Margaret Kalk, BSc, PhD, Professor of Zoology, and John A. Leisten, BSc, PhD, FRIC, Professor of Chemistry, stayed on for twelve and twenty years respectively and both when they left were made 'Professor Emeritus'.

In 1965, with one exception, only tentative efforts had been made to provide staff for a library. Gordon David Hazeldine, BA, DipLib, had been appointed deputy librarian and three expatriate married ladies, one qualified, the others not, all working part-time, had been given temporary appointments. In addition there was a Malawian library assistant who had undergone a short course in librarianship at Makerere, and a typist. These were at Chancellor College where the embryo library existed in buildings of the secondary school.

At the beginning of 1966 a major need was to recruit Malawians with sufficient education to undertake librarianship as a career. Graduates were obviously not available but school-leavers of promise could be found without difficulty at local secondary schools, especially St. Patrick's Secondary School, Mzedi, and it was these who were recruited as our first library assistants in 1966/7.

As the Library grew, and especially after 1.1.67 when it had to develop four other libraries - at Malawi Polytechnic, Soche Hill College, the Institute of Public Administration and Bunda College of Agriculture - it was necessary to find other staff, both junior and senior.

For unskilled jobs there was an inrush of applicants. When we advertised for library attendants (a very junior grade), we received hundreds of applications including some from policemen, telephone operators, timber checkers, forestry fire guards, bus conductors, garden boys, petrol pump attendants, security guards, proof readers, locomotive drivers, a machine operator in a shoe factory and the headmaster of a primary school, besides those who were jobless. The response revealed the paucity of even poorly paid work for young Malawians.

Some of the applicants had names that could only doubtfully have been sanctioned by the missionaries, e.g.

Genuine DDT Kaunde
Tim-Tex Mhango
Lovemore Malata

Brisk in British Empire Mkandawire

Many had wrestled valiantly with the English language:

> I honest to beg apply apost in the university of Malawi as RiBrary atitendants.
> Sir, I will be much greatful if my application meets with your favourite consideration.
> Feelled with confidance that, whether this my sweet application will meet you under your favourable consideration and approval.
> As you know that the missionaries now adays they have got no any responsibilty for sending teachers to course.

One of the young men chosen by our selection committee caused us anxiety after we appointed him. We had a 'rule' in the library that library property, such as scissors, rulers, date-stamps, string, keys, stationery in general should not be taken home. One pleasant and well-mannered young attendant ignored this instruction and 'borrowed' a small Don Gresswell card-cutting knife; he went to a wedding, drank too much, had a fight and stabbed a friend with the library's knife. It pierced his friend's liver, the friend died, and the library attendant was arrested by the Police next day at his desk in the library and charged with murder. He was jailed for four years, the charge being reduced to manslaughter.

Finding suitable senior staff was more difficult than attracting library attendants.

More than anyone else we needed a chief cataloguer at Chancellor College. After enquiries that lasted more than a year we were able to appoint Visualingam Nadanasabapathy, BSc, ALA, a Malaysian who was acting librarian of Njala University College in Sierra Leone. He arrived in Malawi on 11 July 1967 and assumed duty as chief cataloguer three days later.

'Nada' - ancestrally a Tamil - was a prodigious worker and the impression he made on junior staff was dramatic. Besides cataloguing he also took a full share in the course of tuition started at that time for library assistants. He is still remembered for taking a small working party (Rodrick Mabomba, Foster Howse, McNight Kamanja) to Bunda College of Agriculture for the period 2-6 January 1968. He drove 220 miles to Bunda in his VW Beetle and in four days of concentrated effort the working party, with the help of two junior staff at Bunda, classified, labelled, book-carded, spine-lettered, and finished accessioning and pocketing the 1,300 books in the college library. 'Nada' worked straight through the fourth night and then drove back to Blantyre.

In February and March - in Limbe - he regularly started work in the cataloguing department at 5:30 in the morning, arriving before the cleaners, and worked till late at night, cataloguing all night on at least one occasion.

Classification of 26,500 books and serials at Chancellor College was completed on 21 March and a high output of definitive cataloguing was also achieved. On 28 March - after being with us for eight months and twelve days - he returned to Sierra Leone as substantive librarian of Njala University College. (7)

Our next chief cataloguer was Ann Yarr, BA, DipLib, who had worked in the library of University College, London, and later in the library of the Royal Society of Medicine, London. Her husband Brian - BA, ALA - was also a cataloguer; he had been ill in England but in Malawi he quickly recovered and was subsequently appointed to the staff, later on taking Ann's position while she took his, an unorthodox exchange agreed by the University which was only too thankful to have the services of both of them. They arrived with their two small children Lucy and Richard, a large dog named 'Shamus' and a cat who was referred to as 'Nameless', on 16 July 1968.

To find Ann I had written individual letters to 88 cataloguers around the world asking whether they knew anyone suitable who might be interested in coming to Malawi. In 1968 it was futile to advertise for cataloguers as there was a world shortage of experienced people. Ann and Brian worked in the University for 3 years, living in the bungalow in Limbe occupied by Dr Banda when he was arrested by a commando group of the Police Mobile Force on 3 March 1959 and taken - in his pyjamas and dressing gown - to Chileka Airport en route to Southern Rhodesia and Gwelo gaol. (8)

On 19 July 1971 the family returned to England, where Brian became chief cataloguer in the University of Bradford library and Ann worked in that university's Project Planning Centre for Developing Countries.

At the Polytechnic library Patricia M Fiddes, FLA, was appointed librarian on 1 January 1967. She had worked in Uganda for seven years as librarian of the East African Literature Bureau and later, for one year, as bibliographer in African studies at the library of Duke University, USA. On 22 December 1968, she married the development officer of the University of Malawi and in September 1969 moved to Kenya as deputy librarian of the University College of Nairobi. In 1971, after gaining a Master's degree, she became librarian of the Institute of Commonwealth Studies in the University of London.

At various times we were greatly helped by VSOs: at the Polytechnic by John B Greenwood, BA, ALA (1966-1967) who was in charge of that library until the arrival of Pat Fiddes, and by Stephen Thompson, ALA, (1969-1971); at Bunda College of Agriculture by Margaret Gunn, ALA (1968-1971); and at Chancellor College by Moira Woods, ALA (1969-1971).

John Greenwood had worked in Leeds public library and Bradford University library. After he left us he went to Salford University library and later to the Western Australia Institute of Technology. He is now liaison librarian at the Open University, Milton Keynes.

Margaret Gunn was Bunda's first qualified librarian. She married Timothy Ngwira, a Malawian, on 9 May 1970 and went with him to the University of Wales and later to Canada where she obtained a Master's degree at the University of British Columbia. She is now BA, MLS, ALA, and now holds a senior post in the library of the University of Namibia. (9).

Moira Woods was in charge of our acquisitions department at Chancellor College. After completing her two-year stint as a VSO she accepted a contract post as an assistant librarian. She and I were subsequently deported from Malawi on the same day.

It was not until the beginning of 1971 that we began to have qualified Malawian staff.

One of these was Rodrick Samson Mabomba who was the youngest of our library assistants in 1966. He obtained his ALA after going on scholarship to the College of Librarianship Wales 1968-1970; he was in charge of cataloguing in the university library after the departure of Brian and Ann Yarr in July 1971; he moved out of the University to become librarian of the British Council's library in Malawi in June 1975; at the age of 25 he wrote a 25,000 word article on "Libraries in Malawi" at the invitation of the editor of the *Encyclopedia of Library & Information Science* published by Marcel Dekker in New York; he became director of Malawi National Library Service in May 1978. He gained his FLA (by submission of published writings) in 1985 and was awarded the M. Lib after a year's study at the College of Librarianship Wales also in 1985. In December 1986 his post was re-designated 'National Librarian'. He was founding chairman of the Malawi Library Association and there is no doubt that he has done a great deal to help the development of libraries and librarianship in Malawi.

Of the library assistants appointed in 1966/67 six others have secured Masters' degrees and two are now FLAs.

Two assistant librarians have been less fortunate.

Augustine WC Msiska, BSocSc, was appointed assistant librarian on 1 September 1970 and subsequently obtained his DipLib at the College of Librarianship Wales. It was hoped he would become an Africanist in charge of the Africana department. Early in 1976 he was arrested by the Special Branch of the Police and he was not released until May 1978. Not surprisingly, he chose to leave Malawi for the years 1978-1987 in order to work at the University of Zambia library where he became a senior assistant librarian. (10)

Raphael Masanjika, DipLS, a Malawian working in the library of the University of Zambia, was appointed an assistant librarian in July 1972 and placed in charge of the Soche Hill College library. In 1974 he attended a Summer School at the College of Librarianship Wales but on 7 October, only a few days after his return, he was seized by the Special Branch and placed in detention. After five weeks, during which no charge was brought against him, he was released. Then in October 1976 he was again arrested and placed in detention until August 1978. After a period of unemployment he re-joined the staff of the University library in 1980 and secured his MLS in 1981. He became librarian of the College of Medicine in 1993.

Several other staff showed great promise.

Dick Najira was appointed a library assistant on 1 January 1968. He subsequently became a totally accurate catalogue assistant and did a great deal of valuable work, but he moved from the University to the National Archives as Assistant Archivist in December 1974 and became librarian in January 1981. He gained a DipLib from the University of Botswana and has been secretary of the Malawi Library Association and editor of its journal *The MALA Bulletin*.

Godwin B Shaba was appointed a library assistant in May 1968 and later he too became a catalogue assistant. At Bowling Green State University, Ohio, in 1985 he gained a BSc in Education, majoring in Library & Educational Media.

Oswin W Ambali, a very tall young man, was appointed a library assistant in 1972. He moved to the Archives as assistant librarian in December 1980 and became a member of the Executive Council of the Malawi Library Association in 1981; later on he gained his DipLib from the University of Botswana. Although we did not know it when we appointed him to the University, he is the great great grandson of Augustine Ambali who was ordained by Scottish missionaries in 1891.

The library bindery dates from 1 October 1968 when Jeffrey Stickley joined the staff as Bookbinding Officer. He stayed until 1976 when he and his wife Marion moved to James Cook University in Australia where they remained until Jeffrey's retirement in 1994.

When we first advertised for trainee bookbinders 676 applications were received. One of the six applicants appointed was Ellaton B Mkwate, then aged 15. He became the head bookbinder in charge of the bindery.

External Aid

All new university libraries receive a welcome and life-sustaining torrent of grants and gifts, and the University of Malawi was no exception. Our greatest benefactor was the British government which provided three new library buildings (at Bunda College of Agriculture, Soche Hill College and a main library on the university's permanent site at Chirunga); grants for the purchase of books totalling at least £50,000; equipment for a bindery; the services of a bookbinding officer for two years; ten scholarships enabling staff to gain qualifications at the College of Librarianship Wales; the services (through the British Council) of VSO librarians; and last, but by no means least, supplementation to the salaries of British staff employed in the libraries.

The governments of the United States of America, Australia, France, the Federal Republic of Germany, the Netherlands, Portugal and South Africa, and many other countries, were also markedly generous and helped us to get established.

The British Council, the United States Information Service, UNESCO, the World University Service of Canada, the Canadian Book Centre, the Ranfurly Library Service, the Beit Trust, the Schimmelpenninck-Campbell Trust, the Witwatersrand Native Labour Association, the Thondwe Tobacco Company, the Tea Association, the Trustees of the Ewing Bequest, the Trustees of the late Arthur Creech Jones, numerous companies, commercial firms, universities, organizations and individuals were all generous with books, equipment or money.

One small gift in October 1967 was from the Indian Council for Cultural Relations. The High Commissioner for India, His Excellency Mr MM. Khurana, presented 78 books on tropical agriculture and at the presentation ceremony he said:

This is not a gift one can boast about but a mere token of our desire, or expression of our willingness, to share with you our experiences in the fight against a common enemy of hunger, disease, ignorance and poverty. Though my country is large, we are as much a developing country as yours.... I should like you to accept this humble gift in the hope that it will enhance the understanding and feeling of friendship that already exists between our two peoples....

It may have been a routine gift for India but we did not think that it was and those of us in the small audience were touched by the humility and genuine friendship with which it was presented and we appreciated it the more.

Other gifts I vividly recall were:

1. A copy of the thesis of Dr JM Schoffeleers of the Catechetical Training Centre near Phalombe entitled, *Mbona, the guardian spirit of the Mang'anja*, submitted for the degree of Bachelor of Letters in the University of Oxford, a work of unique scholarship - but, again, offered to our library with humility: for us a most precious acquisition.

2. A large packet of papers and photographs from the Executors of Manser William Bartlett, MBE, who died in (I think) 1969. He had lived at Sekwere, near Mtakataka; had been in Malawi for fifty years; was happily married to an African wife; had a thorough knowledge of Chichewa and other local languages; and had written of the Ngoni and the Yao, and testified to the Monckton Commission. Again the material was unique and it will be invaluable to historians of the future.

3. A collection of papers and rare Malawiana given by Canon Edward Maycock who was pastor to some of the students. To receive this last gift I was summoned to lunch at Maycock's house in Maone on 23 February 1969. He was one of the missionary 'characters' of the formative years of Malawi, and I noted in my diary that he was probably 'in his seventies, tall, erect, silver-haired, with a single lock of white hair towards the front of a bald domed head; his face was lined; his eyes magnified by the thick lenses of his spectacles'. I had never seen him wearing anything but shorts and an open-necked shirt. He had been in Central Africa for forty years, perhaps more.

He had planned to leave his books and papers to the University; but on that Sunday he wished to anticipate his demise and hand over a selection of his papers and some of the rarer Africana. He had spent a great deal of time on Likoma Island and latterly as principal of St. Andrew's College, Malosa, which prepares Africans for Church work.

There were original water colours of Likoma on the walls of his lounge and bookcases against every foot of wall space. He had inherited from the Diocese a huge table that was also loaded with books. He was an unrepentant smoker and on one of the small tables were African carvings and in the window-sill a text proclaiming: 'It is better to smoke now rather than in the hereafter'. In the bottom of a built-in cupboard was a stock of beer, lime juice, and Malawi gin: evidently he felt that a supply of these, also, could not be relied upon in the hereafter.

The books and papers had been roughly sorted before I arrived. Each of them was handed over with some kind of exposition and I was asked whether it would be useful. I declined nothing. Even amendments to prayers in the Chilikoma language are likely to have interest in years to come. Many of the papers had been printed at the Mission press on Likoma Island and were primarily of ecclesiastical interest; many were in Chilikoma but others were in Chinyanja (Chichewa) and English. The printed material included Bishops' reports, the very rare Diocesan magazine, lectionaries, translations of the Gospels, instructions to the clergy, school textbooks, a catalogue of the Diocesan library (now, alas, dispersed) and material of linguistic and typographical interest.

The manuscripts, hand-written and typewritten, contained fascinating items. One lays down procedure for questioning about witchcraft (11) and cannibalism during the confessional. Others consist of essays by men prominent in public life.

At Likoma at one time the priests had a small problem. 'We discovered that the Servers were competing with one another to see how many times they could participate in Holy Communion, especially in reception of the Communion wine, each Sunday. Some of them achieved the sacramental wine at least six times'.

It was nearly four o'clock when I left with my loot. Douglas Varley, who was formerly librarian of the University College of Rhodesia, has said that publications of Mission presses of South Africa constitute the 'incunabula' of Africa. I returned to Chancellor College with dozens of the 'incunabula' of Malawi.

'The Cow Barn'
a n d   o t h e r   b u i l d i n g s

Few university libraries start in premises properly designed as libraries and those of the University of Malawi certainly did not. At *Chancellor College* the library had to exist for the first three years in classrooms and offices. In 1968 when an early move to the Zomba site became unlikely it was decided to build a temporary library on the Chichiri site. A very simple one-storey building 150 feet by 60 feet was planned, the architects being Norman & Dawbarn and the contractors Stewart & Lloyd (first phase) and Capitol Construction (second phase). The new building was opened on 15 April 1969. It did not pretend to be an architectural gem and its cake frill fenestration, in particular, did not derive from any known architectural principles: as a result there was excessive dust and dirt, unnecessary draughts in the cold season and temperatures up to 107 degrees Fahrenheit. in the reading room in the hot season. The building was a great improvement, however, on previous accommodation: it provided an adequate easily supervised reading room in which 120 students could be seated without overcrowding, a combined work room for the staff of the cataloguing and acquisitions sections; a serials room; a librarian's office; and a small microtext reading room. The floor area was 9,000 square feet. The total cost was £15,720.

By everyone, except the architects, the building was referred to as 'The Cow Barn'.

At *Malawi Polytechnic* the library was accommodated in a large L-shaped room and two small work rooms on the first floor of the Polytechnic main building which had been designed by USAID planners. The floor area was 5,000 square feet, there was seating accommodation for 94 students, and the book capacity was about 30,000 volumes.

Soche Hill College library was originally crammed into an area of 1,332 square feet at one end of the college dining-hall with a librarian's office built on as an afterthought behind a pleasant shrubbery of *Callistemon viminalis.* Construction of a new building was begun in September 1969 and it was occupied on 13 July 1970. The new library was a gift of the British government. The architects were Norman & Dawbarn. The floor area was 8,000 square feet, the capacity 30,000 volumes, with seats for sixty readers.

The *Bunda College of Agriculture* library was initiated while the College occupied buildings at Dedza Secondary School in 1966. The College moved to Bunda on 20 January 1967 and was officially opened on 10 April 1967. The library occupied spacious classroom accommodation until a new building became available in May 1969. Again it was a gift of the British government and the architects were Norman & Dawbarn. The floor area was 8,000 square feet, the book capacity 25,000 volumes, with seats for eighty readers. One of its architectural features was a small garden of rocks, plants, flowers and a fish-pool in the centre of the building, open to the sky (and to thieves). Night watchmen ate the decorative fish in the pool. There was a pleasant outlook on to Bunda Rock, home of the Rain God.

The *Institute of Public Administration* library was in classroom accommodation, claustrophobic and only barely adequate.

Plans for a new *University library building*, incorporating the collections from Chancellor College at Chichiri, Soche Hill College and the Institute of Public Administration, and including a bindery, to be built on the Chirunga site in Zomba, were finalized at the end of June 1967 and it was hoped that construction would commence in 1968. In fact, it commenced in 1971 and the building was occupied in 1973. The first phase had a capacity of 150,000 volumes and it was planned that the second phase should accommodate a further 150,000 volumes.

* * * * * * * * * * *

I do not remember very much about living at Bvumbwe except that after various hassles at work the district commissioner's bungalow was always a place of peace to which I was thankful to return at the end of the day.

Peaceful - yes! But nevertheless in 1966 burglaries were becoming more frequent in Malawi. The bungalow was burgled twice: the first time on the night before we planned to go off to Zambia, when thieves forced the back door and raided the refrigerator - apart from a Christmas cake the most lamented loss was a cut glass preserve jar given to us as a wedding present in 1939 by Irene and Ted Clark of Durham - and the other burglary occurred while we were away on the same trip.

Smart - who was strong and taller than most Malawians - had agreed to act as night-watchman and sleep in the house. So, armed with an iron bar, an axe, a cutlass, a heavy lathi and my Kashmir sword-stick (the total armaments of our household) he locked himself into the unlit passage between the lounge and the bathroom of the bungalow and was awakened in the middle of the night only by the noise of a curtain rail crashing to the floor of the lounge. When he sprang through the door, half naked, brandishing an axe in one hand and the Kashmir sword-stick in the other, the thieves must have thought he was an apparition and they fled into the night. Smart said he counted thirteen of them in the lounge and the garden. When day dawned, he and Ali the cook shifted all movables belonging to the lounge and the dining area into the second bedroom and locked them up: and when we returned several nights later and I unlocked the front door and turned on the light we were confronted by an apparently stripped bungalow, devoid of tables, chairs, curtains, rugs and pictures.

Smart was so frightened by this encounter with a gang of thieves that he would never again act as night-watchman while we were away. Money would not tempt him, and thereafter we had to ask Ali who was thin and knobbly and liable to get drunk to perform the duty.

One - more pleasant - memory: A fruiting guava tree grew immediately outside the glass window-panes of the dining area of the bungalow and in the guava season, as we sat at breakfast with our toast and marmalade, two loerie birds, purple, green and red and not at all shy, used to hop through the branches, only a few feet away from the breakfast table and us, gobbling their breakfast of ripe guavas.

One of the advantages of working in Malawi was the splendid variety and interest of the landscape almost everywhere, as well as the country's central position - when one had free time - as a launching pad for exploration by road of Zambia, Zimbabwe, Mozambique and even Tanzania and Kenya.

First Explorations

My first one-day exploration was purely domestic and modest - from Bvumbwe to Fort Johnston (now renamed 'Mangochi'), 123 miles away at the southern end of Lake Malawi. In 1966 the road north of Liwonde was already marked on maps as a 'first class road'; but I drove through so many mealie gardens that I do not know whether I followed the main road or, for part of the way, a disreputable 'hoed track' unknown to map makers.

At Easter 1966 I was more ambitious. I decided that the ancient Opel I had bought was capable of probing deeper into central Africa, and I went to Nkhata Bay, 479 miles from Blantyre. I spent Easter Day at Kasungu - quite unwillingly as I had intended to be in Nkhata Bay by then - but the Dwangwa River a few miles to the north was in flood, the bridge was under water, and no vehicles could pass.

Kasungu's rest house was non-catering but the manager must have had a fire somewhere as he kindly heated an emergency tin of steak and kidney pie I had brought with me, and I had that and some oranges to sustain me on Easter Sunday.

The following day the river subsided, leaving six inches of slippery silt on the northern side of the bridge. I skidded through this for one hundred yards at one mile an hour and was then again on the open road.

Between Mzimba and Ekwendeni a huge caravan had broken down at the side of the narrow mountain road. The driver was a grizzled American, and he had been there for three months. His wife had gone off to find a spare part for the caravan in Bulawayo. He was not at all disconcerted or lonely, he said.

'After all, I look out on spectacular mountain scenery; I enjoy the sunshine; I listen to the radio; we are in no hurry; and I'm getting to know some of the local people'.

They intended driving from Cape to Cairo.

Apparently each day a group of small girls appeared from nowhere, bringing him fresh eggs and goat milk - 'which costs almost nothing' - and he had plenty of tinned provisions. The only thing he really craved was a drink of whisky. So I fetched my bottle of Johnnie Walker from the Opel - only frugally dipped into at Kasungu - and we both had a whisky soda. As his need was obviously so much greater than mine I left the bottle, still three-quarters full, with him as an Easter present. His bliss was complete.

'D'ya know', he said, 'I had a buddy back in Wisconsin called "Plumbe". A good pal to me. He was a well-known Chicago gangster'.

The thirty miles from Mzuzu high in the sky and the hills down to Nkhata Bay on the shingly shore of the Lake were more hazardous than I expected. Perhaps the tyres of the Opel were bald - whatever it was, I skidded in a nerve-wracking way on sheets of mud that, in places, covered the good laterite road after a night of storms.

The rest house was delightful. John Kamanga, the manager, could not have been more friendly and he fed me enormous meals. As soon as my luggage was unpacked, two of his sons quickly sluiced the mud off the car with buckets of water. There was even a waste paper basket in my bedroom. (12)

I swam in the clear water at Chikale beach and met two young boys on the nearby rocks who were selling table mats and jug mats of crocheted lace on behalf of the grandmother of one of them. They told me their names were 'Lonely Nyirenda' and 'the Duke of Wellington' - the latter's real name being 'Wellington Alumi' named after Livingstone's servant Matthew Wellington (13) and nothing at all to do with Waterloo.

The two boys ordered me to climb a tremendous hill, almost a cliff, and drop in on the grandmother who had made the mats: She lived in a village of small thatched huts from which there was a prospect of the vast glittering Lake almost vertically below. I bought two mats, and she made a cup of tea for us, and when I left she shamelessly begged from me a further five shillings.

I asked the boys where they went to school; both of them seemed to be about twelve years old.

'We can't go to school', said Wellington.'His grandmother has no money and my uncle has no money, either. We help the fishermen and they give us fish.'

On the way back to Blantyre I stopped for a chat when I reached the American and his caravan. His wife had returned briefly but without the vital replacement that would enable him to repair the engine; she collected a further supply of travellers' cheques and then set off at once for Johannesburg, a thousand miles away, hitch-hiking by lorry to the nearest accessible railhead which was Salisbury in Rhodesia.

* * * * * * * * * *

In December we visited Victoria Falls.

Antony was out in Malawi for his Christmas vacation - as a 'child educated overseas' the University paid his air passage - and we had staying with us a young Nigerian, Olusegun Openiyi, whom we had recruited to the library as a catalogue assistant but for whom official accommodation was not yet available; so there were four of us. We knew that petrol would not be available in Zambia; therefore the back of the Opel had to be crammed with smelly tins and jerrycans of petrol and our luggage strapped to the roof of the car.

At the small village of Lizulu in the Angoni Highlands we bought twenty-two peaches for five pence. On this part of the journey Mozambique lay in sunshine on one side of the road, and Malawi on the other.

It was dark as we approached Mchinji and reached the Zambia Customs and Immigration post. The young officers on duty had brought down and furled the Zambian flag for the night. They had hurricane lamps but these were unlit as they had no paraffin owing to the fuel crisis. I told them we had nothing to declare but they insisted on borrowing our electric torch and in the gloaming they inspected our passports, greeting us cordially:

'We know an old man with white hair won't cheat us!'

'Welcome, African brother!' (This to Olu.)

'Welcome to the friendly country!'

In Chipata we stayed the night at Codrington House Government Hostel, arriving just in time for a late meal, hot bath and a comfortable night in mosquito-proofed double rooms.

On the Great East Road the next day two petrol lorries, one full, one empty, has crashed head-on and completely blocked the road. Other vehicles, trying to by-pass them, had broken down in the attempt and the obstruction across the road was complete. While Gladys, Antony and Olu went on foot, I had to make a cautious detour in the car through bushes and mossy undergrowth at the edge of the forest and the wrecked vehicles in order to continue. The surface of the Great East Road was wet, dangerous and churned up by heavy traffic but we managed to squelch our way 190 miles along it and we stayed that night at Kachalola rest house, a place of history although we did not know it at the time.

On Christmas Day we crossed the Luangwa River by its splendid bridge and - a long time later - came out of the *mopane* forest and into the more open area of savannah and farms around Lusaka. In Lusaka the University of Zambia was under construction, as were the Parliament buildings. We spent the night at the Don Robin Motel in Kafue on the west bank of the Kafue River.

It was an easy journey to Livingstone. A letter to the Fairmount Hotel, booking accommodation, had not been received but they had one double room vacant and were able to put Antony and Olu into a government rest hut for the night.

On the Zambian side of the Victoria Falls we did all the 'tourist' things but white Rhodesian police would not allow us into Rhodesia either by car or on foot.(14)

I had visited the Falls several times before - in 1943-1945 before anything was commercialised, and again in 1964 - but it was novel and exciting to Gladys, Antony and Olu. Even commercialisation had brought benefits - such as a small steamer plying up-river of the Falls and an Open Air Museum on the right bank of the Maramba River.

We spent a few hours visiting a game reserve where a uniformed game guard led us to the vicinity of several white rhinoceros, a lion and lioness, many zebras, hyenas, wart-hogs, bushbuck and several larger antelopes - including a greedy kudu so eager to eat Olu's ginger biscuits that he was in danger of getting his head and even his long spiral horns caught inside the car window.

Returning to Lusaka via Kalomo we ate lunch at a shady lay-by; and at Munali Pass watched the Kafue River from the point where Livingstone first saw it - in fact 'Munali', meaning 'The Red One', was the Africans' name for Livingstone at that time.

* * * * * * * * * *

In July 1967, while we were still living at Bvumbwe, Antony re-appeared in Malawi for his long vacation from University College, London. It was also our long vacation in the University of Malawi so I was able to take local leave that enabled us to go off to northern Malawi. Olu, the young Nigerian, had moved on by then to a small university house at Maone so the trip to the North was purely a family expedition. A few months earlier I had bought from the wife of the Swedish Consul an almost new Volvo station wagon, to replace the elderly Opel, which was not only more powerful but promised to be more comfortable over long distances.

We left Bvumbwe early on 19 July. At Kasupe escarpment beyond Zomba, where we sped 3,000 feet down to the plain, the early morning sun shone like a searchlight into the jagged precipices of Zomba mountain to our left. At Liwonde the tarmac ended, and at the bridge and barrage on the Shire river small ragged boys were fishing with bamboo poles and little girls were washing clothes at the brink of the river. Fresh fish and mats of woven grass were for sale.

Beyond Ntcheu through the Angoni Highlands where the highway skirts the border with Mozambique, the 'spine road' became little more than a rocky track where we crashed over pot-holes, stones and erosion gullies and, at times, we could scarcely see the Kirk range of mountains on account of the haboob of brown dust in which I drove. The Volvo took the first of many batterings over unsurfaced roads.

At Lilongwe - which, a few years later, was to become the site of the new capital city - we took the Salima road, still twisting through very broken country with the grey crags of Golomoti far to our right standing sentinel over the enormous Great Rift Valley in which lay Lake Malawi. Late that afternoon we booked in at the Lake Malawi Hotel a few miles beyond Salima on the western shore of the Lake. From the green cliff and the thatched rondavels of the hotel the Lake stretched endlessly left and right, gently respirant and intensely blue under the afternoon sun. There was a clean sandy beach and a floating platform of logs anchored to the floor of the lake within easy swimming distance of the shore.

Day two: Salima to Nkhota-Kota to Kasungu.

A large area through which we passed had been ravaged by bush fires. One of them, still burning fiercely, caused a cloud to form overhead. At the roadside plucked but unbaled cotton was stacked in white polythene bags.

Nkhota-Kota township has a direct link with Bishop Chauncy Maples. When he drowned in the Lake in 1895 his body was carried to Nkhota-Kota from Rifu where it was washed ashore and was buried on the spot where a chancel for a future church was marked out. (15) That church is today Nkhota-Kota Anglican Church.

Thirty miles outside the town, alongside an extensive game reserve, many of the trees had been damaged by elephants and large balls of elephant dung - said to be excellent for the nourishment of garden flowers, especially roses - lay at the side of the road. But there was very little traffic apart from trundling ox-carts and an occasional lorry carting cotton.

We stayed the night at Kasungu Rest House which, in spite of my experience fifteen months earlier, seemed to have become a catering rest house.

On the Viphya plateau next day the hills were dark with plantations of young conifer, and there were watch-towers on the hill-tops to raise an alarm in the event of Ngoni garden fires spreading to the miles and miles of young saplings. The Colonial Development Corporation had started a scheme here that was intended to result in the establishment of a wood pulp industry.

Ten miles out of Mzuzu, where the Colonial Development Corporation had its tung extraction plant and administrative centre, the young tung trees were protected by wind breaks of conifer, and nuts from trees already bearing lay in bags awaiting collection at the roadside. Apparently tung yields a quick-drying oil that is used in the manufacture of paint.

We stayed three nights at Nkhata Bay Rest House and then went on via Mzuzu, Rumphi and up the Rukuru gorge to Livingstonia. Somewhere in the foothills of the Nyika plateau we overtook a young man whom I recognized as a Chancellor College student. He had seven miles to walk along the road, he said, and then two more miles along a footpath. We gave him a lift in the car for seven miles and when he got out he pointed to a brown speck like a fir cone on a distant hill-top and said that was his destination. His name was Augustine Msiska and in a handkerchief he was carrying half a dozen eggs to his aunt whose home it was at the very apex of the distant hill-top.

It was a narrow twisty stony road with sudden very steep hills and waterfalls sparkling silver and white among dark rocks and the huge Nyika plateau straining skywards on our left. We stayed the night at Kaziwiziwi Rest House. (16)

Livingstonia Mission, at the end of a road that winds along the flank of an escarpment, is 4,000 feet above sea level and 3,000 feet above the Lake. It was established as a Free Church of Scotland Mission by Dr Robert Laws (who belonged to the United Presbyterian Church) in 1894. In 1900 that Church became the United Free Church of Scotland and later again the Church of Scotland.

It had a brick church with a square tower and all its houses and two-storey buildings were constructed of brick. To-day there are primary, secondary and technical schools, a hospital and a post office, and VSOs and Peace Corps volunteers are privileged to assist the regular staff. Ever since it was established its influence on the development of Malawi has been incalculable.

Before leaving the heights and the hills we visited Manchewe Falls where the Chitimpa river reaches the edge of the escarpment and flings itself in veils of white water a thousand feet into the forest below.

I had then to ease the car in bottom gear down a narrow, nerve-racking descent with more than twenty terrifying hairpin bends - known as 'The Gorode', presumably deriving from 'Go-road' - to the lakeshore lane at the bottom of the escarpment. In seven miles we trickled, yard by yard, down 3,000 feet of leaf - strewn unsurfaced forest track: it took an hour and at the bottom we were in a different climatic zone, hot, humid and tropical.

We planned to follow this lane along the lakeshore to Karonga. It was shown on the maps as a dry season road and it did exist although very little motor traffic could have used it. The grass shack which was the terminus of the Chivwati Bus Services - the 'buses' were open lorries - was several miles to the north. Our first task was to remove a rotten tree that lay across the grass in the middle of the lane and across the wheel ruts made when lorries actually used the road in the past. The tree trunk must have been gently decaying for at least several rainy seasons as a footpath made by dusty bare feet passed over the top of it.

Later we had to negotiate, very gingerly, half a dozen semi-rotten timber bridges that enabled us to cross small ravines, and one of us - Gladys or Antony - had to walk in front and 'test' each bridge before I risked the weight of the Volvo on it.

We stopped to eat our lunch in a patch of shade at Deep Bay, looking across the Lake to the high and rugged Livingstone Mountains in Tanzania. It is off shore from this peaceful coastline that the Lake attains its greatest depth - 2,200 feet.

The 'dry season road' by now had greatly improved and had become, indeed, a 'Lakeshore highway' with, alongside it, inlets, lagoons, baobab trees, dom palms and occasional small villages.

Karonga, we found, was on a marshy plain surrounded by mountains that rise to 7,000 and 8,000 feet. The township is not on the Lake but several miles inland, built around an airfield so that planes take off and land in the middle of houses and shops.

It is a cotton growing area and in July the leaves of the cotton plants were green and the bolls beginning to form. Bananas, finger millet, maize and rice were also plentiful and there were many herds of cattle. The people in the villages were mostly Nkhonde (Wankonde) who are said to have lived in the area for hundreds, or perhaps for thousands, of years.

It was near here that Mlozi, a half-caste Arab slave trader, had built his stockade and resisted the African Lakes Company. He was eventually bombarded into submission by Sir Harry Johnston in 1895, immediately freeing over 1,000 slaves and virtually ending the slave trade in the far north of Malawi. In the nearby hills Stone Age artifacts have been found, and precursors of modern Malawians and the Akafula evidently lived here 50,000 years ago.

We spent the night at the palatial Rest House in Karonga.

The plain stretches inland from the Lake for ten or fifteen miles and the road then enters a gorge, becomes very humpy with short steep hills and it climbs into a mountainous, desolate, uninhabited region. About sixty miles out of Karonga it turns sharply to the south, passes into Zambia and re-enters Malawi near to Katumbi. It is a lonely road: in a hundred miles we saw only one other car and one lorry.

Rumphi was our destination for the night.

On the Nyika plateau, next day, reedbuck, roan antelopes and duikers were grazing in the dambos and near the patches of relic forest; a side-striped jackal trotted in front of the car, and there were wattled cranes, Stanley's bustards and unexpected small flocks and flights of francolins and ducks.

Large areas of grassland had been deliberately burned, mainly on each side of the grassy lanes that criss-cross the high uplands and around the plantations of conifers where fires have to be strictly controlled. Mr Thomas, the friendly Forestry officer at Chelinda, told us it was the policy to burn the grass once in three years. Another ten thousand acres of conifers were due to be planted within the next year which might prove too ambitious a target as the Tumbuka people who live around the foothills of the plateau and comprise the labour force do not like the cold nights they experience if they remain overnight in temporary accommodation at 7,000 feet.

It was intended that the Nyika should provide timber for a pulpwood scheme but eventually the Viphya was chosen instead. (Twenty-five years later Chelinda had become the centre of a hugh pine forest).

On 27 July we retraced our route across the hills to the main Rumphi to Blantyre road and spent the night at Mzimba Rest House. Following that I had a long day's drive over rough roads down to Liwonde, after which there was blessed and welcome tarmac all the way to Blantyre and out to Bvumbwe - where the house was unburgled, no real calamities had occurred, and what we needed most in all the world, with the dust of the North still clinging to us, were large cups of tea splashed with brandy, followed immediately by hot baths.

* * * * * * * * *

These small excursions, and others which followed, were snatched from work whenever the University of Malawi closed for an official university holiday, as at Christmas and on public holidays or when I was able to take local leave. I was supposed to work a 37 hour week and to take three months overseas leave after completing 21 months service, but for most of my time in Malawi I worked at least 80 hours a week as the library was grossly understaffed, and it was not until 39 months had elapsed that I was able to take overseas leave.

All this overwork reflected no credit on me. Librarians should not work longer than other people, although many of them do so in the tropics. Some of my academic colleagues in Malawi thought - without doubt - it was my own incompetence that caused me to work so many hours and to postpone my overseas leave. In fact, I had no wish to be a workaholic; I had many interests to which I would have liked to devote some energy. If one had a clock-watching trade union attitude and was prepared to exchange only the number of hours of work prescribed in conditions of service in return for one's salary, I suppose libraries and universities might still be created but not at the speed with which some of them were created in the 1960s and 1970s.

In my case, I think it was sheer obstinacy that allowed a desperate personal situation to develop: I was not willing to allow a service I was establishing with the help of other library staff and for which I was responsible, to collapse for lack of official support. There was nothing missionic, altruistic or even egotistical, about it.

In Malawi, half a dozen professors - including the three women professors - had much the same attitude and worked similar hours (although I would not wish to suggest they were unpleasantly obstinate). Their attitude towards their students was stimulative, possibly paternal - or maternal - which some people would regard as reprehensible, but they were practical educators who established academic standards and carried out research that was valuable. I merely tried to create an effective university library, in a short period of time, irrespective of the difficulties that we shared.

The journeys of exploration, the many friends of different tribes and different nations, the discussions and parties we enjoyed in each others' homes, the picnics on mountains and beaches, were all part of a process of integration with 'our' part of Africa where the 'wind of change' was blowing like a force ten gale. The background, however, was always prosaic work in the small libraries my colleagues and I were struggling to create and guide into existence.

To the Luangwa

On 20 November 1967 we moved house away from Bvumbwe, about a dozen miles downhill to Chirimba at the foot of Ndirande mountain. On the day of removal we found - rather late - that the servants' quarters of our new house swarmed with bed bugs which, upon our urgent appeal, Blantyre City Health department (using 'Sevkol') swiftly eradicated.

The railway line from Beira in Mozambique passed near the back of our new garden, and locomotives snorted like dragons as they tugged heavily laden coaches marked 'Bagagem' up the gradient towards Salima.

When our friend Jean Johnston wrote from her retirement home in the Yorkshire dales that she would be passing through Malawi in 1968 en route to Australia, the University of Malawi reached out and grabbed her for three months as a temporary cataloguer to help bridge the gap between the lamented departure of 'Nada' and the anticipated arrival of Ann and Brian Yarr. Jean had been children's librarian at the Middlesbrough central library and I suppose it must have been there we first met her. At the time she had been plump with impressive contours, sandy red hair, a direct piercing glance that could be intensely serious: a sensitive, thoughtful, brave, humorous person, with a kind of inner stillness and full of delight in living. Later, after her marriage, she left Middlesbrough to go as pioneer first librarian of Edge Hill Teacher Training College in Lancashire where, sadly, her husband died.

It was at the Chirimba house that Jean stayed with us while she did her stint of cataloguing in June, July and August - after which it was agreed by all concerned she should experience the real wildest wilds of central Africa.

For a preliminary week Gladys took her to Rhodesia - this was before the Unilateral Declaration of Independence - flying from Chileka to Salisbury and then on to Victoria Falls. Thereafter they travelled by train to Fort Victoria and Zimbabwe ruins, and came back by air to Chileka.

I had a fortnight's local leave due to me but I could not take it before September, and Jean's further introduction to Africa took place 4-19 September 1968. We planned to visit Lake Malawi, Lifupa Game Camp, Nkhota-Kota, Livingstonia, the Nyika plateau, Nkhata Bay and the Luangwa Valley Game Reserve in eastern Zambia.

So, with the usual accompaniment of clothes, bedding, food, medicines, crockery and cutlery, petrol, demijohns of drinking water, a pocket of 100 Rhodesian oranges, and including this year boards for my bed (I was recovering from an attack of lumbago and had to sleep on a hard bed), we left Chancellor College on 4 September. Before setting out I telephoned the Lake Malawi Hotel near Salima and obtained reservation of three beds there for the first night.

Tremendous road construction work was taking place north of Zomba and north of Ntcheu and we were thickly bedizened from head to foot with red laterite dust by the time we stopped for lunch at a vantage point in the Angoni Highlands where Lake Malawi can be glimpsed thirty miles to the northeast.

We reached Salima in darkness and the Lake Malawi Hotel (formerly the Lake Nyasa Hotel) seemed to have vanished utterly; there was no signpost to it but after driving around a few patches of forest we found it had been re-named 'The Fish Eagle Inn' - and that we were expected.

Jean was eager to see as much as possible of Africa's animals in the wild and at Lifupa the next day - with game guard Edward in his clean khaki uniform and bush hat, and armed with a .303 Lee Enfield rifle - we drove slowly along grassy tracks skirting the dambos in search of them. Reedbuck, roan antelope, sable antelope and oribi quickly appeared among the trees; eight black buffalo stood stock still without moving a horn while we inched past; and there were elephants moving like shadows on the edge of the forest.

A little before dusk, returning to the Game Camp, a herd of enormous elephants - surely the biggest in Africa? - was crossing a dambo and our track. Edward told me to stop the car while he got out, and he made a noise that was partly a roar, a bellow, a shriek and a honk - it sounded like an order in Elephantese - directed at a bull elephant eighty yards ahead. When the old tusker moved off we drove in complete darkness between walls of *mapelele* grass, and the night seemed to be full of galloping elephants: two of them, pale in the car headlights, hurtled across our path not more than forty feet distant. I began to feel that the Volvo and its occupants could be flattened at any moment.

Next morning we went out early and encountered hartebeest, wart-hogs, duikers and some more sable antelopes. Some of the sable bulls had fine black pelts.

At the camp we were accommodated in rondavels, some of them brick, others aluminium, all of them thatched. There was a thatched dining room in the open air and baths and flush toilets in a separate building. Against a grass fence lay an array of elephant skulls and the bones of animals killed by lions.

We stayed two nights at Lifupa. There were no other visitors, so it was pleasantly peaceful with only Jean, Gladys, me and the game guards - and the animals munching, belching, prowling and calling to each other in the bush as their ancestors had done for the past million years.

On 7 September we drove on to Nkhota Kota which has a population of 27,000 and is the largest traditional town of thatched buildings in central Africa. We found the Rest House where I had arranged for us to spend the night and paid the necessary courtesy call on Mr Mkandawire the District Officer. The Rest House was a modest affair consisting of two chalets and two other buildings, one of them the dining-room, the other the kitchen. The caretaker in charge was Awakilo Musa who looked as if he might have been an askari in World War I.

In the chalet that was the dining room a 'Suggestions Book' was conspicuously displayed. Visitors in the past all seemed to have been government officials and their visits infrequent, but correspondence as well as comments was kept in the 'Suggestions Book' and there was an unexpected exchange of memoranda dated 2.6.60 to 23.2.68 on the subject of bats, e.g.

The Nyasaland Museum,
PO Box 512, Blantyre.
11th October, 1963.

The Government Agent,
Kota Kota.

Dear Mr Government Agent,
It has come to my knowledge that an extremely interesting bat (Ansorge's Free-tailed Bat) has in the past been collected from your Rest House. The species is known from Angolo (sic), Congo and Tanganyika but not hitherto from Nyasaland. Unfortunately we have no specimens in this museum and have no knowledge whether your Rest House still has this distinguished

tenant and if you could possibly collect a few we should be most grateful. If you can help I shall be pleased to send jar of preservative and pay expenses.

Needless to say, if this species still occurs, it may well prove to be of considerable attraction to tourists and worth including on your brochures.

Yours sincerely,
(sgd.)
P. Hanney.
Curator.

The reply to this was:

Government Agent,
Kota Kota,
Nyasaland.
21st October, 1963.

The Curator,
The Nyasaland Museum,
PO Box 512,
Blantyre.

Sir,

Bats in the Nkhota Kota Rest House

1. Thank you for your letter No. Mus/NH/355 of 11th October, 1963.

2. I am unable to confirm whether or not the bats which are inhabiting the Nkhota Kota Rest House are of the Asorge's (sic), Free-tailed species or not, or whether, if they are, they are to be found elsewhere in Nkhota Kota township. I therefore suggest that you send me sufficient jars of preservative, with notes on how the creatures should, ideally, be killed, and I will then try to have specimens collected from various buildings in the township, and I will return these to you, marked.

3. I have recently had a similar request form a Government Officer in Northern Rhodesia, but I will give the Nyasaland Museum first priority, when distributing the creatures.

4. Unfortunately, although the bats in the Rest House many be of interest to the zoologist and natural historian, their habits are obnoxious to the majority of guests, and the Ministry of Works and Housing recently tried to clear all of them out of the dormitory roofs. However, I will see if any stragglers remain, and will ask the Ministry to delay further clearing exercise until the specimens which I shall send you have been positively identified.

I am, Sir,
Your obedient servant,
J. Radcliffe,
Government Agent.

Other comments included:

25.2.66. Officer i/c Police Central Region: This suggestion book does not appear to have been seen by the Administrative Officer i/c District since February 1964 - two years! The Rest House is gaining an unpleasant reputation outside the district for 'bugs' and other 'biters'. Suggest that early remedial action is taken.

5.3.66 The Medical Officer, Kota Kota, have searched for the alleged 'bed bugs' in the Rest House and have not found even a single one. If the reputation is spread outside, it is spread by people who do not really know anything about the Rest House. E.O.

In spite of such intimate revelations in the 'Suggestions Book', we were perfectly comfortable at the Rest House and were not molested by bats, bugs or 'other biters'.

The District Officer, Mr Mkandawire, was most helpful and that first afternoon he took us around some of the villages that comprise Nkhota Kota. Firstly there was the Boma where he was building fine new administrative offices and a new Rest House looking out towards Lake Malawi, landscaped with a crescent of pineapple gardens. Then we visited the African township, the Asian township and the Republic Day Memorial where Dr Banda had addressed the people of Nkhota Kota at the first political rally he held after returning to Malawi in 1958.

At the port jetty fishermen who were total strangers gave us a present of newly caught fish - which we ate for our supper.

Near the Mosque is a huge old fig tree with a board bearing the legend:

This memory indicates the arrival of Dr David Livingstone in the year 1863. He camped at the foot of this fig tree. He sailed through Kaweya to meet Chief Malenga of the Achewa and awarded him with an umbrella.

In Malawi an umbrella is something of a prestige symbol. Can its distinction derive from this occasion in 1863?

To-day the Mosque is painted green and stinks of bat guano. There is a pierced screen at the end opposite the *quibla* behind which women can pray; the door to this has been intricately carved - possibly by one of the Jumbe chiefs himself - but unfortunately it has been painted over. Outside on a corner of the verandah youths and boys sit with their wooden tablets engaged in learning the text of the Qur'an.

It is near the Mosque that Salim bin Abdallah, the first Jumbe, is buried. His grave consists of a heap of earth with stones littered around it, shaded by a tree. The graveyard is clean as far as grass and bushes are concerned but the grave itself is uncared for and the District Officer allows it to remain so deliberately, as he does not wish to start or strengthen a Jumbe cult.

A hundred years ago this area was the slave market and from this point on the lakeshore the first Jumbe sent thousands of slaves across the Lake to Losefa in Mozambique. They were packed like animals under the deck planks of dhows and then made to walk from Losefa to the coast of the Indian Ocean where they were transferred into sea-going dhows for the journey to the main slave market at Zanzibar.

It was only in 1889 that slavery was abolished in Nkhota Kota when 'the Jumbe, Tawakali Sudi, made a treaty with Sir Harry Johnston and placed his country under British protection in return for subsidy of £200 a year.'(17)

Most of the people of Nkhota Kota seemed to be Muslim.

Of the population in 1968 at least 6,000 were refugees from Portuguese rule on the other side of the Lake. Many of the newcomers were skilled carpenters, bricklayers and builders; when they arrived they were each given £1 and were expected to find work within a month. This was not easy for them as most of the public works - the construction of the new rest house, the Republic Day memorial, the upkeep of the roads - were all carried out by use of penal labour.

Formerly the town had possessed a flourishing Co-operative Society which had good buildings and many vehicles and employed many people, but that had been closed down by government order and the vehicles and buildings were now unused.

On 8 September game guard Paul Nyoka, kindly 'seconded' to us by Mr Mkandawire, shepherded us around and we were able to visit Chief Malenga.

A short unobtrusive figure wearing a plain white cap and a faded European jacket over his white Muslim gown, Malenga was brought up in the household of Jumbe I. He is the grandson of the Malenga to whom Livingstone gave the umbrella. (The board on the fig tree does not tell the full story. Besides the umbrella, Livingstone gave Malenga a china plate; and Malenga (or Marenga) gave Livingstone a sheep).

The chief asked questions about the University which I tried to answer: obviously, he knew nothing whatever about what the University was trying to do and one couldn't help wonder whether this ignorance was universal among the traditional chiefs of Malawi, and what the cause of it might be. Probably we should have disseminated news about the University in Chichewa, Chitumbuka and Chitonga to a much greater extent than happened at that time. Malenga said his people wanted to adopt European ways instead of the old African ways and they wanted more help from Europeans.

The Chief has had seven wives and, with an effort, he could recall the names of seventeen of his children. His younger brother, Ahmadi Tambala, acted as interpreter. We also met his second son, Sefu Malenga - obviously highly intelligent - who, at the age of seven, looked like a future student of Chancellor College.

Malenga had not yet been given a house by the Government; he was living in the end of a Court house a few miles down the Salima road. Before we left his senior wife gave us cups of tea and also eggs and a packet of rice, presumably home-grown, which lasted us for four days. At the Rest House we left a reciprocal present of tinned meats suitable for Muslims: Awakilo assured us that the government messenger would deliver it.

Paul took us to visit ivory carvers, but they seemed to have little natural talent in their craft and, especially, they needed much more practice in observing and copying animal anatomy.

At the jetty where we awaited the arrival - off-jetty owing to shallow water - of the lake ship 'Chauncy Maples', I talked to a 25-year old policeman who had been at St. Patrick's Secondary School, Mzedi, along with Rodrick, Foster and some of the other library assistants, who was studying for 'A' levels but could not get books, so I offered to lend them to him from the university library. (Paul Nyoka, the game guard, also wanted to borrow books on Biology and English).

At the end of the day we visited the hot springs from which hot water is piped, ingeniously, to public bath houses in various parts of Nkhota Kota: this was my first encounter with natural hot water being captured in this way.

All-in-all, we thought Nkhota Kota had distinct possibilities of development: it had an energetic District Officer; a good beach of fine white sand; many historical associations; traditional crafts (we did not see them all); public hot water from the hot springs; pineapples and rice; a port of sorts; and Chipata Game Reserve only thirty miles distant - not to mention rare Ansorge's Free-tailed bats in the Rest House!

The journey next day, Nkhota Kota to Rumphi, consisted mainly of dust and hard driving over 256 miles of laterite corrugations.

On 10 September we visited the office of the District Commissioner, Rumphi, where the chief clerk gave us permission to use the Rest House at Kaziwiziwi which is towards the top of the Rukuru gorge. The timber Rest House was still under the charge of Labson Banda whom we had met in 1967 when we brought Antony to northern Malawi; he promised to find us another chicken for our supper and said he would boil it before roasting so that it would be less 'hard' than its predecessor the

previous year.

The Rest House was very much like a fishing lodge. It had four beds, comfortable, elementary, pleasantly rustic, with a fast flowing trout stream pouring over brown rocks to contemplate from the front verandah. No electricity, no catering, and the thatched lavatory, dark and buzzing with flies, suitably remote among the rocks.

After depositing our 'loads' we continued up the rump of Mount Waller to Manchewe Falls. Near the main road an African 'Hotel 1968' had been erected and much other building with large mud bricks was in progress. The family of builders said their name was 'Fraser' which established an immediate link with Jean whose middle name was 'Fraser'.

So that we might all marvel at the view across the Lake, I drove the car, cautiously, down the escarpment to the fourth hairpin bend and we ate our lunch with leaves fluttering on to us from the forest trees.

At Livingstonia on the scalp of the headland our exploration of Africa included the Kandodo shop, the secondary school library and the famous brick church erected by Dr Robert Laws in 1894. Deliberately, we did not call on Mkandawire the Principal as I knew he had received many visitors from the University in recent weeks and probably had no desire to receive any more.

A member of staff was with some of the boys who were playing soccer. The library was closed but a clerk let us in. On the library walls were colourful posters from the British Information Service. The book stock on the shelves consisted mainly of items received as gifts from the Ranfurly Library Service and the United States Information Service and there was no evidence of book selection by a trained librarian or of adequate records of stock.

A qualified librarian or teacher-librarian in each of the secondary schools of Malawi would probably have a greater educational impact than some of the teaching

staff, and I would be more favourably impressed by Livingstonia if the library were open in the afternoon so that boys could read, if they so wished, instead of having to play football or wander about in state of obvious boredom.

John Banda, assistant registrar at the University of Malawi office, who was formerly a teacher at Livingstonia secondary school, has told me that while he was there many books were stolen from the library and that on one occasion at the end of term when he was accompanying a lorry taking boys the 49 miles to Rumphi it was decided to teach the thieves a lesson. Midway to Rumphi the lorry was stopped; the boys were required to dismount and reveal the contents of their cases; many had stolen library books with them; the books were retrieved and the thieves were left at the roadside to walk the rest of the way to Rumphi through a landscape where they might encounter lions and other dangerous animals.

The stained glass window in the Church is impressive. It depicts Dr Livingstone with Susi and Chuma (no sign of Sudi, Majwara and Wellington) with Livingstone's sextant, medical instruments and a bale of cloth in the foreground, together with a family group - a man with assagai, his wife and child definitely over-dressed for that period -and the escarpment, Florence Bay and the Livingstone mountains as background. Under the window is an inscription:

This window was gifted by Dr J.C. Ridge in memory of her Father. 5th December 1952.

Kaziwiziwi Rest House, on the edge of the *mopane* forest, proved a minor nightmare after dark. For some reason our electric torches failed to work and our only light after sundown came from minute oil lamps. There were legions of mosquitoes and we went to bed at 6:30 p.m.

Next morning, while Gladys washed clothes and the Rest House verandah looked as if it had been transformed into a laundry, Jean and I went for a walk up the valley of the Kaziwiziwi stream. Soon it came on to rain and we thought - to keep dry - we would cross the stream at a shallow point and seek shelter at African houses on top of a small hill.

I found a spot where the water looked fordable and where, on the opposite bank, several substantial trees had fallen into the stream. About forty feet of water had to be crossed and at once we took off our shoes and socks and started paddling across. I tied my shoes together and slung them around my neck, together with my camera, and I stuffed my white stockings into the breast pocket of my shirt. Jean tucked her frock into her pants, hung her camera round her neck, carried her shoes in one hand and paddled rather uncertainly with the help of a stick.

I crossed safely and sat astride a fallen tree trunk at the brink of the stream, waiting to help Jean. The water had been a little above my knees. As Jean approached, I leaned forward and took her shoes from her, placing them on the tree trunk behind me; then I took her right wrist to help her firmly across the last three or four feet where there was a deep cleft in the rock and the current was very strong.

Almost at once, she lost her footing and fell full-length into the torrent between us, completely submerged except for her arm which I still held. I tried to drag her up on to the tree trunk but it took a great effort to bring even her head out of water. I wriggled lower down the tree trunk and struggled my hardest to pull her on to it but all I could do was get her head above water for about half a minute at a time. Owing to the tremendous force of the current she was unable to stand but lay extended under water like a wind-sock in a high wind, nor could she grasp the tree trunk, either with her free hand or her legs. Her lips became blue and I was afraid she might drown so I let myself down into the water, still clutching her wrist, threw myself across the torrent into shallower water and dragged her up beside me. She had lost all strength and I had great difficulty in getting her head out of water.

I suppose all this took only a few moments but it seemed a very long time. In the end I hoisted her on to a small rock, got off my knees and on to my feet and lifted her by the strong girdle at the top of her skirt, a foot or less at a time, back to the other bank from which we had paddled. The water in the torrent was up to my chest but it was only a few inches deep across the rest of the stream.

By this time Jean was only semi-conscious. As soon as I knew she was conscious I dumped her ungallantly in a patch of comfortable mud and threw myself flat on the grassy bank nearby until I had more breath and my heart beat became tolerable. After perhaps fifteen minutes we were both rested, although Jean was still semi-exhausted and shocked, and we began to pick our way back to a footpath on higher ground.

Suddenly a Traditional Authority policeman appeared ahead, I hailed him and he dashed down to us. He took off his tunic and cap and he carried Jean on his back up the slope to the path and supported her all the mile or so back to the Rest House. For the last hundred yards, near Labson's house, I ran ahead and asked Gladys if she could make some hot tea quickly. Probably I gave her a fright as I was very muddy and my bare legs bruised and bleeding; anyhow, Jean, supported by the policeman, arrived almost at once and Gladys gave us tea with plenty of brandy in it.

We put Jean to bed for the rest of the day to recover from the exhaustion and shock. I was quickly all right apart from a few bruised toes and cuts on the legs, and my right arm was strained by the pulling and lifting. Jean weighs nearly eleven stones when *dry* and she doesn't remember being dragged out of the torrent and across the stream so she thinks she was unconscious most of the time; certainly I have never before lifted anything as heavy.

In this episode, both our cameras were submerged and mine no longer functions; Jean lost her spectacles, her pants which were swept downstream, and her shoes which we did not attempt to retrieve from the tree trunk; I lost only a new pair of white stockings that were swept out of my breast pocket when I had to throw myself across the torrent. Fortunately Jean had another pair of spectacles and other pairs of shoes; she did not inform me about her stock of pants.

The name of the Traditional Authority policeman who appeared so providentially was Benson R. Kumwenda of Phoka Tax Office, P.O. Rumphi.

When we came to leave Kaziwiziwi, Labson could not cope with the demands of modern bureaucracy but he had an account book with a piece of carbon paper, he was determined that propriety should be preserved, and he insisted I should issue an account to myself.

Kaziwiziwi   Rest   House,
Rumphi   District,
12 Sept. 1968.

Received from Mr W.J. Plumbe, University of Malawi, Box 200, Limbe, the sum of 36/- for 2 nights accommodation (3 persons using own bedding). Also 2/6 for 3 bottles of Fanta.

- to which Labson, whose name is perhaps 'Robson', appended a wobbly signature; 'R Banda'.

Still feeling rather battered, we went on next day from Kaziwiziwi to Chelinda on the Nyika plateau. Jean had apparently recovered although she had huge bruises on her elbows and knees. I was very stiff but able to drive the car.

We passed within one mile of Nchenanchena, an idyllic place surrounded by blue mountains, home of one of our library assistants.

Driving into Nyika National Park there were roan antelopes, eland, zebra, bushbuck, reedbuck, duikers and wattled cranes. In the late afternoon and later in darkness game guard Jackson conducted us around the hills which, in fading sunlight, were tawny brown like sand dunes, and we saw more of the same species of animals, plus a wart-hog and three Stanley's bustards. Near the house of Mr Thomas, the Forestry officer, were zebra and a variety of antelopes but no leopards which we had hoped to see.

Chelinda camp is at 7,500 feet and cold at night. The sheer comfort of the cottage (No.1) was a pleasure after the rigours of Kaziwiziwi: a large lounge with a comfortable settee in front of a blazing fire of half a hundredweight of pine logs; euphoric beds in two bedrooms; a large well-appointed kitchen; clean toilet and bathroom; a servant (Dickson) to care for our needs; and a big welcome from Mr Thomas who said he was working hard to get more timber away before the rains broke.

13 September: Chelinda to Nkhata Bay where we stayed two nights.

When we stopped for lunch somewhere along the Ekwendeni road a very robust and muscular man of about thirty greeted us in Chitumbuka and called his old mother over to the car. He informed us in English that he was her twelfth child. The old woman looked worn out with child-bearing and begged without shame. We gave her three sixpences - all the change we had - a bottle of Fanta and some shortcake. She clapped, ululated and lay on the ground at my feet. I felt that Fanta did not merit such an exhibition but I expect the old mother's behaviour was a revelation of the abject poverty in which some people of this area exist.

The road down to Nkhata Bay was as rutted and dangerous as ever. Although the valleys on either side of the road are well populated with people of the Tonga tribe, there is no African township on the shore of the Lake -mainly the Boma, the prison, the mission hospital, a post office, a few shops owned by Indians, a cemetery containing graves of the Martyrs of 1959, and the Rest House standing back a little from the beach. It is, however, an important port, one of a number of delightful small bays. The sands are sandstone yellow and fine black biotite - a tourist paradise without the tourists. There is a bus service to Mzuzu and Lake steamers are able to berth at the floating pontoon.

At the Rest House, John the caretaker took one look at our dust-coated car and - as on a former occasion - called one of his sons to clean it. We sat for a while on the beach, watching fishermen mend their nylon nets. Some of the fishing dug-outs, we learned, were axed and carved several miles inland and were dragged to the Lake on small rotating boles of timber: they cost up to £6 each upon arrival at the Lake.

Later, William Banda, a Chancellor College student, turned up and we had cold drinks together at the Rest House.

The road to Chikale beach had been greatly improved and I was able to drive down the hill and park the car in the shade of trees. The cemetery at the edge of the beach had been fenced and now looks properly cared for. (18)

I asked a young fisherman named Barton Mamfwe whether he knew Lonely Nyirenda or Wellington Alumi. He said that Nyirenda was his cousin and Wellington lived nearby. He offered to take me to them so I followed him up the hillside till we came to Bwelelo village where I sat outside a house while Lonely and Wellington were found. Wellington had grown quite well and looked better fed this year. When I asked whether he remembered me, he said: 'Yes - you are Wilfred'. Lonely was thinner and did not look as well as I remembered him. Both boys seemed to have done well at school. Wellington obtained second place in his standard. (I had paid the small school fees required to keep them at St. Augustine's F.P. School and St. Maria Goretti F.P. School for two years). To help them with books, I gave them £1 each, but it was apparent they meant to spend it on shoes, not books. We gave them a lift to the Indian shops.

On the beach in the afternoon we talked to a family of fishermen; the father was a refugee from Portuguese territory and had come to Nkhata Bay via Likoma Island. His younger brother offered to show me another beach and after walking only a quarter of a mile we came to it, a very charming little bay with houses on a bank, a dug-out canoe in the shade of a tree and a stretch of fine silver sand that contrasted with the grit at one end of Chikale beach.

On the way back to Gladys and Jean, this boy asked whether I could find work for him in Blantyre as a cook or houseboy; he had previously worked in South Africa for five years. His name: John Longwe; address: Bwelelo, Headman Dinga, P.O. Nkhata Bay.

That evening the 'Ilala' came into harbour and a brother of William Banda allowed us on to the jetty so that we could see the ship at close quarters.

15 September: Nkhata-Bay to Lundazi.

A short distance out of Nkhata Bay we met the Tangri family from Chancellor College. Roger, a research associate in Sociology, with the help of students, had been discovering materials of historical interest that were the property of old people in local families. I told him about Chief Malenga at Nkhota-Kota.

From Mzuzu we crossed the Viphya to Mzimba - long winding hills, much afforestation, with more look-out posts than I remembered on the hill-tops. From Mzimba we went to Loudon along a forest road where we saw no other traffic. At the Customs and Immigration and Health Office in Moocha they had run out of forms in the Immigration building and asked us to report to the Immigration department in the government offices in Lundazi which - rather straggling and inadequately signposted - was our first town in Zambia.

We stayed the night at Lundazi Castle Hotel, a rest house built to look like a (highly pseudo) mediaeval castle, complete with turrets, crenellated walls and arched doorways. It was built totally of brick, incredibly ugly and ill-planned, especially inside, but the view from the windows was of great beauty - a peaceful lake with reeds and trees beginning a few yards from the water, and fish eagles and water birds flying and crying as the sun set. One of the main entrances was through a bathroom.

One of the first people we met on the domestic staff of the Castle was a former cook named Lackson who had been employed at Chancellor College; he was now a 'castle-boy', responsible for cleanliness of the rooms and Cardinal-redding of the floors; there was a distinctly mediaeval look about him.

This was a 'catering' castle but the meals, costing full hotel price, were vestigial and we ate them with disgust. The food was as unreal as the surroundings, but then, whoever expected to find Camelot, deserted by King Arthur and his knights - but inhabited by a rapacious caterer and a mediaeval Lackson - on the shore of a beautiful lake in the heart of central Africa?

I had asked the Zambia National Tourist Bureau to send to the 'Lundazi Rest House', for collection on 15 September, our entry permit granting permission to enter the Luangwa Valley Game Reserve. Nothing had arrived, however, at the Castle, or the equally mediaeval African Rest House, or at the Post Office, so on 16 September we continued hopefully, but illegally, into the Reserve.

From Lundazi we crossed a stream by a 'diversion' and set off for Luambe where we aspired to stay the night. To begin with the forest road was good but later we came to elephant country and through the hills it was stony, sandy and occasionally dangerous. Elephants had wrecked the whole forest, tearing down the small trees, stripping off the bark, leaving on the road enough droppings to nourish all the gardens of the University's rented houses. At one point where one could not easily force a way through the surrounding bush, a torn-down tree completely blocked the road.

While the three of us were trying to drag the heavy tree aside, a pickup - as if we had pressed a magic button - rattled up behind us and an Indian capitao and half a dozen Africans sprang out. This was an official road-clearing team which operated from Lundazi. We had been seen entering the Luambe road and someone had realized we should find it blocked. The Africans quickly macheted sufficient branches for us to pass, and again we set off.

But the road was only barely passable to a Volvo station wagon. Somewhere the engine broke partially out of its mounting; the heads of retaining bolts were shorn off; and we tore a large hole in the silencer. I did not know exactly what the damage was until 24 hours and 250 miles later when we clattered into Chipata.

Meanwhile, we reached the road barrier beyond which lay the Luangwa Valley Game Reserve, I showed the correspondence we had exchanged with the Tourist Bureau and we were allowed in, but we were told that Luambe Camp was closed.

We thought, however, we would call there, if only to see it. Several rondavels were empty but there were no beds. The trees were full of monkeys and scores of assorted antelopes walked nonchalantly along the sandy margin of the river. The forest was swarming with animals. But we had to go on to Nsefu, another 46 miles.

We passed several small herds of elephants and then, a few miles beyond Luambe, a new bicycle was lying at the side of the road and an elephant fifty yards away with rounded ears and raised trunk, was trumpeting at us and stamping its feet in anger. There was no time to see what had happened to the cyclist: simultaneously the elephant charged us and I accelerated hard and we tore off at forty miles an hour, leaving the elephant in a cloud of ochre dust.

Half a mile along the earth road, we heard a shout and an African youth, in a distressed state, ran out of the forest. His lips were parched almost white.

'*Njobvu!*' he said. '*Njobvu*, Bwana!'

The elephant had charged him but he had managed to run away into the forest. We gave him water and sat him in the car and I backed the car warily for half a mile till his bicycle was in sight. The elephant had gone; the bicycle was undamaged; and for the eight miles out of the Reserve he rode it in front of us till we reached a road barrier and the policeman there gave him more water.

At the next barrier - to Nsefu Camp - we were again allowed in, and told which earth road to take. We soon ran into animals - graceful impala and delicate fox-brown puku leapt in waves only a few yards ahead of the car; then there were zebra, and clouds of green-headed guineafowl and hundreds and hundreds of green love-birds in whizzing and whirring flocks. It was like driving through a ballet or symphony of animals and birds that poured away, quite unalarmed, as the car slowly advanced. We passed several elephants, some with calves, but all at a safe distance. But soon we realized that the road ahead was writhing with elephants. I backed behind bushes out of sight but they were not passing quickly and the daylight was going and I was anxious to get on. We therefore took an alternative 'road', only to find it blocked by a fallen tree; but we were able to make a rather scratchy detour, and within five minutes we were safely at Nsefu.

Rondavels were available, hot water was hissing in the water tanks connected with the bathrooms, but members of the Plumbe/Johnston safari were too exhausted to wash until we had drunk some hot tea. As we sat drinking it, a large bull elephant ambled out of the trees fifty yards from the open-air dining room and casually ate the seeds that had fallen from a *chikuyu* tree.

That night, after a large dinner to compensate for the frugality of Lundazi Castle, we retired early to our rondavels and, as I tried without much success to sleep, hippos and crocodiles burped in the river, a miscellany of unidentifiable animals snarled, whined, grunted and sniffed outside the good solid walls of the rondavel, and during the night an elephant tore down a branch with a tremendous crash that sounded only yards away but was actually at least eighty yards away. There were balls of elephant dung six feet from the rondavels and comments in the 'Visitors' Book' mentioned that a few nights earlier elephants had tried to get in at the door of one rondavel and had scraped the mosquito wire with their trunks.

When at last I slept I had a nightmare in which we were being charged from all sides by trumpeting elephants.

At 6:30 a.m. next morning Patrick Nguni, the game guard in charge of the Camp, took us walking in the forest. There were a great many antelopes and also wart-hogs and elephants and many birds ; a leopard coughed across the river; a lion called to his mate or mates in the long grass. Patrick told us that baboons take the partially digested seeds from elephant dung and eat them. Elephant dung looked so delectable - from a strawberry and tomato point of view - I wished I could carry a few sacks of it back to Blantyre. Alas, we saw no cats, although a week earlier twelve lions had been seen and a few weeks before that no less than twenty-four, one of which had charged the party of visitors.

On 17 September I drove to Chipata and Consolidated Motors examined the car, kept it for several hours and claimed they had repaired it. We stayed at the Crystal Springs Hotel in Chipata which was very comfortable so that we felt we really were back in 'civilization'. Before leaving, we visited the Regional Library which was charming and swarming with members, especially children: we thought it might be taken as a model by Malawi's National Library Service.

In Chipata I paid my debts and made my peace with the Chief Game Warden who seemed shocked we should have got into the Game Reserve without an entry permit.

Thirty miles out of Chipata the Volvo engine broke loose and the noise was worse than ever. In Lilongwe I took the car to Hall's garage but they referred me to Constantini - who actually mended it. But we had to stay a night at the Lilongwe Hotel.

19 September: Left Lilongwe very late. Had lunch at Maciel & Filhos Hotel near Dedza. Came back via Zomba and arrived in Limbe about 7:00 p.m. Called on Ann and Brian Yarr to let them know we were back; then came home; unpacked the house; scraped a jigger out of one of my toes; Jean and Gladys had baths but I was worn out and had only a wash before going to bed.

Next day I collected a fortnight's mail from the Library and spent the day convalescing in preparation for work on 21 September.

* * * * * * * * * *

Jean went off to Australia. A whole year passed. I went to UK on long overdue leave and visited Lusaka on my way back to Malawi in August 1969. Gladys stayed on in UK for two months and arrived back on 4 November 1969.

From my diary 1969

7 September 1969

The Commonwealth Foundation Conference of Commonwealth Africa University Librarians, held at the University of Zambia, Lusaka, 25-29 August, was very successful, and I greatly enjoyed meeting the other participants. I had not previously met John Ndegwa of Kenya, Tucker Lwanga of Uganda, Martin Mvaa of Tanzania, Rita Pankhurst of Ethiopia and EY. Amedekey of Ghana. President Kenneth Kaunda (recipient of seven honorary doctorates) opened the new Library building on Wednesday afternoon. I submitted my paper on 'Classification and cataloguing of Africana' on Thursday morning. There were numerous parties and it was quite the most alcoholic conference I have ever attended. After one party some of the delegates sang songs in English, French, German, Russian, Latin, Swahili and Amharic, Jim Pearson of the School of Oriental and African Studies and Rita being the chief songsters.

We stayed in students' hostels which were spartan but quite adequate for a few days, and on Saturday Tony Loveday, the convenor, moved Jim Pearson and me into his house. He took us out one evening to the Blue Boar - now re-named 'The Copper Chalice' - and on Sunday we drove to the Kafue River and watched a dozen hippos in the river, some of them young calves.

I also had dinner one evening with the Krishnamurthys (he is an historian) who were formerly at Ahmadu Bello University. The new University of Zambia library building is colossal, ugly outside - until trees grow up around it, as intended - but functional inside except perhaps for a 40-foot high fountain in the light well which tends to become clogged with cigarette ends and several species of frogs.

Jim Pearson and I left on Monday and flew straight to Blantyre. I had to pay £5.16.0 for carriage of my Moroccan carpet which British Airways had transported free of charge from London to Lusaka but at Chileka airport I claimed it was my 'household effects' and paid no duty to bring it into the country.

Ann and Brian of the library staff met me at the airport, together with Marion and Jeff Stickley from the bindery and Liz Berreen also from Zomba. Ann had kindly bought in provisions for my pantry and as it was lunch time when we arrived the Zomba contingent brought me to the house in Jeff's car and - once we had carried all essentials out of my locked study and dumped them where they belonged - Million the cook (who succeeded Ali) hastily improvised lunch from tins and the provisions Ann had deposited. Lunch (and conversation) lasted till about 5:30 and then Marion, Jeff and Liz went back to Zomba.

The house was perfectly all right. Million had washed all the floors and I got everything completely sorted out by midnight. The strawberries are still alive in the garden; Million says Smart has eaten them, so far, but probably they are only just beginning to fruit. Peas and beans are growing well but not yet ready for eating, and later there will be cabbages. The Jeffreys - my neighbours - have erected a grass fence between their garden and ours, opposite the servants' garden. There is a good deal of fencing to be done and Smart has already started collecting the necessary grass. (19)

On Monday I dealt with library matters.

Then on Tuesday Jim Pearson moved out of the Shire Highlands Hotel and came to stay with me. On Tuesday I took him to Zomba to visit the library bindery and the Government Archives. We had lunch with Marion and Jeff at Ku Chawe Inn on Zomba mountain, then drove and walked around the mountain. Notices have been posted up at the Inn and at Chingwe's Hole stating that lions have been seen and that children should not be allowed to stray from paths. There are also lions at Kasupe and one child has been eaten. (In 1993 the Ku Chawe Inn was severely damaged by fire).

On Wednesday Gordon Hazeldine took Jim to Bunda. He had chartered a plane but it failed to turn up so he had to use the Leopard Air Service. That evening I gave a party for Jim, the guests being Marion and Jeff, Joan and Richard from Domasi, Swanzie and Fulque, Gordon, Isaac Lamba an administrative assistant, Mupa Shumba a lecturer in English, Dick Najira, Elias Kambalame, Fred Johnson the Director of the Malawi National Library Service, and Peggy Robinson. Ann and Brian were invited but Brian had malaria so they couldn't come. I borrowed their cook Kananji, however, to cope with the sweets, and we had five chickens, savoury rice, green salad, cheese in green peppers, three delicious pastries a la Kananji, cream and ice cream, and some South African wine.

On Thursday I took Jim to the University Office, the Polytechnic, Soche Hill College, the Institute of Public Administration at Mpemba, and the National Library Service, and we had lunch with Fred Johnson. I did a little work in the afternoon but it was midnight before we went to bed.

On Friday Jim left at 5:30 p.m. for Rhodesia.

Now that I have had time to re-collect my wits, I find that at work things are no more calamitous than I expected. My secretary has resigned and gone to Bonn with her husband. The bright young men I found for Soche Hill College and the Institute of Public Administration - Kenneth Wheeler for the SHC and Gaaffar Hassam for IPA - have both left and two new assistants have been appointed, one of whom does not have the required qualifications. The building of the new library at Soche Hill College has begun. Pat Larby has resigned from the Polytechnic and taken a job in Nairobi.

The house that was being re-built on the land next to us at Chirimba is now occupied.

Smart has killed two snakes in the garden.

14 September

Yesterday I was out to dinner at the Agnews. Swanzie wore a scarlet dress with a gold and scarlet Indian scarf and looked magnificent against a background of Agnew heirlooms. The other guests were the Uttings (John Utting is Dean, Chancellor College) and the Luckhams (he is the new Director of Extension Services and his wife is Guyanese). Swanzie's cook was too drunk to come into the house and the other servants dropped cutlery half a dozen times.

It was at this party Swanzie told me that when she and Fulque stayed at Nkhata Bay Rest House, one of the hens belonging to John Kamanga, the manager, came into their room each day and laid an egg in the waste paper basket.

While I was on leave a large number of murders were perpetrated in Zingwangwa, the township near Limbe. Other murders have taken place in villages between Mulanje and Zomba - all because of a rumour that the President has promised to repay a £4 million loan from South Africa with the blood - for medicinal purposes - of Malawians. Three policemen have been killed by Youth Leaguers; officials of the Malawi Congress Party have been made to *eat* their party membership cards. One day last week McNight Kamanja (ex library, now employed on the Lake Chilwa Research Project) turned up at my office saying he had come in from the Lake as he was afraid of being murdered since people thought he was involved in the collection of blood for South Africa. (20) The 'Blood' rumour has been denounced by the President who says it was started by rebels outside Malawi. According to Kamanja police reinforcements have been sent to villages around Mulanje in order to maintain public order. Certainly there has been a curfew in Zingwangwa.

I have bought a hundred yards of nylon fishing net from Horace Hickling (for 22/-) to cover the 450 strawberry plants. The birds have begun to eat the fruit. Each day Jim Pearson was here I managed to find enough strawberries for his breakfast and I have eaten several handfuls myself this past week. The mulberry tree at the corner of the strawberry plot is fruiting profusely. In the flower garden there has been a flush of carnations and I have taken some to Ann Yarr and Marion Stickley.

To-day there has been a flurry of rain. Ndirande mountain is still russet and gold and umber and burnt sienna and half a dozen shades of blue, all the winter tints of grass and foliage.

Small yellow wagtails and the neighbours' dogs are drinking from the bird bath.

27 September

Lonely Nyirenda from Nkhata Bay turned up on Saturday and stayed until Wednesday instead of departing on Monday as I expected. Then on Wednesday Hilary Fry, a lecturer of the Zoology Department, Ahmadu Bello University, Nigeria, turned up on one of his international expeditions in search of bee-eaters and I had him to lunch at one hour's notice. To-day, with Ann and Brian, I have been to Zomba and we had lunch with Marion and Jeff. We drove up Zomba mountain so that Ann and Brian might see Chingwe's Hole. I think they enjoyed it although with no railings and precipices dropping 3,000 feet, almost under one's shoes, it is a terrifying place in which to have small children running around.

At home Smart has continued fencing of the garden and he has made a small internal fence to keep our neighbours' dogs off the flowers. Million has washed all the blankets; I shall now see whether he can tackle numdas. I have equipped both servants with new tailor-made uniforms, Million in white, Smart in pale blue. Million, aged about sixty, is really the most reliable and faithful - and by far the thinnest - servant we have ever had: totally honest and a remarkable source of forbidden news and gossip. (A Sena from Mozambique, sadly now gone to his rest. One hopes that in his hereafter he is still allowed to drink his full on Sundays even if he allows himself only a frugal consumption of local beer during the rest of the week.)

4 October

On Tuesday our two VSOs for Chancellor College library arrived on the VC.10. They are Kathy Pain, 21, tall, strawberry blonde, who claims that her hobbies are swimming and fencing; and Moira Woods, 25, Irish, round faced, who has been a journalist before becoming a librarian. Both have obtained an ALA after passing through the College of Librarianship Wales. Bruce Nightingale, Representative of the British Council, was also at the airport to meet them and he carried them off to tea at his house. Later I transported them to their flat and organized a welcome party at our house in the evening, the guests being Margaret and Willie Kalk, Sir Fulque Agnew (Swanzie is away), Fred Johnson, Ellen and Vim van Zanten, Dick Najira, Godwin Shaba and Owen Kalinga. We had curried rice, three roasted chickens, savoury rice, strawberries and ice-cream and some wine.

On Thursday the temperature in the library reading room was 102 degrees Fahrenheit.

8 October

Staff meeting of senior and intermediate library staff at 2:00 p.m., lasting till 4:00 p.m. Attendance: Gordon Hazeldine, Ann, Brian, Kathy Pain, Moira Woods, Dick Najira, Peggy Robinson, Stephen Thompson, Margaret Gunn, Jeffrey Stickley, Ken Rawlings, Boniface Semu and Jenny Jarvis (IPA). Too much a monologue by WJP, but I hope it will help as far as staff cohesion is concerned.

At the end of the day I received a note from the library messenger Joseph Thom. He had not paid his rent and the landlord had locked him out of his house. He wrote:

> Know what I am going to do? I am going to sleep out side to-day and I am going to sleep with hungly too. My lod don't live me to die with somethings this night.

Of course, I handed over the necessary 30/- that will enable him to get back into his house and buy some *nsima*. I shall never see this again - or ask for it, I suppose.

During the week Smart has continued building the grass fence around the garden of the Chirimba house.

On the frangipani narrow leaves have uncurled like red claws.

This morning a raven was wiping its beak on an exposed root of the rain tree after it had eaten some ghoulish object on the edge of the bird bath.

On Tuesday Owen Kalinga, who has just graduated, joined the library staff as a trainee assistant librarian. On Wednesday notification of his postgraduate scholarship to Birmingham to study History was received - and he vanished again.

Tomorrow afternoon I plan to take the Yarr family and the two VSOs to visit the family of Dick Najira at Luchenza near Mulanje mountain. I have bought a plastic container of 'Fruit Cup', comb honey, pilchards, pickles, tins of curried beef, and tinned fruit instead of the traditional gift of poultry or a sheep.

9 October

The jacarandas are in magnificent bloom all over the Shire Highlands, even in our garden, and the frangipani is about to flower.

There are bishop birds, sunbirds, bulbuls, wagtails and ravens in and around the garden, and some of the birds are so tame they fly down to the bird bath as soon as Smart has filled it with clean water.

11 October

I am still struggling to write my book of war-time experiences in East and Central Africa. It has reached 45,000 words, but running the Library and running this house - not much less than operating a rest house - sometimes leave me limp. It has been so hot I have little energy, even in the very early morning and late at night.

This afternoon we had a thunderstorm and the sky spat enough rain to lay the dust.

The glory of the jacaranda - whole avenues in bloom - is fading now and tarmac roads and dusty roads are hyacinthine blue with fallen flowers. Frangipani is in flower, coral pink and waxy cream.

12 October

This house is more historic than I realized when we moved here on 20 November 1967 (almost two years ago). It was built by Ishmael Surtee, the present Speaker in Parliament, after the firm he owned in Balaka went into liquidation. The actual bricks were baked from clay dug out of the pit between this plot and Jusab's. In 1954 Surtee was leader of the Coloured community. From 1959 he supported Dr Banda and according to my neighbour Jeffreys there was a great deal of feeling against him during the disturbances of 1959, so that it was feared the whole Surtee family might be murdered. They all took refuge in this house and for several nights a friend of the family, Cliff Wintle a Coloured man, mounted guard on the roof of the house with a machine-gun.

On Thursday the father and sister of Dick Najira turned up at the Library, so I felt obliged to have them to lunch along with Dick. There wasn't really enough meat but Dick and I went a bit short and we coped. I think the Najira contingent enjoyed the visit - they are a delightful family. (21)

19 October

On Wednesday I had supper with our neighbours, Jeff and Rubia Jeffreys. They have added a dining-room to their house.

It was a pleasant meal with Raymond, the eldest boy, sitting at the table. They have offered me a dog - one of their ten Alsatians - but I feel quite safe at night and, as tactfully as possible, I have not accepted.

Friday was a public holiday and I took most of it off in order to get on with my book. I have ground my way up to 58,000 words. My only spare time is in the early morning. I sometimes get up at 3:00 a.m., sometimes at 4:00 a.m., but I haven't always the mental energy required so I have started taking Multivite.

27 October

Some of the seeds I planted a week ago are now coming up. Agapanthus and other lilies will soon be in flower. Smart should finish the fencing today: it greatly improves the garden and if we can persuade flowering creepers to establish themselves on it, there should be pleasing patches of colour quite quickly.

Blantyre and Zomba have both had rain, but here in Chirimba we are in the rain shadow of Ndirande mountain and we have had only a few drops.

Am still plodding away at my book. Have done 69,000 words and I hope to finish it before Gladys arrives on 4 November.

3 November

The garden, thanks mainly to Smart, is now in a fit state to be seen by Gladys.

On Wednesday I bought a load of rooted perennials - cannas, geraniums, white daisies, verbena, a yellow creeper that attracts birds, and several other flowers I like but don't know the names of - so that one triangular flower bed is full of orange, yellow, mauve, gold, cerise, carmine, pink, various blues, white and purple, with several plants about to flower. On Friday we had rain which lasted half an hour and did a great deal of good.

The writing of the book is finished. It is about 78,000 words in length and I finished it at 4:00 p.m. yesterday. I have only the preliminaries and perhaps an index to complete, and the latter can only be done when, and if, it gets into print. It is the story of my introduction to Africa.

My sleeping hours have been very erratic this past week. Yesterday I had lunch at 6:45 p.m.

5 November

Gladys arrived safely from UK yesterday afternoon.

30 November

My book will have 33 and perhaps as many as 50 photographs as illustrations. Peter Morgan, a young chemist working on the Lake Chilwa Research Project, has kindly made more enlargements from the negatives I have hoarded for twenty-five years. To bring it to completion I had to reduce my work for the University to the official (revised) 42 hours a week.

The last few days have been HOT. Yesterday, just before dark, we had fifteen minutes' rain. For several days the ants in the garden have been migrating, looking for water. Several billion of them have disappeared into a hole in the ground above the septic tank. This morning there appeared to be a zigzag crack in the lawn - but it was moving, and it was merely another million ants from the Jeffreys' land en route to our septic tank.

The uncle of one of our bookbinders has been killed fighting with the 'rebels': I am not clear whether this is the anti-Banda 'rebels' who have been driven out of the country or the Frelimo who are in Mozambique. It is not known (at least to me) whether the fighting took place at Nkhota-Kota or across the Lake in Mozambique.

The death penalty can now be imposed by District Courts and as a result four expatriate Judges have resigned.

7 December

The rains have come - at Chirimba nothing violent so far, but the lawn is growing grass and more than fifty *Cossum spectabilis* have burst into golden flower and their large saucer-shaped leaves, edged with gold, have been flattened by the rain. Blue agapanthus, white and yellow daisies, salvias, petunias, zinnias, verbenas and various lilies - all are in flower, and the morning glory vines have produced shimmering capes of brilliant cobalt flowers.

In the vegetable garden the cabbages have been ravaged by locusts. We have begun to pick mangoes from the garden trees as well as buy them in the market.

Ndirande and all the other mountains are transformed: the sky is washed clear of dust and smoke from fires; mealies have begun their upward spurt; the whole countryside is green; the evening air is fluttering with termites, every street light is bombarded by beetles and sausage flies. Makanjira Road is already grooved by water channels.

17 December

Last Friday Gladys and I and Margaret and Willie Kalk and Blodwen Binns went to Bunda, returning on Monday this week. There was a tour of the College farm on Saturday morning and a meeting of Senate on Saturday afternoon. We all stayed in the Women's Hostel in the flat occupied by Margaret Gunn and Gill Copeland; students and members of the Peace Corps drifted in and out of the flat; the girls have a large dog named 'Usiku' (22) whose tail scimitared everything within range.

On Sunday we all went to Salima. Blodwen collected plants, seeds and fungi; Gladys rested in the rondavel at the top of the beach; Margaret and Willie and I swam in the Lake. (23)

The new library building at Bunda has been occupied and in use for eight months. Bunda is now the best developed of the University's colleges. The buildings are attractive and well-spaced, housing is very good, and the setting on the plain with Bunda Rock - home of the Rain God - nearby and hills on the horizon is very pleasant. There are obvious financial advantages to staff living at Bunda. The College Farm produces beef and pork which is sold at 1/6 a pound (c.f. 5/- or 6/- in Blantyre) and locally produced vegetables are also incredibly cheap. Petrol is available from the College pump at less than the local price in Lilongwe. On the whole, one detects a sense of purpose - even of drive - at Bunda which is totally lacking in Chancellor College.

On Monday we set off from Bunda at 7:30 a.m. and arrived back in Blantyre at about 3:30 p.m. after making short halts - to collect butter yellow orchids for Blodwen at the northern end of the Angoni Highlands, to buy peaches and potatoes from a line of dirty under-nourished children at a roadside village and to inspect the small stucco pyramid that commemorates the death of Jedere on 23 February 1953. We made a longer stop at the home of Joan and Richard Allen in Domasi upon whom we descended without notice in the best African tradition - and Richard at once provided drinks and Joan miraculously produced an impromptu light lunch in the lap. (24) The roads have been greatly improved by long stretches of excellent tarmac along which one can speed at 85 m.p.h.

28 December

The 'Cow Barn' leaked in fifty-one places during the storm on 24 December: it was found later that the bolts holding down the roof had not been provided with collars to keep out the rain.

Transport lorries - i.e. "Swift" lorries that normally bring Rhodesian fruit, especially peaches, to Blantyre and Limbe at Christmas time - this year stuck in the mud twelve miles short of Chileka. It is not known what became of the drivers - or the peaches.

In the great Christmas orgy in Blantyre five people died in road accidents and others were trampled to death in a mad fight to get on to buses at the bus station.

One night there was a disturbance in our garden as two heavy animals thudded around the bungalow under the bedroom windows. In the morning we found the spoor of a hyena. An Alsatian dog from next door had evidently chased it and the hyena went out of the garden through the grass gate like a circus performer through a paper hoop; the spoor led into one of the big erosion gullies. It must have been a very old hyena as it left scratches from its long toe nails on the brick path.

From my diary 1970

7 January

The rains have made it possible for every part of the garden to be put to use. Smart had planted 750 mounds of groundnuts on the Jusab side of the bungalow, and the waste land between the lawn and the vegetable garden has been box ridged and planted with beans, cucumbers, groundnuts, pumpkins and custard apples. As seed I bought the large variety of groundnuts that is available in Lunzu market. We are now eating our own beans and cabbage and there should soon be another crop of peas.

16 January

Thanks to the rain maize is four feet high in the Shire Highlands. Farther south the Shire river has overflowed, the Chiromo ferry has been closed and flood relief measures have been taken. There has been an outbreak of mass murder at Ndirande which is rather near to us at Chirimba. The Malawi Broadcasting Corporation and the newspapers have not reported it but we have several library staff who live in Ndirande and they say that ten nights ago houses were broken into by the 'rebels' and ten people were hacked to death and six others wounded. As a result there has been a riot situation and the Police have used tear gas to disperse demonstrators. The Army moved in and a platoon of soldiers camped in tents near the Police station in Chileka Road.

Since then everybody goes to bed at night with cutlasses, iron bars and whatever other weapons they possess lying at their elbows; and we lock the back door of our bungalow early in the evening.

Two nights ago there was a scare a few hundred yards from this house, but with my capacity for sleeping through riots, gang fights and civil insurrections I had a particularly good sleep that night.

At the other side of the railway line is an empty house belonging to Brown & Clapperton, an engineering company. Six men were seen at this house and someone rushed to inform Jeffreys our neighbour. He reported at once to the Police in Chileka Road but the Police are alleged to have wasted four hours composing a report and only when that was available was a platoon of thirty-five soldiers armed with Sten guns and three Bren guns and their officers armed with revolvers and hand grenades, rushed to Chirimba where they surrounded the house concerned, all in bright moonlight. Of course, by that time the 'rebels', squatters, axe-gang, or whoever it was, had melted away into the ravines of the mountain and nobody was caught, although the following morning I was told privately that a Sena man had been captured. According to rumour the 'axe murders' were committed by ZANU or Frelimo or terrorists organized by Chipembere.

In the night, while I slept, an Army lorry was parked outside our bungalow and Smart chatted to the local Commandos. Now the tented encampment at Chileka Road Police Station has been dismantled and we don't know where the Army has gone.

20 January

A small alarm about 8:00 p.m. yesterday evening. After hearing a noise somewhere in the African darkness I switched on the yard electric light which revealed a group of strange men armed with heavy sticks standing outside the back door (which was locked). It was a relief to see that one of them was Smart the gardener.

They had with them an unknown man from a hut on the mountain whose primus stove had exploded when he was lighting it. His face was badly burned, he had lost his eyebrows and some of his hair but much worse were his arms and hands. Burnt flesh hung in grey strips from the raw flesh of his forearms. The men with the sticks had already taken him to a nearby bungalow occupied by Europeans but they had been driven away, probably because they looked like a gang of nocturnal murderers.

All we could do was get out the car and rush the man who was burned to the casualty ward at Queen Elizabeth General Hospital in Blantyre. Gladys hastily draped her Shetland shawl round the man's naked body to keep him warm - his teeth were chattering with cold - and we gave him aspirins to swallow but he showed no sign of pain - so Smart and one of the 'stick-men' came with me in the car and we dashed four miles through the darkness to the hospital. There the 'stick-man' remained to guard the patient, who was at once taken away for treatment, and Smart returned with me.

(Several months later this man - his name still unknown - came to thank us and return the shawl. The hospital doctors had patched him up very skilfully with skin grafted on to his forearms, his eyes were uninjured, his eyebrows had grown again, and he was pleased with himself. Gladys gave him her shawl as a memento of the incident.)

24 January

A life insurance policy I have paid for many years has matured and with the proceeds, plus a gratuity from the University in respect of my first three years work in Malawi, we have enough money to contemplate buying a house as an investment.

There are several properties available at prices far below those demanded by estate agents in Britain.

One we have looked at belongs to Mrs Rosie Bell, just out of Chigumula along the Thyolo Road. It is a seventeen acre plot half a mile from the main road, fringed with eucalyptus trees, with a superb view of Mulanje mountain. The bungalow is at the top end of the plot, it has five bedrooms, a lounge, a dog room, an office, two kitchens, a dining-room, a scullery, various stores and two guest houses, one of them attached to the main house, one detached. I think there are three bathrooms, maybe four. There is mains water and electricity, a bore-hole which provides overhead irrigation for the garden, and in a kind of paddock several plank buildings that formerly housed 5,000 hens and twenty pigs, some of which now accommodate white turkeys. In front of the bungalow is a flower garden. The vegetable garden is spurting with green stuff and the fruit trees include peach, William pear, tree tomato and the usual tropical fruits. Rosie says that in times past she grew half a ton of grapes a year, and she doesn't know of any vegetable that will not grow in her garden. I believe her acres, enriched by the offerings of 5,000 poultry and other livestock, must be among the most fertile in Malawi, which means in Africa.

There must be several hundred gum trees.

All this she is willing to sell for £6,500 freehold. I have had to say 'No' although if I had twice as much money I would buy it without a second thought.

This part of the Shire Highlands seems to be sprinkled with charming old ladies most of whom, outside Africa, would be regarded as 'eccentric'. They are all widows, neither poor nor - with one exception - fantastically rich.

One of the less wealthy is Mrs Grace Hilda Snowden, widow of the former Chief Engineer of the Imperial Tobacco Company. She has been in Malawi since her marriage 57 years ago (in 1913) and she must be around 84. In appearance she is slightly bent by age and weather-beaten by the tropics, but she dresses smartly, has over thirty pairs of shoes, makes regular visits to a hairdresser and wears 'Albert', her hearing aid, on all convivial occasions which she obviously enjoys. In the past she and her husband lived rather grandly with many servants and a dinghy, cabin cruiser and a yacht on the Lake, and she still uses her Crown Derby dinner service for parties. Her eyes are chips of blue ice but she has a kind heart and a wide circle of friends. Now she feels she can no longer cope with her three houses and gardens and wants to move to another house and would be willing to sell her private Shangri-La to us for £5,000.

The plot is two miles out of Limbe, on the side of Mpingwe Hill, at the end of a steep dirt road, and again the property is fringed by huge gum trees. The bungalow is much smaller than Rosie Bell's having merely a diningroom, a large bedroom, a dressing room, a bathroom, a second bedroom, a third bedroom which could be used as a writing room, a kitchen and a store. The servants' quarters are good, and there are wattle and daub out-buildings some of which act as potting sheds, garden stores, or else accommodate an ever varying number of ducks some of which end up as the local equivalent of pate de foie gras. At the back of the house is a garage for the Snowden Vauxhall. The bungalow is not beautiful outside but it is well-built and above average for Malawian houses inside. There is a fenced garden and a prospect of Mt. Mulanje and the Luchenza plain.

If Mrs Snowden - whom we refer to as 'The Old Lady' -can move we have agreed to buy this house. It was the sight of 3,000 strawberry plants, still fruiting in January, and the atmosphere of utter peace surrounding the house, that really decided us.

The Old Lady has another house - Plot 7, Senga Bay - that she is willing to sell to us for £4,000. This 'holiday cottage' is right on Senga Bay but constructed twelve feet above the highest known level of the Lake. The foundations of stone and brick cost £2,500; it has large rooms, including two bathrooms. There is a kitchen, a laundry room, a workshop, an engine room, a store and three 'quarters' for servants, all detached from the house. Inland is a prospect of the Senga Hills. The Old Lady says it is the best built house on the Lake. We shall go up to Senga Bay and inspect it and, if Gladys likes it, we shall buy that, too, as an investment. Of course, I don't have an extra £4,000 but the Old Lady would be quite happy to take a deposit and monthly payments for the balance.

At the Library I am gradually plodding through arrears of work. Moira Woods has taken over the acquisitions section and it seem likely she will be a success at it, which will be one job off my mind. The use being made of the library is terrific and I feel we are making a very solid contribution to the work of the University.

31 January

On Friday, Gladys and I attended an exhibition of Malawian traditional dances at Chancellor College Hall. The dances were: Ingoma (which means 'war dance'), the Malipenga, Nyau, Ndingala and Masikitiko. The show was organized by the University Cultural Society. One sees more spirited dancing in the villages where the sexual theme of most of the dances is allowed to be much more apparent, but it was a colourful spectacle and it cannot be often that expatriates are permitted to catch a glimpse of the Nyau dance without being a member of the semi-secret society of that name. (25)

We have had the Old Lady and Margaret Kalk to lunch. The O.L. ate hardly anything as she had to go out to dinner later on; Margaret did better even although her colon gets knotted if she over-eats. All rather a pity as Gladys had excelled herself with chicken cooked in wine and a meringue fantasia of fruit, ice-cream and cream. Snowden reminiscences included:

Coming up the Zambezi in a house-boat, i.e. a canoe partially roofed with thatch, surrounded by 'naked natives';

Being carried up Mulanje mountain in a machila, borne by eight men, in three relays;

Refusing to seek refuge on islands in Lake Malawi, as the District Commissioner wanted, at the time of the Chilembwe Rising in 1915;

Sleeping with nuns and other European women and men in a tobacco barn on bales of tobacco during the 'troubles', presumably in 1959;

Having to charter an aeroplane to get food to Salima when three weeks constant rain in some past year cut the railway in three places, washed away the road, washed away the chickens in the villages - and, indeed, some of the villages.

Apparently the Cottage at Senga Bay cost £1,500 to complete after the foundations had been laid. When it was first built lions regularly prowled round the house at night and there was no road to it; it had to be approached by a track running near the present Fish Eagle Inn. One lion used to sit outside the cook's quarters for the first hour of daylight and prevent servants coming to work at 6:00 a.m. The builder of the Cottage, in the 1920s was a man named Warren who was known to have spent £10,000 (not his own money) in one year; he was once seen chasing his mistress with a knife along the street beside the present Co-op. shop in Limbe. (More reminiscences).

Of local land prices, the Old Lady recalled that it was the father of Bill Fiddes and Margaret Fiddes (whom we have met) who once owned Bangwe, Mpingwe and Limbe, having bought the whole area for half a crown an acre. In more recent years land sold by Ruth Partridge for £7.10.0 an acre is now being offered for re-sale at £1,750 an acre.

1 February

Various aspects of the Library service are being criticized.

On 24 January I received a note from Blodwen enclosing a copy of a circular which two social scientists at Chancellor College had sent to academic staff

throughout the University. It invited everyone to comment on whether he or she found 'the Bliss system of cataloguing'
a) Very satisfactory
b) Satisfactory
c) Neither satisfactory nor unsatisfactory
d) Unsatisfactory
e) Very unsatisfactory

(The 'a' to 'e' categories had been lifted from an elementary text-book on sociology). A second question asked recipients to state whether they preferred the Bliss system of 'cataloguing', the Library of Congress system, or the Dewey Decimal system. A third question was about 'books on reserve', and the same questions as in the first section were asked.

I was not sent a copy of the questionnaire by its originators, nor was the Vice-Chancellor or any member of the library staff. Blodwen had completed her copy, coming out solidly in favour of the Library's methods. Bridglal Pachai, Professor of History, told me he had torn up his copy as he considered the questionnaire ridiculous.

There were several developments:
1   I was invited to attend a meeting of the Social Sciences and Administration Group Board;
2   I discovered that a member of the English department staff has asked students to complete another circular encouraging them to criticize the Library;
3   Three of the editorial staff of the students' magazine *Expression* came to interview me and I talked to them for three-quarters of an hour. At first they were rather 'anti' and trying to make mischief but I gave them quiet answers that were factual and financial and they subsequently published a fair report that may have helped to calm what was becoming an inflammatory situation. (Maybe they will help to inject a little sense and courtesy into some of their lecturers).

8 February

I appeared before the Social Science and Administration Group Board on Tuesday, 3 February, feeling rather like a prisoner in the dock. There should have been 34 people present but only 13 turned up. The two social scientists (one of whom had been in the University less than a month), the lecturer from the English department (whose circular was supposed to be a 'Social Psychology research project'), a lecturer of the Institute of Public Administration, and a member of Soche Hill College staff were the principal critics. Two of them made an emotional attack on me personally, accusing me of inefficiency; the others asked questions which they hoped, presumably, I would be unable to answer satisfactorily, but they were so naive that I felt reassured.

After I left - so I was told - the meeting developed 'into hysteria' and was inconclusive, although the minutes included eight recommendations - mostly that we should do things that have been in practice for months and, in some cases, years.

One needs a good nerve and the capacity to remain calm and factual on these occasions: they are not mentioned in books on library administration and yet they occur in academic libraries from time to time.

At Senate last Thursday the minutes of the Social Science and Administration Group Board should have been considered but before the meeting started the Chairman came to me and said he proposed to have the recommendations of the Board referred to the Library Committee - which is what I had told him, in writing, was the correct procedure to follow. In Senate this referral was made in the nick of time. I knew that several professors in the natural science departments were poised to 'tear the social scientists into shreds' if they had half a chance. The Vice-Chancellor, who had more experience of universities than the social scientists, warned their Chairman: in Senate, referral to the Library Committee took place adroitly and at top speed.

After the meeting the Vice-Chancellor called at my office to express his regret about the questionnaire; and I was told separately that two of those concerned received written reprimands for their part in the matter. Let us hope that this unsavoury episode is now at an end. (26)

9 February

It is now Tuesday morning and after a night's rain and thunder the whole world - even our garden at 3,300 feet - is swathed in *chiperoni*. We were at Domasi on Sunday, visiting Joan and Richard. Their home is unbearably hot. Last week the rains were so heavy that the road between Liwonde and the Lake was cut; the radio announced that 120 people were homeless on Likoma Island as the result of a rainstorm there; and owing to enormous floods there is chaos in the Lower Shire Valley.

16 February

The University's Administration has had to manoeuvre with unaccustomed speed this past week. Although the Chairman of Council had asked John Utting to continue as Dean and Professor of Economics at Chancellor College for another year, it became known that Utting had declined.

This means that pressure for a Malawian Principal by many of the academic staff cannot be ignored. Much of the last Senate meeting was concerned with proposals for 'Malawianization' which had been asked for by Senate but which had been diverted to the General Purposes Committee. Felix Mnthali of Chancellor College and Lewis Mughogho of Bunda College of Agriculture had prepared a memorandum which some of us had not seen; the Vice-Chancellor had to yield to clamour at the meeting that it be made available to all members of Senate, and at the end of the meeting Felix stood at the exit - like a newsboy with a Late Night Special - handing copies to all who wanted it.

It suggests that the vice-chancellor should be a Malawian, that all the principals should be Malawians, that Malawians should be on all important committees, that the Administration should be totally Malawianized, and that the teaching staff should be Malawianized as soon as possible. It points out where suitably qualified Malawians can be found.

Not all the memorandum is accurate and the paragraph about the Library is almost wholly inaccurate. I hope I can get it corrected.

The memorandum was not officially presented to Senate as the General Purposes Committee - on which there is only one Malawian - had not concluded consideration of it before the meeting of Senate.

Earlier that day Dr Peter Mwanza, who is the obvious candidate for Principal at Chancellor College, had been promoted from lecturer to senior lecturer; and immediately before the meeting of Senate the Administration added to the agenda a note that John Banda would be made deputy university registrar in September this year and university registrar in September 1971.

As John Leisten put it, the memorandum had obviously 'scared the pants off the Administration'.

22 February

We have received an anonymous letter informing us that one of the students was forming his own private collection of books stolen from the Library. John Banda and I, together with the Warden, examined the room of the student concerned and we retrieved fourteen books and one journal which should not have been in his possession; many of the books had book-cards still in them. This University is too soft and permissive to expel any student but I hope the Principal, Chancellor College, and his disciplinary committee will take reasonably fierce action.

To-day I walked into a swarm of wild bees on the campus; by some miracle I was able to beat them off with my hands without being stung while I fled at my top speed of 9 m.p.h.

A pretty blue aster is in flower. Golden zinnias are six feet high and dominate the flower bed. A sulphur yellow dahlia is also in flower. The cucumber plants have garnished themselves with a few pigmy cucumbers, round, oval, egg-shaped, some studded with spikes, others quite smooth.

Esnath, wife of Million the cook, is drunk again and as we retire for the night I can hear her shrieking at the servants' quarters.

3 March

It is the cicada season. Before going to bed each night G. and I go round the garden and lawn with an electric torch and my Kashmir sword-stick, trying to slaughter the murderers of sleep. The insect has a burrow in soft soil and after darkness falls it emerges and squats defiantly at the mouth of the burrow, watching with beady eyes; when you locate it, it sits grinning, dilated and stridulent. If you don't smash it with the first swipe, it is too late; it scuttles like lightning down the burrow which may be two feet deep.

I have discovered that Kachalola, where we stayed in 1966, is named after Dr Spencer 'Kachalola' Broomfield who was born in England in 1847 and arrived in

Rhodesia in 1892. Originally Mr Spencer, it is said that he acquired a doctorate for five dollars after following a correspondence course and that he took the name 'Broomfield' from an entomologist of that name who left him his estate.

He was deported from Nyasaland - the first of all the deportees. Some time later he turned up in Nkhota-Kota and walked from there to Serenje in Northern Rhodesia. Later, he acquired a band of African followers and attacked slave caravans, releasing the slaves but keeping the goods and ivory for himself. Later still, he became well-known as an elephant poacher, but he also became a prospector for gold, a miner, a hunter and a farmer. In Fort Jameson (now Chipata) he used to shoot the bottles off the shelves of the bar in the Victoria Memorial Institute Club. He owned farms at Mile 195 on the Great East Road (site of the Kachalola Rest House) and traces of the foundations of his house can be found in the bush at the back of the Rest House. He grew cotton at Mile 195 but had another farm nearby and another on the Lunsemfwa river, and yet another just below the Luangwa Bridge.

On one occasion he tried his hand at being a train robber, cutting a hole beneath a safe loaded on to a train so that it would fall out on to the track - but it lodged on the chassis of the coach.

He had at least eight or nine African wives and, in between times, two European ones; in the Feira district he fathered 36 children. As *lobola* settlement for the first of his African wives he paid two donkeys.

To-day we have been to Zomba to accompany Marion and Jeff up Zomba mountain to Chagwa Peak from the side of which there is a fine view of the Mulunguzi Dam. There were small blue and pink orchids in the undergrowth.

At their house Marion and Jeff have a huge avocado pear tree growing above the garage. The fruit is now ripe and every few minutes a pear crashes down on to the corrugated iron roof and slides to the ground. We brought away about forty of the pears to give to various friends.

Smart has killed a banded cobra and two other snakes in the garden. He and his wife recently had a fight in a public bar and two of Aswan's fingers were broken.

15 March

A sunbird has made a minute nest and hatched some minute offspring in one of the *Delonix regia* rain trees.

One evening I found on our bougainvillea a beetle that resembled a jewelled brooch. It had a black convex proboscis like a clip, its thorax was glossy emerald green and it had three green stripes down its rectangular wings; the hind legs ended in metallic looking c-shaped claws.

Some of the balsams have burst into pink, purple and carmine flowers, and the dwarf portulaca that Smart transplanted bears tiny brilliant cups of crimson, gold and cerise, again like little jewels, almost devoid of leaf, projecting on small stalks from the infertile soil.

5 April

On Easter Monday Joan and Richard came through from Domasi and Marion and Jeff and family from Zomba and we went on a picnic to Murchison Cataracts on the Shire river. (These were encountered by Livingstone in 1858 and named by him Murchison Falls after Sir Roderick Murchison of the Royal Geographical Society).

The Government's efforts to attract tourists have not included keeping the track to the cataracts in good order, and the signpost on the Matope road had vanished. Richard and I built up some of the most eroded patches in the road with large stones but even so I had to drive round a small tree in a mealie garden rather than risk negotiating the gully that was the 'road'. At the edge of one mealie garden a rubber tyre had been placed on a rock with a large stone on top of it to keep the tyre in position. Apparently at night the rubber was set alight and the acrid smoke kept baboons and monkeys away from the mealies.

There seemed to be more lime pits beside the track than formerly and one wonders if there is not sufficient lime here for it to be exploited on a larger scale.

Children from Matope followed us to the 'Falls' and took us in search of hippos which were said to be present near the bridge. We drove four miles in the direction of Ntcheu, then nearly four miles along a field road leading through a small cotton plantation where there was a village. The Shire river swept past very full and swift and smooth, and there were islands of green bulrushes and a woman cleaning her saucepan with sand on the edge of the river - but no hippos although the banks were marked by their four-toed spoor. When we got back to the road and the Matope children departed, one of them apologized, like a village grocer temporarily out of stock; 'Sollee! No hippos to-day!'

20 April

The main event to record is a visit to Salima. We left the Maison Snowden about 8:30 a.m. on Friday; had coffee by the roadside somewhere this side of Ntcheu; had lunch at Lilongwe hotel and arrived at the Fish Eagle Inn, near Salima, about 4:45 p.m. At present, unfortunately, the hotel is infested with bats; the roofs are full of them and the stink of their guano almost makes one sick.

On Saturday we visited the Old Lady's cottage at Senga Bay, built on its small knoll on a base of rocks and concrete at the top of two paved terraces, facing the Lake, in three acres of grounds.

The present tenants use the plot as a small-holding: pigs leapt all over the place, sheep shuffled across the back yard; cows invaded the garden from the next plot; hens and turkeys strayed from their enclosure; there were baby ducklings in a small pen. A thatched store, detached from the house, had been converted into a pigsty, much to the indignation of the Old Lady. Dogs ran freely in and out of the house.

We were given cups of tea on the verandah and then shown round the cottage (or bungalow). The rooms are very spacious with a wide verandah on three sides. There is a tamarind tree by the back door and many beautiful shade trees in the grounds. On the beach is a boat house built of planks and grass. The water pump is above a well on the edge of the beach and water is pumped up to a 1,000 gallon tank perched on a brick water tower with a store below it. A separate Honda engine generates electricity.

In the past when she herself lived in the Cottage for fifteen years the Old Lady used to have a hundred citrus trees in fruit and she provided the Grand Beach Hotel with grape-fruit, oranges and lemons. The arm of a lagoon, now full of weeds and blue lotus flowers, supplied the water.

I have offered to buy all this for £4,000 plus £250 for some of the old but well-made furniture.

On the return journey on Sunday we had lunch in Dedza at the Green Corner Hotel and we had to wait awhile to leave as the Ngwazi was starting a tour of the Central Region and was addressing a crowd under the tall trees by the market from his semi-military motorcade. We arrived back at the Snowden eyrie at 7:30, after dark.

23 April

A few more showers of rain but in some areas the rains have failed and there may soon be hunger. The Farmers' Marketing Board seems to have no maize left. Around Lilongwe there have been bumper crops but at Mangoche the crop has failed. In Salima market the price of imported Rhodesian maize is £3.6.6 a bag.

6 May

In the Northern Region three hundred children have died of starvation. Nothing of this in the press. Such news is transmitted only on the African grapevine.

Mrs Snowden's solicitors have applied to government for permission to convey the Senga Bay bungalow (i.e. Plot 7, Salima) to us. There is a 99-year lease of which 78 years are left. The annual rent to government is £15.

I took Smart and Million to Lunzu market on Sunday morning and we bought a sack of maize for each of them. A sack weighs more than 200 libs, a 'lib' being the local word for one pound avoirdupois. At 8:00 a.m. the market was busy. A huge quantity of maize was available in sacks and many people were buying it in bulk. It had been brought in by rail from Lirangwe where there had been a good harvest. Every seller of bulk maize had a customer; but the women selling *ufa* in small enamel bowls sat in a long line mostly without customers. Smart, who is very strong, carried the 200 lib bags to the car on his back. A peaceful scene - not a policeman in sight - we were told they had all been summoned to Blantyre to man the road intersections when the Ngwazi ventured out to Mulanje where he was to close an annual conference of the Southern Branch of the Malawi Congress Party.

To-day Gladys and I and Margaret and Willie Kalk have been to Zomba to inspect the plumbing in the Biology laboratory which is now being handed over to the Bindery. Marion and Jeff fed us on local pork and strawberries from Changalume where apparently they fruit almost the whole year round as in the Old Lady's garden in Limbe. It was pleasant to get away from the University for a while although I found it difficult to drive and take in at the same time what Margaret was saying about the split-ring structure of genes and chromosomes.

17 May

On 14 May we went up to the southern end of the Lake with Marion and Jeff and their children and had a picnic on the edge of the beach where the Nkopola Lodge - latest of Malawi's hotels - has been built. The hotel is at several levels and appears to climb the rocks. A strong wind was blowing, the Lake was choppy and cold and neither G. nor I attempted to swim. A crocodile watched Marion and Jeff who did swim but it did not attempt to molest them. A little fawn dik-dik ran out of the rushes and grass at the edge of a nearby swamp and came and ate berries fallen from one of the trees; it was very tame and allowed Marion to stroke it. There were vervet monkeys in the trees; fish eagles flying in arcs over the Lake; a crested hawk eagle on a swamp tree; and we found turtle or crocodile eggs - or rather, egg-shells - on the edge of the sand. A big fleshy crimson petal from a banana flower seemed tough enough to be used in lieu of leather for book binding.

One setback to our hopes and plans; the Old Lady has decided to stay in her house on Mpingwe Hill. So, once again, we are house-hunting in Blantyre/Limbe.

19 May

It is turning cold now at night; one needs two blankets. The tulip trees are in flower; the grass is brown but not yet black after grass fires; avocado pears and citrus fruit are plentiful in the markets; and we have had several days of *chiperoni*.

26 May

After a week's late afternoon house-hunting we have agreed to buy a house. It is in the heart of Blantyre, almost opposite the Queen Elizabeth General Hospital in Mahatma Gandhi Road, two plots from the corner of Mandala Road. The plot - no. 479 - is of one and a quarter acres. The bungalow has large pleasant rooms: lounge, dining room, two bedrooms, small kitchen, lavatory, bathroom, two store-rooms attached to the house on the rear *khonde*; and there's a lock-up garage and servants' quarters. The asking price was £5,500 but I haggled in a vulgar way and got it down to £4,850. Howard Downs, the agent, says the land is worth £1,350. We plan to live in the house as soon as we can move - so far, I've done no more than pay £500 deposit - and then let it when the University moves to Zomba.

Of course, we saw several other attractive properties:

1   A modern house at Mitsidi, with six acres of land in front of it. Within ten minutes of seeing it, I was already in my mind populating the empty acres with cascades of jacaranda, vivid blue *petrea volubilis*, bougainvillea, cup of gold, and at least an acre of strawberries. Alas the owner was willing to let it but not sell it.

2   Also at Mitsidi, the very first house in which missionaries lived in Blantyre. It was built on a five acre rocky kopje with one of the most wonderful outlooks I have ever seen - the Kirk Range, Zobue mountain in Mozambique, at least a hundred miles of Africa in several directions and not another house in sight;

it was like being in the sky. But all the doors and window frames had dry rot, the kitchen was impossible, there were no servants' quarters, and two missionaries were buried in the garden. Asking price £3,000, probably available for £1,500. But we did not feel we could live in a graveyard. (27)

3   Up the Thyolo Road, the house in which John Carver the deputy registrar used to live. Unusual interior including Moorish arches; magnificent views of Mulanje mountain; steeply terraced two acre garden; eminently lettable.

Anyhow, we can now finalize the purchase of the Senga Bay cottage. The Old Lady will be happy if we pay £2,000 initially and the rest by monthly instalments completing in two years time. All being well - and if the Balaka-Ntcheu road is passable - we'll spend Christmas there.

In this country the value of money decreases or devalues faster than it can earn interest in a Bank, so it seems best to have one's savings in the form of property which doesn't lose its value.

2 June

One of the library assistants has asked whether I could get him a £20 advance of salary from the University until the end of July. He has been given a young girl to look after while her father is in Zambia and her mother working for a European who won't have her children around. By day the girl works at the Cafe de Paris; at night she comes and sleeps with him at the ultra-respectable Anglican Hostel - presumably in a single bed in a room he shares with three other young men - and he thinks he ought to move out of the Hostel and find a room in Ndirande village, and, if necessary, marry the girl. I have advised him to send the girl to friends for three weeks until his next pay-day when he will receive £28, after which they can get to know each other with less publicity in a small house of their own.

4 June

Jeffrey rang up to say that one of his bookbinders (the second this year) has disappeared. The young man is apparently a dagga smoker and was involved in a fight last Monday so he may be hiding from the Police.

Million has been off work for a couple of days with a 'flu cold. Several more of his front teeth seem to have fallen out or been knocked out by Esnath.

15 June

We expect to move from this rented house in Chirimba on 20 June. I have already moved all the books, archives and bric-a-brac to my office at the University, and Gladys has cleared the small bedroom and started on the kitchen store. Moving the contents of the garden may prove a bigger task. I have bought six dozen flower pots at the Ceramic Co. in Chileka Road, and we have dug up and potted the geraniums, montbretia, carnations, bougainvillea, cup of gold, petrea, *Celosia plumosa*, salvias, white daisies, michaelmas daisies, and a half a dozen flowers the names of which I cannot recall: there remain the agapanthus, day lilies, Orange lilies, madonna lilies, freesia, yellow daisies, and my 700 strawberry plants which are threatening to fruit this very week.

The lakeshore Cottage project is going ahead. I have approved draft agreements that - grandly - give us the right to build a jetty and use the Lake for the landing of flying boats. We shall have to stock the garden there as well as at the house in Blantyre.

There is more trouble at the Bindery. When Jeffrey got back to Zomba last week he found that one of the bookbinders had attacked Harry Tembo with a hammer. That evening at their 'quarters' he attacked him again and slashed his face open with a *chikwanje* so that he had to go to hospital for treatment. I have caused the offender to be peremptorily dismissed as we cannot staff our Bindery with homicidal maniacs.

It is 5:50 a.m. and Million has just peeked round the study door, saluted (is he drunk?) and indicated that the morning cup of tea is on the table outside. So I had better get up and start the day.

21 June

The house removal started at 7:15 a.m. yesterday and the university transport arrived at 8:00 a.m. All the morning until after 1:00 p.m. I ferried loads and people in the Volvo and G. packed at the Chirimba house and unpacked at this one.

The only thing that failed to go as planned was the transportation of Million's loads and family. Esnath got drunk, abused the university labourers and Namate the maintenance officer who was in charge of the transport, so that Namate refused to transport Million, his family or his goods. So I had to take Million to Limbe market where he hired a lorry for £3.17.6.

We have now had a closer look at the house and the out-buildings of our new home. They are all old; the servants' quarters are more like accommodation for goats than humans and will have to be re-painted at once; their lavatory is disgusting, and I shall have to build better accommodation for them as soon as possible.

The house itself has a good many small cracks, is grubby inside and will need complete redecoration. The main rooms are: lounge 19 feet by 19 feet; dining room 19 feet by 17 feet; front bedroom 18 feet by 15 feet; back bedroom 15 feet by 14 feet; hall 22 feet by 7½ feet. Attached to the main house is a small building containing two rooms, one of which was a kitchen in the past, and the other an ironing room. There is a wide verandah along the front and one side of the house, and a smaller verandah in front of the ex-kitchen and ironing room.

The garden has been neglected but Smart and the rains will cope with that. It is one acre in extent and contains about half a dozen mature guava trees, two mature peach trees, a lemon tree, several avocado pear trees, and some flowering bougainvillea. Juniper and cupressus line the drive, and there's a cupressus hedge at two sides of the garden, a jasmine hedge at the back, and a wire fence on the fourth side.

Mineral rights remain with the African Lakes Company. The view from the front window is of Mount Soche and, until the hedge grows, of a legend on its flank, 'Long live Kamuzu'; from the side of the house a shoulder of Ndirande mountain is visible.

At a meeting of Senate on Monday I managed to have it removed from the record that staff returning from the College of Librarianship Wales would not be eligible for senior posts until they had undergone a further period of training overseas. I took to the meeting a list of 139 ALAs employed in senior posts in university libraries in five continents.

28 June

Gladys has been hard at work trying to get the Blantyre house clean. My spare time has been spent on improvement of the servants' quarters and making a start with the garden. The first job was to get the City Health Department to pump out the appalling mess of excreta and maggots two inches long in the servants' pit latrine; this was done on Tuesday. We are having to put ceilings in the four servants' rooms and their verandah, and the walls will then have to be cleaned up, the scabs and nail holes filled with alabastine, everything sealed, undercoated and painted - they want shamrock green paint. Simultaneously we shall build a new lavatory and bathroom for them. I have bought the paints required, the alabastine, the nails, twelve sheets of softboard for the ceilings, sixty-three sawn lengths of wood, and have hired the university carpenters in their spare time to do the work. They started yesterday and have continued to-day; so far only one room has a ceiling but a second has the completed wooden framework for it. The cost so far is about £42.

I had to order timber at the sawmills and then collect it, using Smart and five labourers and the long-suffering Volvo. The sawmills are very large, there is a great variety of timber available and huge quantities of it, and the sawmills will undertake joinery if orders are placed with them. Firewood is available on Tuesdays and Fridays at 4/- for as much as one can cram into one's car.

In the garden there has been less progress. My strawberry plants have been carefully planted out and if they don't die they should still be fruiting next Christmas. But from a Ministry of Agriculture leaflet that arrived unexpectedly at the library I see that my system of applying fertilizer is wrong, so I am not too hopeful. Also, we have been held up for manure - 'ripe' chicken manure in plastic bags from Mrs Brereton's farm at Bvumbwe, pig manure from elsewhere, sludge from the Health Department, or chemical fertilizers from the garden shops - all are available.

During the past week I have had letters from Foster Howse and Rodrick Mabomba who both want me to buy maize for them in advance of their return from the College of Librarianship Wales. So to-day Smart and I went to Lunzu market and brought back about 4 cwt. of maize. We bought from Yao women who measure the quantity with an enamel bowl; each time the bowl contains a shilling's worth they pop one grain into their mouths and then when the basket or sack contains twenty shillings' worth they spit out the twenty grains into their hand. Smart counted in the same way but kept the grains in his hand or pocket. The controlled price of Farmers' Marketing Board maize is 45/- a sack and each sackful is supposed to weigh 200 libs.

30 June

The new library building at Soche Hill College is finished and has been handed over to us by the Architects this morning.

5 July

To-day we've been to Domasi on a visit to Joan and Richard. They have greatly improved their garden; the whole area has been carefully re-planned and re-stocked, with a thriving vegetable garden inside an Alsatian-proof fence.

We went up the valley between Zomba and Malosa mountains - a rough road, with splendid views of Phalombe plain and the mountains between Domasi and Kasupe, and small family farmsteads in clumps of fruit trees, the vestiges of a development scheme started in 1948 but not continued after Independence. The old Mission station is up this road: an enormous brick Church, a school most of which looks structurally unsafe and with almost no equipment, and a few clusters of huts. The population has moved down the valley towards the main road and Domasi Teacher Training College. A mile or so beyond the school the track becomes very eroded and although it continues for another eight miles, until the watershed is reached, it is only accessible to Land Rovers.

This week-end we have Independence Day celebrations on Monday, but yesterday (Saturday) was also a holiday. At night the Malawi Congress Party Headquarters is a fantasy of coloured lights; the city of Blantyre is decorated more tastefully, I think, than in other years, and the Kamuzu Highway is lined with white-painted gum poles carrying flags in a way that, when driving, I find hypnotic.

6 July

Antony is now in Tanzania. He left England on 10 June, spent a few days in Ethiopia en route, and arrived in Dar es Salaam on 14 June. Almost at once he went up-country by Land Rover to Mwanza on Lake Victoria, 800 miles from Dar. He has also been into Geita and was expecting to return via Dodoma. On one occasion his Land Rover broke down thirteen miles from a road and he had to walk in through the bush at night. Elsewhere he had a minor accident and ran into a hole in the road also at night; in pouring rain and in his underpants he had to dig the Land Rover out of the hole. We hope he will come here for Christmas.

When the Old Lady came to lunch on Saturday she had come straight from the hairdresser and her hair looked like tinted candy-floss. She knows more about the private lives of Malawi's early white settlers and residents - I would guess - than any other person still living. A friend of hers, Ruth Partridge, who is 82 and phenomenally rich, still drives her car to Mangoche if there is a rabies tie-up order in Limbe and her large Alsatian 'Rui' needs exercise on the beach - or if she wants to play bridge there. Malawi is not only the 'Land of Lake and Sunshine' but also the 'Land of Tough Old Ladies'.

At work, lettering of book spines with the electric stylus was falling behind so I have had to bail out the library assistant concerned from the local Court so that he could come back and continue his lettering instead of waiting for a paternity suit to be brought against him.

The carpenters working on the servants' quarters charge from 1/8 to 2/6 an hour for their services.

13 July

We have a plethora of parties ahead: on 15 July a party organized by the students for departing staff and students; on 16 July a farewell party at the Shire Highlands Hotel for the departing Dean, John Utting and his wife; on 17 July Marion will be leaving on the afternoon plane for England and she and Jeff will be here for lunch; on 18 July Dr BS Kirshnamurthy and his wife will come to stay with us; on 20 July there will be a cocktail party for the forthcoming Early History of Malawi Conference; on 23 July we plan to hold a buffet supper for twenty people; and on 28 July there is to be an At Home at the residence of Ian Michael the Vice-Chancellor and his wife. On 30 July we hope to collect the Old Lady and escape to Senga Bay for the week-end.

3 August

The Early History of Malawi Conference was opened by HE Ngwazi Dr H Kamuzu Banda. He was supposed to speak for one hour but, instead, he spoke non-stop for three hours. I was supposed to meet the plane on which the Krishnamurthys were arriving from Zambia but, of course, no one could leave the Conference room until the Ngwazi had finished.

Once I could leave without discourtesy I quickly checked the three hotels, questioned the driver of the Air Malawi bus, rushed down Chileka road to the airport and back, and eventually found our friends unloading their cases outside Ryall's Hotel. It was too late to go back to the conference so after bringing them home we decided to go off to Jeffrey (who knows the Krishnamurthys) in Zomba. He drove all of us up the mountain so the Krishnamurthys had an early panoramic view of eastern and southern Malawi.

On 23 July, so that K. could meet a few people socially, we held our buffet supper. Those who came included Bridglal and Leela Pachai; the Colin Bakers from the Institute of Public Administration, Paul Cole-King the Director of Antiquities, Swanzie and Sir Fulque Agnew and their house guests the Lintons (he is Professor of Geography at Birmingham), Felix Mnthali and his wife, Jeffrey Stickley, Joan and Richard from Domasi (the last three knew the Krishnamurthys from Zaria days), Dr DB Gupta an economist, Dick Najira from the library and Augustine Msiska who will join the library staff on 1 September and hopefully evolve into being an Africanist.

On 25 July I took the Krishnamurthys to Mulanje; I think they were impressed by the expanse of tea plantations, so green and tidy, and by the rugged mountain around the precipices of which floated wisps of white mist.

On 26 July we drove to Cape Maclear; the Lake was at its best, blue and calm, with a warm breeze blowing. We visited the graves of missionaries and K. took photographs of rock hyraxes. The next day the Ks returned to Zambia.

On 30 July we collected the Old Lady at 7:30 a.m. and went to Salima, having lunch en route at Maciel's near Dedza. There are now only fourteen miles of diversions between Liwonde and Balaka and all the road is tarred except through the Angoni Highlands where there is a terrible stretch of rocky dusty track; but tar begins again fifteen miles out of Dedza and continues all the way to Lilongwe and on to Salima. We stayed at the Fish Eagle Inn.

On 31 July the three of us and Chintambo, Mrs Snowden's faithful retainer, met the Da Costas who have been the tenants at the Cottage. Our take-over is going to be difficult because;

a   There is no water pump as the Da Costas have taken away the existing pump which belonged to Mrs Da Costa's father;

b   The Honda generator for electricity is not suitable for the existing wiring which was installed years ago by Mrs Snowden, so we do not know whether there will be electric light or not;

c   The kitchen stove is broken, so there is no means of cooking;

d   Some years ago Mrs Snowden told Mrs Da Costa she could have the dining room chairs, so there is nothing to sit on when eating;

e   The dogs, pigs, sheep, hens, ducks and turkeys that rampaged all over the property for five years have left behind them an incredible number of fleas, mostly outside the house but also inside it.

The Cottage itself is in good condition although a great deal of cleaning will have to precede total redecoration. I have taken on a Chewa gardener-cum-watchman at the magnificent salary (for Salima) of £1 a week. At present there is no garden worthy of the name and Abisai (the g-cum-w) has first to dig a large pit and then dump in it all the litter of tins, bottles and other rubbish that are strewn about the grounds. Then we will try to have a garden.

At the far side of the lagoon is a neighbour Heston Tandaza who has cows, sheep, geese, ducks and chickens, all more or less under control; he supplies milk to the hotels and lakeshore cottages, and also vegetables from his flourishing garden on the edge of the lagoon; he also has transport available and has promised to bring things from Salima. Heston is about the size of Idi Amin of Uganda but he smiles more readily.

As we returned in darkness along the sandy tracks between the Cottage and the Fish Eagle Inn, a cyclist without lights wobbling along on the wrong side of the 'road' dithered across to the lefthand side. Chintambo, in the back seat, perhaps feeling himself to be in an English-speaking environment, muttered a curse that ended indignantly in English: 'That bloody stupid boy!' (Chintambo is supposed not to know English).

Back in Blantyre, the painters have been at work on the servants' quarters, painting the walls shamrock green.

In the garden, Smart has placed dried grass between the strawberry plants which are now beginning to fruit, although so far only the bulbuls and yellow-breasted thrushes and the children of Smart and Million have benefited from his efforts. The french beans and spinach have grown, the petrea has thrown out six spikes of intense dark blue flowers, and a bush in front of the house is now covered with a delicate lilac flower consisting of tiny bells.

At work, we have received £2,500 worth of reference books given by the British government.

16 August

I am on local leave this month. From now onwards, probably for the next year, we shall have to visit the Cottage as often as possible in order to carry out, bit by bit, the renovation and improvements that can be made. There is bound to be a great deal of rushing by car between Blantyre and Senga Bay.

Our second visit this month started on 6 August and consisted of three cars. First the Volvo, grossly overloaded with a dining room table, two chairs, two foam mattresses and cartons of food and bedding. Second, the Old Lady from Limbe, in her Vauxhall, carrying our cases of clothing and some bedding with her own luggage, Chintambo driving. Thirdly, at Zomba, Jeffrey and his dog joined the motorcade, his Ford station wagon loaded with a new paraffin stove, a new lavatory cistern, four picnic chairs and garden tools, all of which I had off-loaded at Jeff's the previous evening.

We took a short route, allegedly known to Chintambo, leaving the main road fifteen miles north of Balaka, wriggling down to the plain and the railway and then continuing via Bilila, Penga-Penga, Sharpevale, Kasinje, Golomoti, Ntaka-taka, Chipoka and Salima. The Old Lady and Chintambo led the way in and out of dry river beds and, with the OL sitting up very straight, plunged hopefully through running rivers the depth of which they did not know. Chintambo got lost somewhere near Ntaka-taka and took to the hills; later we took two wrong turnings ourselves near Chipoka; but eventually we all met again at Salima.

Of course, along this route there are a great many steep descents into river beds, a few of them bridged in ways that are picturesque and precarious, but most of them without bridges of any kind. During the rains it would still be possible to get to Golomoti but all the small rivers would be impassable.

At dusk we arrived at the Cottage, unpacked the contents of the three cars into the hall, and immediately I drove back to Salima to buy two more beds so that we might each have a bed for the night.

The first few hours at the Cottage were fairly basic; we had only electric torches and candles; there was no water in the house; the refrigerator was not working; the new paraffin stove emitted clouds of smoke and flame; there was no working sanitation. When essentials had been located in the mounds of chaos on the hall floor, miraculously we had a splendid three-course dinner of hot soup, roast duck and asparagus and fresh strawberries; I had lots of brandy; and we then slept as soundly on our assorted beds as the hundreds of fleas would permit.

That night there were two rats in the bath adjacent to the bedroom in which Jeffrey and I and Jeffrey's dog were sleeping; the flicking of their tails against the bath as they fought each other kept me awake; and by morning one rat had killed and partly eaten the other. Outside the house there seemed to be rats everywhere, especially in and around the outdoor kitchen.

By the end of the next day I found out how to operate the generator that produced electric light; without mercy, we poisoned a great many rats; as the water pump was not working we carried water up the beach into the house and became so well organized that we could each have two hot baths a day. In Salima I bought more buckets and a large supply of Rattex and Gammetox bombs. With dieldrin, Gammetox and pyrethum powder encircling the house in three lethal bands, and with sprays and bombs inside the house, we waged chemical warfare on the fleas. An elderly sitting room suite and an equally ancient lion skin on the dining room floor (the lion had been shot in the garden) were alive and hopping with fleas so we carried these out of the house, dumped them in a small store and bombed them with Gammetox.

Jeffrey took his dog into the Lake and drowned the hundreds of fleas that were tormenting it.

The garden, too, was infested, especially the former duck and hen houses and their vicinity. I was wearing white stockings and so many fleas hopped on to my legs I could wipe them off in swathes. I imagine that in those first few days we had to kill tens of thousands of fleas, both in the house and outside in the grounds. (We learned later there was also a plague of fleas in the nearby village).

Inside the house Gladys cleaned the various rooms sufficiently for them not to be a health hazard, and the process was continued with quantities of Jeyes fluid the
following day. The Old Lady, feeling sick at all the filth that had been uncovered, and badly bitten by fleas, departed for Limbe on 9 August.

I engaged eight labourers at 2/6 a day - the standard local rate - and started cleaning up the garden. We scraped all the dirt off the stone terraces and paths, re-laid a path to the engine house, gave each of the citrus trees twelve buckets of water, sprayed the former hen houses and the garage with Gammetox, chopped up a fallen tree for firewood, and made more pits near the perimeter of the plot and filled them with all the old tins, bottles, broken glass, broken machinery and other rubbish we picked up from the three acres of 'garden' and the beach.

On 13 August we returned to Blantyre, taking the Lilongwe rather than the Golomoti route.

23 August

On 18 August - still on local leave - we set off again for Senga Bay, carrying in the car a new Dover stove, four dining chairs, a chimney for the kitchen stove, and our usual clothes, bed-boards, drinking water and oddments. We arrived at dusk and were able to get the Honda going at once so that we could unpack by electric light.

The next day I hoped to buy a water pump from Walter Stansfield who owns the Grand Beach Hotel round the next headland, but it proved to be unsuitable and, in any case, the sand point in the well, when we excavated it, was found to be broken.

We have found several people, however, who are helping us. One of these is Kandulu Chintambo, son of Mrs Snowden's old servant, who lives a few hundred yards inland from the Cottage. He is a big friendly carpenter who, in his spare time, is taking down the unhygienic mat ceilings in the Cottage and replacing them with rectangles of modern ceiling-board, all of which will be painted white. Kandulu, who works at the Grand Beach Hotel, also builds boats and there is a large sailing boat under construction in the shade of trees near his house.

We have also found a Cook who will be in charge of the Cottage in our absence. He is Aisa Wazikili, a Yao, who approached us seeking employment with one half of a copy of Mrs Beaton's 'Complete Cookery' in his hand (he had given the other half to his brother); he said he knew all the recipes in the half of the book he possessed and he could remember many of those that were in the other half. He is an ex-askari, six feet tall, with a slight limp from a war wound, aged 75, and speaking twelve languages (English, Arabic, Yao, Swahili, Chichewa, Chibemba, Chilozi, Chilala, Chinsenga, Sindebele, Shona and Zulu). His elder brother whom we already know is Chief Malenga of Nkhota-Kota.

Most of my time at the Lake I take on a small gang of casual labourers to help clear the beach, clean the environs of the lower stone terrace, fetch black soil from the edge of the lagoon and start preparing a vegetable garden. Many of these men have no money, no work, only the clothes they are wearing, and they sleep on the beach at night. Their names are Hassan, Saabwe, Lion, Dim, Jeros, Musa, Idi, Shabiayt, Kambani and Frank. Shabiayt has an umbilical hernia under his vest like the funnel propping up the pie crust in a pie dish. Frank understands English and chops wood from the fallen tree. They start work at 6:00 a.m. and finish at 2:00 a.m.

31 August

We are back in Blantyre.

On Sunday we had a farewell meal for Ken Rawlings and his wife who are leaving Soche Hill College. As so many people are away on leave we could find only Blodwen Binns and Jeffrey for the farewell luncheon.

The Rawlingses were late in finding Plot 479 so while we waited for them Blodwen (who is a well-known systematic botanist and illustrator with several books to her credit) inspected the garden and identified some of the plants and shrubs of which we did not know the names. The blue shrub with tiny bell-like flowers is *Iboza riparia*; a yellow flowering bush is *Heliotropum*; a spire of blue florets is *Anchusa* and the small bush with blue daisy-like flowers is a Namaqualand daisy or *Felicia;* the red-leaved pink flowering shrub is Roselle (*Hibiscus sabdarifa*); the three trees at the corner of the house are *Dombea*, a wild pear; a shrub with white and purple trumpets is *Datura metel*, very poisonous; and another shrub with leaves like purple velvet, having yellow flowers like thistles, is *Cestrum*. Malawi must be Paradise to a botanist.

I have returned to work to-day.

9 September

Two of the junior library staff were in jail when I returned. Jeffrey Nyambose had been involved in a fight at the International Hotel where most of his clothes were torn off him after he had been hit on the head with a Coca-Cola bottle by one of the hostesses. Stamford Kacisa had been attacked by a bus conductor when travelling with his wife to Balaka; the conductor had bitten him, and when he came back on bail he had on his hand teeth marks like stigmata.

Since 2 September I have had to take over Soche Hill College Library. Thirty-five small processes have to be carried out before the library will function properly. After the mindless period on leave at the Lake, the mental strain, as well as the physical strain, have been quite a challenge. I just hope that Soche Hill College achieves a well-ordered library as one of the products of it all.

At home, Million our cook has developed pneumonia and is now in Queen Elizabeth General Hospital. We take food to him.

I have bought an Atalanta water pump for £67; dealt with insurance of the Lake cottage; paid the rates for this house; and failed, so far, to trace a sand point (or well point) that, alone, will enable us to pump water from the Lake into the raised water tank at Senga Bay.

In the Blantyre garden weaver-birds are building their nests in a corner of the garden hidden from the house; under the roof of the house itself two hoopoes are nesting - beautiful dainty black, brown and white birds with a long sharp beak and a serrated crest, a pleasure to watch.

4 October

At Chancellor College we have to provide a library service for an Extension Studies course. At Soche Hill College there have been conferences on History, Geography and Education, and in spite of much chaos in the library we have remained open.

Freshmen arrived a Chancellor College on 28 September. Term begins tomorrow.

The Yarr's cat (they are still on leave) died on 28 September 1970, the same day as President Nasser of Egypt.

Limbe has been blue with jacaranda.

Last week-end we went to the Lake to see what progress had been made in putting in softboard ceilings and to try to get the Atalanta water pump installed. I had, after all, been able to buy a new sand-point. We left Blantyre at 6:00 a.m. and arrived at Senga Bay about 12:30. There was no sign of the servants: Aisa was at the mosque; the gardener, perhaps, had gone to look for beer. The doors of the Cottage were wide open to all comers and we walked straight in. Kandulu had constructed the framework for the ceiling of our bedroom but had run out of timber and had been unable to continue.

On Saturday I contacted Walter Stansfield about the water pump and on Sunday morning he came along with his plumbers and fitted that and the new sand-point, much to my relief. From having no water in the house we suddenly had too much: in one bathroom there was a leak behind the bath and in the other the lavatory cistern overflowed. I have to buy a copper connector and a copper socket for a prehistoric length of piping originally fitted for Mrs Snowden, in the mists of history, by Manser William Bartlett; then the next time we are at the Lake maybe all will be working correctly.

The Cottage was full of the perfume of Afzelia trees.

On Sunday I agreed to employ a young man who said his name was 'Green Charlie' to paint the house inside at the rate of £3.10.0 a room - more if I liked his work.

We left the Lake again at 6:30 a.m. on Monday morning; in Lilongwe I ordered timber and paint; and we got back to Blantyre at 1:00 p.m. I spent three hours of the afternoon at a committee meeting at Soche Hill College.

In the Blantyre garden Smart has excavated trenches that we hope will become flower borders. We went to Tuchila on 24 September and bought fruit trees - one lime, one seedless grape-fruit, one Jaffa orange, one navel orange, one Neno lemon and a tangerine. Smart and I have carefully planted these. This morning there were two libs of strawberries. One day we had rain and it suddenly became piercingly cold.

19 October

I paid another visit to Senga Bay 11-13 October. Gladys was recovering from 'flu-laryngitis-tonsilitis and wasn't well enough to come, so I took Dick Najira of
the library as a companion (and interpreter). I had not heard from Kandulu and I suspected that the timber, paint, paint-brushes and nails I had ordered from Lilongwe Hardware Centre had not been delivered to the Cottage. I found that part of the main consignment had left Lilongwe on 2 October and I was told that the ivory white paint for the walls had been sent by road on 10 October.

At Salima Road Motor Services I found that the first load was still in the railway shed; and the goods office claimed that the second consignment had not arrived. They promised to deliver on Saturday afternoon or Sunday morning and, true enough, on Saturday afternoon a Railway clerk appeared at the Cottage to say that the goods had arrived. What he should have said was that the lorry had sunk in sand on the hump in the track between us and the Salima road. It was such an ancient lorry it couldn't wheeze its way over the sand, so we had to off-load it and have the goods carried the last three hundred yards to the Cottage. Thanks to this contretemps a case of paint-brushes and a tin of Solignum went astray, and when I paid the carriers there was another small clamour because two of the men had made three journeys to the house and claimed 2/- each instead of 1/6 as agreed: but I felt cross because somebody had 'nicked' the paint brushes and Solignum, and I told them to go to the District Commissioner if they were not satisfied.

The Cottage itself was not much different from a fortnight earlier except that the dining room mat ceiling had been taken down and bits of electric wiring were hanging from the roof. I started the Honda but failed to get electricity into the house owing to the state of disorder the wiring was in. Nor could I get any water into the house: when I unscrewed a nut to pour water into the Atalanta (it sometimes needs to be primed) a strong jet of water shot out into my face, blinding me and drenching me from head to foot, so that I had to screw the nut back in the middle of what seemed an erupting volcano of water. Fortunately the Aladdin lamp - with a new mantle brought from Blantyre - performed well and Kandulu kindly lent us a Tilley lamp.

Dick had to sleep in the lounge in the big bay window where there was plenty of breeze; most of the Cottage furniture was stored in the other parts of the same room.

On Saturday the Lake was calm and in the late afternoon we had an enjoyable swim. On Saturday night a high wind blew up and the Lake became very rough; we swam again on Sunday but the breakers were strong enough to knock people over and it was less pleasant. Sunday morning we walked along the sands as far as the Baptist Mission which has a large house and maintains a big power boat. It was very hot. Fishermen had a four-foot catfish in their net.

On Sunday the local headman, Dalamkwanda, came to visit us. While Dick interpreted I fed him on Smith's crisps and tinned peaches and he drank Fanta, and when he left I gave him 5/-.

On Saturday evening the gardener was drunk and on Sunday Dick and I carried bath water up from the Lake until some of Aisa's women came and helped. On Sunday evening we visited Kandulu so that Dick might see the 18-foot boat he had built.

On the return journey to Blantyre on Monday the heat between Balaka and Liwonde was so intense that I almost fainted as I drove. It was a relief to get back into the coolness of the Shire Highlands.

On Friday Ann and Brian Yarr and family returned. I met them and broke the news about 'Nameless' their cat. Gladys fed them; and I took them shopping and installed them in their house.

Smart has finished the long flower border parallel to the main road. Under the house roof our hoopoes have chicks. Margaret and Willie Kalk have given us four orchids for the garden. To-day, rain and cloud.

6 November

Last week-end G. and I went again to the Lake. It was a blessing we made the effort as some of the paint supplied from Lilongwe was not the shade we wanted so I had to get it changed. Creeping up the track to the Cottage from the main Salima road the Volvo stuck in sandy holes made earlier by the Road Motor Services lorry and had to be dug out.

I managed to get electric light into the house quite easily but no water until Sunday morning when Member Matora, a plumber, came and dissected the water pump, removing about two pounds of sand from the suction unit. Eventually the water pump went like an oil gusher so that water spurted all over the bathrooms and the water tank on its tower quickly overflowed after imbibing 1,000 gallons.

The balsams were in full bloom - red, pink, mauve, cream, cerise and white.

We swam on Saturday and I swam again on Sunday.

Following heavy storms on the Lake last week two fishermen were drowned; and on Friday night there was another high wind.

On Saturday we were visited by Mdalamdoka Nkuti, the local sub-chief under Maganga, who brought us a present of eggs. We hadn't much to give him in return, merely Fanta and Coca-Cola to drink and some shortcake biscuits and oranges that he could take away with him. He planned to go to a nearby shop so I gave him a lift in the car. In the confusion of folding him into the car alongside Green Charlie the painter (who acted as interpreter) and surrounded by empty cans and drums to contain paraffin and petrol which I had to fetch from Salima, I forgot that I had placed my briefcase on the car roof. It was only when Green Charlie and I arrived at Salima that I realized what had happened - I had no briefcase in the car.

In panic we tore back to Senga Bay along the rutted and dusty road at seventy miles an hour, Green Charlie enjoying the unusual speed, me very conscious that the briefcase contained my passport, birth certificate, driving licence, car insurance, Cottage insurance, office keys, camera, all correspondence concerning the Cottage, plus other documents.

There was no sign of a battered briefcase along the road so I went to the Cottage, enlisted Aisa the cook as chief interpreter, and despatched Stephen the gardener, Sanudi the carpenter's mate and James a painter's mate to question people up and down the road, letting it be known that I would give £1 reward to the person who returned the briefcase to me intact. I also informed Dalamkwanda the headman and a Detective Inspector of Police who was investigating firing of some grass shacks, so the whole neighbourhood was quickly alerted.

Within five minutes James discovered that the case had been picked up by a woman on the road who had taken it into a nearby shop. So I got back the briefcase, found it intact, handed over the reward; and the headman's son and James, Sanudi, Stephen and other helpers all trooped back to the Cottage to be refreshed with Fanta and Coca-Cola. Then Green Charlie and I rushed back to Salima.

It was so hot at the time of this visit that for the return journey to Blantyre Gladys and I got up at 3:00 a.m. and left at 4:30 a.m. as dawn began to paint the eastern sky with beams of red, orange and yellow and the mountains of Mozambique were silhouetted against the sunrise.

Somewhere along the twisting tarmac road that led up to the plateau, we met a completely naked man - an unusual sight in Malawi - dancing homeward and alone down the middle of the road, obviously in a state of euphoria after a particularly good *ngoma* and totally oblivious of early morning traffic from the Lake. He was not drunk - merely a human being blithe and completely happy.

21 November

Another week-end at the Lake, leaving Blantyre at the crack of dawn and arriving at Senga Bay about 1:30 p.m. I had to drive slowly as the car was grossly overloaded with two bags of maize and twenty gallons of paint, plus all the usual impedimenta - about seven hundredweight in all. When we unloaded at the foot of the terraces of the Cottage the tail end of the car rose at least six inches on the springs, as if with relief.

While we were there, Green Charlie painted the walls of two rooms and Kandulu constructed the wooden frame to carry the new ceiling in the lounge. The water pump worked and so did the Honda generator. I had sent by train from Limbe a new bath for the second bathroom and a bundle of timber, and had arranged for more timber and ceiling board to be sent from Lilongwe. Everything was at Salima station except one bundle of timber, but although the Manager in charge of transport promised to get everything out to me at the lakeshore on Saturday, nothing arrived and when we came away I had to leave all the documents with Kandulu and ask him to secure clearance.

It was very hot and there had been no rain at Salima since our last visit.

In Blantyre the garden is flourishing after several good rains. There are masses of tomatoes and we have picked over two hundred peaches which are delicious whichever way you eat them. Guavas, oranges, lemons and avocado pears are beginning to form.

At work I seem to have many small worries at present owing to a shortage of senior staff and too many inane committee meetings. We had meetings of Chancellor College Library Committee on 10 November and again on 19 November, a meeting of the University Library Committee yesterday, followed by a meeting of the Student Affairs Committee at which the theft of books from the library was discussed. (The Chancellor College student who stole fourteen books was fined a paltry 10/-; as a result he became a students' hero.)

The University Library Committee includes, at present, so many inexperienced and irresponsible people - as well as some who are experienced and most helpful - that at yesterday's meeting I asked for several important matters to be deferred for a year, until Malawian staff at present in Britain have returned, since it seemed wrong to me that a bunch of young expatriates, with only a few older and wiser people trying to restrain them, should attempt to determine policy that qualified Malawian librarians would have to execute.

Yesterday evening Gladys and I were out to a party at the Indian High Commissioner's - the Khuranas are going to South America, and I think they had invited all their friends to say goodbye to them. Many, of course, belonged to the Diplomatic Corps or were Indians who lived locally. The Indian High Commission has the largest house in Mahatma Gandhi Road; ours, six plots away, is the smallest. I enjoyed the party although both G and I were reeling with fatigue.

1 December

I seem to write this record immediately after our trips to the Lake. We went there again last week-end, taking Moira, the VSO in charge of acquisitions work at Chancellor College, with us. I couldn't get away until Saturday morning as I had to appear at the General Purposes Committee in connection with the 'returning Malawians' on Friday evening, so we left about 6:00 a.m. on Saturday. Again, I couldn't drive fast as we were overladen, mainly with a lavatory cistern, several heavy 4-foot ridge-tiles for the roof of the Cottage, plus tins of paint and boxes of plants for the garden. In any case, there was rain at the northern end of the Angoni Highlands and beyond the tarmac the road was pure pap, with more slippery slush on the Salima-Senga Bay stretch.

Kandulu had finished the lounge ceiling except for the top of the bay window and the painters Green Charlie and James had put on another coat of ivory white paint in two of the rooms. While we were there Kandulu took down the mat ceiling in the hall, the painters painted the lounge ceiling and Matora, the plumber, installed the new bath and the lavatory cistern.

On the beach, Moira was trying to explain to Stephen the gardener and Sanudi, Kandulu's assistant, that she was a VSO.

'So you are a present from the British government!', Sanudi concluded.

12 December

The past two weeks have been varied but not very stimulating. I had to appear at the Appointments Committee on 2 December about the 'returning Malawians'; there was a meeting of Chancellor College Library Committee on 3 December, a meeting of Senate on 8 December, and meetings of the Polytechnic Library Committee and Soche Hill College Library Committee on 9 December. Nothing is more stultifying to creative work, or just plain work, than attendance at committee meetings.

On 5 December I was out to a 'Heads of Department' lunch on the occasion of the visit to the University by Ian Maxwell, Secretary of the Inter-University Council for Higher Education Overseas, and Frank Thistlewaite who is Vice-Chancellor of the University of East Anglia. There was sherry before the meal and *vin rose* with the roast chickens; a typical academic gathering but quite pleasant.

The following day we had Margaret, Willie and John Kalk to lunch. John is working in South Africa at Baragwanath hospital, the big hospital for Blacks. His description of conditions there was enlightening: Whites and Blacks are not only treated in separate hospitals but they get different drugs - the cheapest kind for Blacks.

Clemence Namponya arrived back yesterday from Aberystwyth in advance of his colleagues. His plane was three hours late. I was the only person at the airport to meet him so I brought him up to the house, gave him tea and then took him to his home. He lives in a cluster of huts - scarcely a village - thirty miles from Limbe. I had to go up the Midima Road, then branch off on a gravel track, then drive on earth tracks for several miles between newly planted gardens where the maize was a foot high.

His mother, in a orange *chirundu,* was the first person we saw but she didn't greet him till she had called to other women working in the gardens and women and children came rushing from all points of the compass. I think most of the women were his aunts and sisters; there was only one adult man who arrived after the rest. All of them shook hands first with me and only then with Clemence; there was a little mild buttock waggling but not much evidence of excitement at his homecoming. The aunts gave me nine eggs, quickly rounded up from the huts. I didn't want to take them as they probably had little food themselves, but to avoid giving offence I had to follow the custom and accept.

As it was late and rain was threatening and I didn't want to get stuck on any of the footpaths, I soon followed my wheel tracks back to the gravel road and on to the Midima road again. I wondered how Clemence in his dark suit with a brilliant eggshell coloured shirt with matching tie would settle down for the night on his mat (if there was one) on the earthen floor of a hut. (28)

There has been a great deal more rain. Every night, under the street lamps in Mahatma Gandhi Road, women and children stand in clusters, carrying tins, basins, enamel bowls and paraffin lamps, to catch the big fat termites that have hatched and whirl in their thousands round the lights.

Esnath, the cook's wife, is in hospital with bronchitis. Her children have taken her a tin of fried termites as a special treat.

The University of Malawi had to contend with difficulties that were greater than in most universities: it had to be created within the context of a political situation that started as something like democracy and became something quite different. Many of us accepted the political situation. An autocracy is not always bad; at least the time-wasting processes of having to hear the views of every ill-informed minority, and the elevation of nincompoops, can be avoided.

In any case, we were not in Malawi to participate in politics; we were well content to consider them the affair of local people. Our job was to carry out a professional function which included the training of Malawian staff. If we did our job efficiently, the political situation might change or it might stay the same - but it was not part of our function to try to influence matters. What we hoped we could influence in the long term was the standard of living, health, education, prosperity and security of the nation.

By 1970 some people claimed that Malawi was a Police State. The Special Branch of the Police was said to have developed a network of informants - or informers - that existed in every part of the public services and every institution, including the University, and which received reports from a 'listener' at every public gathering, even to arguments in pubs and at Church services.

It was no accident, five years after it had been established, that the University had no statutes. It is not too difficult to draft statutes. (The largest University in Africa is still using statutes that were expertly drafted by its vice-chancellor's wife within days of that university being opened). In Malawi the university administration and Council were not free to draft and implement statutes in the normal way. The Chancellor Dr Banda determined most important policy matters, making standard university administration impossible. He felt no urgency to 'malawianize' either academic or administrative posts; salaries of support staff were kept unnecessarily low; censorship of books, outside the law, was applied to the library; the powers and duties of college principals were not defined - so we floundered on from year to year without statutes and, in a university with five colleges, I was not the only head of department who found this a nuisance. Their absence affected the library in many ways. After I had worked for almost five years I assembled, therefore , seven pages of remarks I thought ought to be made and submitted them to the Vice-Chancellor. Alas! - they had no effect and we continued to fumble on as before.

MOROCCO

Chileka - Johannesburg - Lusaka - Brazzaville - Libreville - Douala - Lagos - Accra - Robertsfield - Dakar - Las Palmas - Agadir: it seemed an indirect route but it was the best I could achieve for my leave to Morocco and England 1969.

I had no visa when I arrived late at night in Congo Brazzaville and the police at the airport confiscated my passport and told me I was *illegitime.*

Inevitably they lost the passport. But the next morning while they were looking for it elsewhere it fell out of an accumulation of litter on the bottom shelf of a steel cupboard in their little airport office, and I was able to snatch it back.

At Brazza airport facilities for making onward bookings did not exist but airline officials said I could fly whether I was booked or not - so I did. The flight to Libreville took off one hour before the scheduled time.

The River Congo, swollen with flood water, broken trees and other debris, swept silver under the sun; Kinshasha sprawled on one bank, Brazzaville on the other. The absence of boats on the river reflected the diplomatic *froideur* between the two cities.

In Gabon the River Ogowe coiled through marshes and equatorial forest like a gratified anaconda.

Douala in Cameroon had three impressive arts and crafts shops: Ali Baba's, Madame Charmian's and the Musee des Arts Africains. At an open-air arts and crafts market an ancient Citroen drove in from the bush crammed with carvings from the villages.

At Lagos airport Dennis Gunton, who was British Council Library Adviser, met me and wove his car with great expertise through the tangle of taxis, trucks, buses, cyclists, pedestrians and all the honking and clangour of the streets, to Okoyi where he lived. The Nigerian Civil War was 'on', we were stopped by soldiers outside the airport and a few soldiers in battle-dress were camouflaged among the crowds. Two Tuareg from the Sahara - 'Blue Men' in indigo robes - strode unconcernedly beside the rush of traffic heading for Carter Bridge. Dennis and his wife Mildred were kind enough to put me up for the night.

Lagos story: Early in the Civil War a drunken Federal Air Force officer took off one night in his military plane with his girl-friend as a passenger; light-heartedly, he dropped a few bombs on Lagos and then the plane blew up. His body fell down the night sky and crashed through a roof-top on to a bed occupied by the wife of the Czechoslovak Consul.

On 20 May, travelling by air from Lagos to Kano, I narrowly escaped seizure by the Nigerian Army. After the plane landed at Jos and took off again, I was about to take a photograph of the town through the plane window when the small camera was snatched from my hands by a young man with tribal marks on his face who sat in the seat across the aisle. The fierce young man demanded to know who I was, where I was going, what I was doing in Nigeria. I showed him my passport, explained my presence, and asked whether he was a police officer. He said he wasn't a policeman but was 'also a somebody' and showed me his identity card which revealed he was an Army officer. He seemed to think he had captured a Biafran spy, and at Kano airport I had to accompany him to an Army office.

Other people there soon said I could go but he insisted on confiscating the colour film in my camera and carried it off to be developed. It contained only one exposure - of a fishing village, complete with dug-out canoes, taken in Douala.

In Kano the telephone at the Central Hotel was out of order, which didn't surprise me, so early in the morning I went by taxi to Abdullahi Bayero College about seven miles distant. Goats on top of the mud wall of the city grazed the dust; donkeys laden with charcoal and firewood trotted in from the Zaria road; a very dusty naked man ambled beside the roadside ditch; beggars sat at culverts and at the city gates, all of them blind. My friend Zaki Badawi, Professor of Islamic Institutions, had gone to Zaria at 6:00 a.m. so I left a note telling him I was at the Central Hotel.

Back at the hotel I decided to have my hair cut by the hotel barber. The temperature was 115 degrees Fahrenheit in the shade. The barber came from Warri in the South and we both dripped with sweat while I was shorn.

In the late afternoon Zaki turned up at my bedroom, which was like an oven since the airconditioner was broken, and insisted I should stay with him instead of at the Hotel. So we went back to Abdullahi Bayero College where he had a corner house near the road. He tried hard to grow flowers in his garden but the plot had no hedge or wall and whenever he was away camels lurched in from the road and munched his petunias.

At Dakar airport, Jean Rousset de Pina, Bibliothecaire en Chef, Universite de Dakar - another friend - came in his car to meet me. Pan-Am had booked me into the Grand Hotel de N'Gor, a skyscraper palace on the edge of the sea, for the night. I was not accommodated in the palace part of it, however, but in a chalet in the gardens. The walls were of woven grass but it had a wooden floor and a private bathroom. The bed sagged so badly that I lifted all the bedding on to the parquet floor and slept on that, quickly lulled to sleep by the roar of the sea.

Jean was most kind, making his car available the next morning, having me to lunch, providing the car again in the afternoon and inviting me to a cocktail party in the evening. He took me round the University Library which has a central position at the end of an avenue in the University City. There was a reading room for each major subject; impeccable catalogues; a large administrative area on the ground floor. The bulk of the books were in a stack in the centre of the building; eventually this could be fifteen storeys high.

At the cocktail party, held in the Library several floors up the central stack, about half the guests were Senegalese and half French. The occasion was to honour a library colleague who had received an award for her academic work. The Senegalese girls were beautiful, vivacious, chic and gorgeous in dresses and head dresses of silver, gold, blue and purple. One of the five people in the room who spoke English was Amadou Alain N'Daiye who was in charge of the Sciences section of the library, a tall young man in a black suit with a kind of Chinese jacket; he had a degree and a diploma from the Dakar Library School. Also present was the Library's Head Bookbinder, a huge man weighing perhaps twenty stones. After having a few drinks he insisted on demonstrating a tribal dance: on the steel shelves the books around us danced in time to his pounding feet.

There was no traceable air flight from Senegal to Morocco so I had to travel via the Canary Islands. I spent the next night at Las Palmas, surrounded by geraniums, tourists and flamenco dancers.

Agadir (at last)

From Las Palmas we flew over the sea, full of turquoise shadows, to the sun-baked desert of the Rio de Oro; north to Tiznit, with neat walled gardens shaded by palm trees, the town looking vaguely like a fortress or the last outpost of life and vegetation on the edge of the southern sands; north again across a few valleys, sprinkled with green; and then down to Agadir, warm with sunshine and bright with bougainvillea.

On 29 February 1960 Agadir had been destroyed in an earthquake. Only trees were left standing. In fifteen seconds almost every building collapsed and at least 15,000 of its 35,000 inhabitants were killed. After the earthquake, while the Army was in charge of the town, it was realized that it would be impossible to find and dig out most of the dead so the ruins were bulldozed flat, quicklime was added to the rubble to dispose of corpes and prevent an epidemic; and the King ordered massive relief work. A new Agadir was built.

To-day, it is a splendid clean town of strong concrete buildings, with tarmacked roads, a beautiful mosque, excellent shops and hotels, and it still has its incomparable beach, said to be the best on the West African coast, a modern harbour, and a climate so mild - without being too hot - that swimming and sunbathing are possible in midwinter.

The souk is high above the town on a hill, and everything that one would expect to find in well-established shops is there displayed in tents, open on the leeward side. On the grass mats are silver and brass trays, tea-pots, the biggest copper kettles in the world, canakas for brewing Turkish coffee, lamps, candlesticks, urns, bells, water containers; gaudily striped blankets -red, yellow, green and blue - or in more sober colours, black, white, umber and silver; a coruscation of bangles, rings, brooches, necklets, pendants and ornaments for the forehead; saddles and bridles; bags, pouffes, cushions, sandals; warm hooded djellabas, guftans, shirts, silk scarves; stools, trays, caskets inlaid with mother-of-pearl and ornamented with silver and brass.

Then there is the vegetable and fruit market with great heaps of green-striped melons and plums, figs, dates, tomatoes, potatoes, and corn and grain.

There are snake-charmers fluting to cobras; and fortune-tellers whispering the future; and medicine men with purges and aphrodisiacs; and conjurors and magicians.

The people using the market are all Moroccans, women in charcoal grey or drab *haiks*, mostly yashmakked, men in guftans and small multi-coloured skull-caps, boys in European shirts and trousers and pullovers.

The people of Agadir all seemed to be friendly. That first evening, when I visited arts and crafts shops in town, I found that the young assistant in charge of each shop shook hands as soon as you entered the doorway and seemed to enjoy showing you his wares even if you didn't buy; again when you left the shop he would shake hands again, or stroke your forearm in both of his hands, or even give you a friendly hug.

Some of the boys around the shops were obviously ready, in fact eager, to go further. I was asked by several of them whether they could come and sleep with me at the hotel. After dark there were also a few girls around the small restaurants; they were too shy to speak directly but while I was having a drink at a bar two of them sauntered up and tentatively tapped my vertebra and a man standing beside me enquired in French - did I want either (or perhaps both) of them? There was nothing importunate about any of this or about the overtures from the boys - everything was open and honest and sometimes hilarious.

The welcome to tourists could not be more complete.

The Anti Atlas

The bus next day, coming from Tiznit, was late but the clerk at the bus office shared his glass of mint tea with me while I waited and as soon as the luggage had been secured under a net on the bus roof I waved goodbye to the wrinkled old man and the Berber boy selling popcorn who had come and sat, one on each side of me, on the bus company's bench, and we were off like an Arabian mare.

For the rest of the day we undulated through Zaouia Tamrat, Taghazout, Amesnaz, Tamri, Ain Oufra, Tamanar; plunging to the Oued Iguezoulen and bounding up again over Djebel Amssiten;   on then to Dar el Cadi, Tidourine, Essaouira (formerly Mogador), Ounagha, Et Tleta des Hanchene, Ain Taftecht, Sidi Moktar, Chichaoua, Mzoudia, Sidi Athmane and finally, long after dark and via the unromantic railway crossing, Marrakesh.

This was the coast road as far as Essaouira.   At first, after leaving the harbour of Agadir, we hurtled along the cliffs, waves from the Atlantic creaming on the empty sandy beaches or splashing into rocky coves on our left, open moorland and soft eroded rocks on our right.   Pink oleanders clustered thickly over narrow deep ravines cut by torrents from the higher moors.

I was the only non-Moroccan in the bus.   There were four or five yashmakked ladies, one of whom had to lower her yashmak so that she could be sick into a tin kept for that purpose by the conductor - we swept and yawed down startling hills and round precipice corners and the tin had to be constantly in use - there were also a few sleepy children; maybe a dozen grizzled and prickly-faced farmers in woollen djellabas; a few portly traders; and a tall and handsome Mauretanian boy with rosy cheeks: ethnically, the bus load comprised people who were Berber, Arab, Mauretanian, possibly Jewish, and some probably with French, Spanish, Targui and Negro ancestry.   Every seat was taken.

After a long time we stopped at one of the villages for communal urination in the bed of a ravine and the drinking of mint tea in a small roadside restaurant and I ate goat's liver kishbebab in a bread split (like a hamburger).   The Mauretanian boy and his friend came up to talk , and one of the men I thought must be a merchant; and back in the bus, after we started moving again, the farmers asked questions and beamed and smiled as if I had been a long-awaited brother.   My fragmentary French proved useless but my pidgin Arabic came back swiftly and was understood, although I could rarely grasp easily what was said in return.

When we turned from the sea into the Anti Atlas the valleys were full of olive and argan trees, and I learned later that juniper and jujub and tuya grow near Essaouira.   On some of the hillsides fortified farmhouses frowned like miniature kasbahs and in the meadows sheep, goats, cows, donkeys, mules and camels munched the rich herbage and spring flowers.   Many of the donkeys and camels carried loads, camels being used to transport hay and stubble.   It looked as if one crop had been harvested.

It cost 75p to travel the 345 kilometres (215 miles) from Agadir to Marrakesh.

Marrakesh: a touch of ta'wwadit

I stayed the first night at a respectable hotel recommended by an ecclesiastical friend. It cost 28 dirhams (c. 93p) for bed and p.d. I had a comfortable room, a double bed with a long narrow bolster, and an attached bathroom; but the hotel clientele seemed to consist of blonde Aryan couples and elderly French ladies engaged in complicated knitting; its atmosphere, with a few Byzantine touches, was exactly that of a railway station; and the stink of the waiter's feet when he bought my restorative *mahia* (a local liqueur made from figs) was nauseating.

In the Banque d'Etat du Maroc next morning I met a young Scandinavian who was supposed to be studying archaeology in Bulgaria but who had somehow side-slipped and become more interested in anthropology in Marrakesh. His name was Stjordal; he was golden-bearded, long-haired, bespectacled, wearing a Marrakesh shirt with tasselled borders, jeans and sandals, and he carried a shoulder satchel of camel-skin. While I waited in the cool ornate tegular hall of the Banque for my Spanish pesetas to be exchanged for dirhams - a procedure involving several printed forms, three authoritative Banque officials, a *moshani* (messenger) and a numbered metal disc, and which took at least three quarters of an hour - we chatted. He said he would be happy to accompany me to the souks and that, if I wished, I could probably get a room at the Hotel de l'Oued Issil which was situated deeper in the medina. He himself had previously stayed at the Hotel for four dirhams a night but he was now sleeping in the open with some friends who had a car and camping equipment.

To begin with, we went to the main souk, the Kaisariyah, approached from a corner of the Place Jemaa-el-Fna. There is no signpost: one has to know where to go.

First, there are small shops each selling several kinds of dates, olives, dried figs, dried ginger, fresh green mint, various kinds of grain, and spices. Nearby are undecorated earthenware pots which are possibly water-jars as they have stoppered spouts and huge earthenware handles at the top that would fit over a wooden pole carried by a mule or borne on the shoulders of two men (or women).

In the same shop is a collection of gaily decorated baskets with cone-shaped lids - these are presumably containers for food - and painted earthenware and pottery. Farther on are flutes, rattles and stringed musical instruments made of bamboo and the skins of goats and giant rats and tortoise shells, plastron and carapace unseparated.

From this point onward the lane narrows but it is still the main street through the big souk and swarming with people, bicycles, hand-carts, donkeys, all of whom manage to compress themselves into the ten or twelve feet between the *boutiques d'artisanat* which huddle together on both sides. The thoroughfare is cobbled, cool - thanks to the stratum of tattered palm branches with which it is partially roofed - full of deep shadows, and brilliant with yellow and scarlet hanks of dyed wool strung to dry across the upper part of the lane. The proprietors sit at the entrance to their shops, chatting with friends, drinking Turkish coffee and mint tea, anxiously waiting to shake the hand of every tourist. Many of them already knew Stjordal.

The shops are bulging with beautiful things. Rugs and carpets are sumptuous and their colours pure and clear; rose red *tapis* from Chichaoua; golden yellow, green, blue, crimson from the High Atlas; Persian styles from Fez; Berber black and white; soft-piled treasures from Rabat; and a residuum of antique carpets fabricated in styles unknown for two hundred years.

Blankets of camel hair or sheep wool, also dyed in bright colours, patterned in stripes or lozenges; and gorgeous guftans and djellabahs in hues from pigeon grey to gaudy silver and gold; and embroidered waistcoats and caps and capes and silk scarves and clothes for women (under their drab *haiks* one catches glimpses of pink and peach yellow and pale green and vivid blue); and brilliant yellow sheepskin babouches and Persian slippers with turned-up-toes - all these spill from the shelves and decorate the walls of the shops.

Then there is the leatherware, silverware, copperware, bronzeware, brassware, woodware, basketry, jewellery, pseudo-antique daggers and pistols and powder horns, flint-lock guns and splendid swords; and rows of long-necked pots and cascades of plates and dishes and bowls, jade green, ultramarine, Nankin blue, and burnt sienna, sepia and umber.

We went to the far end of the souk and entered the labyrinth of alleys where the craftsmen work in narrow streets of small mud-brick cubicles, unhindered and unheeded by tourists. There are said to be six thousand artisans and forty guilds.

The hammering of red copper, nickel silver and brass, the soft thud of shuttles on the hand looms, the muted clank and clink and chime of a dozen different trades, and the endless passing of people, probably has not changed much in five hundred years. An occasional bushy grape-vine shaded a studded wooden door; date palms thrust stiff branches above the grey plaster of courtyard walls; in order to pass at one point I had to fold back a donkey's furry ear.

We were quickly lost. There were big vats of dyes in dark misshapen mud rooms like dungeons; whole families at a single loom deftly and swiftly weaving rugs or carpets; camel and sheep and goat leather being pared and cut to shape for babouches and cushions and sandals; 'antique' brass ornaments being screwed to the stocks of guns that truly were from ancient wars; iridescent chips of mother-of-pearl being glued to jewel boxes and caskets of tuya wood; pots being painted; small wooden blocks being turned by a lathe operated by a big toe into handles for kishkebab skewers; blacksmiths battering decorative iron gates and grilles; acres of people working; no one idle. Stordal, after much bargaining, bought a star-patterned camel-skin bag and a quadri-corded black silk lanyard on which eventually, in Oslo, he hoped it would hang from his mother's shoulder.

It took about twenty minutes to find our way out of the maze of alleys to a lane we recognized.

Then we went to the Hotel de l'Oued Issil. This was in another part of the medina.

You entered the Riad Zitoun Kedim through a horse-shoe arch leading away from the Place Jemaa-el-Fna, passed through another two arches and the Hotel was on the left, simply a big wooden door in the cement wall of the lane. Stepping inside, there was a small patio with green and blue tiles where the receptionist, Nejnaoui Abdelghani, sat at a little wooden table and the Berber bedroom boy, Wafi Lahoussein, just sat and talked and , at night, the watchman lay across the heavily bolted door in his woollen djellabah with the hood pulled over his head.

My room was up two flights of tiled stairs, round a few corners and across another small patio. It was wedge-shaped, like a segment of cake, and it contained a large double bed, a table and wooden chair, a wash basin with running water (cold only), and a cracked mirror, and it had a green shuttered window looking out over the rooftops to the minaret of the Mosquee de la Kasbah; below was a bird's-eye view of the alley.

You had to provide your own towel, soap, toilet paper and share a WC that was communal to the patio; somewhere there was a shower. If you wanted to, you could dry your washing or sleep on the flat roof. Abdelghani asked seven dirhams a night, payable in advance, but Stjordal reduced this to six dirhams (20p), and I paid the night before I left. It wasn't particularly comfortable; cockroaches got into the bed one night and bit me; but I felt it was a corner of Marrakesh and not an imported part of any other country.

There were less reputable hostelries in the area.

The Hotel was occupied solely by *les etudiants*. Marrakesh seems to have attracted its own share of these, a small, individually changing, but semi-permanent population of hippies and junkies. I had seen them in the town; young men with fashionably uncombed hair, dishevelled beards, open-necked food-spotted shirts, stale jeans, dirty finger nails, dirty feet, their necks and wrists garnished with heavy beads and metal bangles; the female of the species somewhat similar in appearance, with unkempt waist-length hair, faded jeans, Moroccan jewellery and no make-up - one I met carried a whisky bottle full of drinking water and a painted three-stringed violin (lacking its bow), which she wanted to sell.

They were French, German, Dutch, American and probably a few English.

All of them were said to smoke *kief* which was sold openly in the form of cigarettes or in little patties brought round on trays in the Place Jemaa by a couple of hawkers. Every room at the Hotel appeared to be occupied by these representatives of Europe and America: some of them as picturesque as anything in the medina. Stordal warned me to lock my bedroom door since they were impecunious as well as Bohemian: some of them had already sold most of their clothes to buy hashish, others obtained money by begging from tourists.

We took our lunch sitting outside a little restaurant fronting the Place Jemaa-el-Fna. A burly old man in a djellabah grilled kishkebab over a charcoal fire outside the door, and you could go inside, lift the lids of the various metal containers, prod about in the gravy with a long spoon, and select which dish you wanted. We had salad, followed by a sort of soup containing vegetables and pieces of mutton, and a French loaf and butter - the remains of which I asked them to keep for me in the refrigerator till the following day - and Moroccan fruit squash and mint tea to drink. It was very cheap. The restaurant was a good vantage point from which to watch the scene on the Place and I subsequently ate all my meals there.

The Place Jemaa-el-Fna is mainly a market by day. The shoe blacks sit in a row, some of them under coloured sunshades, opposite the little restaurants. The taxis and calashes (two horse carriages) line up elsewhere. There are two bus offices at opposite sides of the square. And there are two rows of semi-permanent booths selling everything from yogurt to second-hand clothes. The surface of the square is used by small traders; it was here *les etudiants* had spread their clothes and sold them for hashish.

Towards nightfall everything changes. The water-sellers- much photographed - wearing tasselled hats, dressed in scarlet, brass drinking bowls hooked to the decorated leather straps that pass over their left shoulders, goat-skins of water slung behind their backs, still tinkle their bells; and amongst the motley *djellabahs* and bright shirts small yashmakked girls thread their way, hand in hand. But a great many men and youths come in from the souk and the fondouks and the square is largely taken over by entertainers; musicians playing the *ud-er-rhab,* a two-stringed violin, or the *ta'wwadit,* a kind of flute, or guitars, or other instruments weird in appearance and sound; and there are singers, story-tellers, buffoons, acrobats, snake-charmers, handsome Chleuh boy dancers, fortune-tellers, medicine-men, magicians, old men with tame monkeys and obedient, possibly hypnotized, pigeons. Each entertainer has his own audience in a circle around him.

The crowd is mostly Moroccan but it is very varied as it is in Marrakesh, and especially in the Place, that people congregate from the oases of the southern desert, Sus, and Ifni, the Ait Ouaouzguit, the High Atlas and Mauretania, to find their entertainment and pleasure.

The whole square resounds with merriment; singing, dancing, clapping, tinkling, shouting, half a dozen kinds of music.

Tourists take photographs by day from the high flat roof of the Hotel C.T.M.; they process in 'crocodiles' led by official guides, into the souk; in the evening they venture out in groups.

If you walk alone in the evening, you are quickly accosted by youths or boys and although they genuinely like to talk to and enjoy the company of anyone from another country, every conversation, sooner or later, includes the same invitation.

One group of three who started a conversation with me proved quite interesting. Apparently, there is an organisation known as Jeunnesse et Sports which has a Connaissance du Maroc section (or a C. du M. organization which has a J. et S. section); this organizes tours and camps and sends boys to them in the summer months. The trio had come from Essaouira to take part in swimming competitions in Marrakesh. One of them, Abdal Rasheed al Riyad, an Arab whose father had come from Baghdad via Algeria and then died, leaving his family without support, wanted to earn money in the usual way - which I think may have been his only means of survival - but after I had given him a few dirhams for food he escorted me pleasantly and courteously back to the door of the Hotel where he vanished discreetly into the shadows; he seemed an intelligent and well mannered boy.

That night there was some kind of merry-making in a nearby fondouk and I fell asleep to the faint strains of singing and the plangence of a *ribab* stroking plaintive notes out of a two-string fiddle while a seed rattle, the muffled thump of a dancer's bare feet and occasional chanting provided accompaniment.

One morning I walked down the Riad Zitoun Kedim to its far end and an unsolicited 'guide' attached himself to me and led me to the Palais de la Bahia where, with a few other tourists, Dutch and German, I strolled through various ornate reception rooms, the extensive harem court-yards and bedrooms (empty of life) and a pleasant shady garden.

Then to the Dar si Said, a museum of Moroccan arts and handicrafts where antique carpets line the walls and fine pottery and impressive brassware are on display; but, preserved in a palace turned museum, and guarded by uniformed attendants, it all seemed inadequate like trying to view the fierce pageant of Moroccan history through a dusty lens. I could not help recalling, all the time, that only a kilometre away sprawled the pulsating souk, a vital living exhibition where everything was for use and sale, a sufficient magnet, one would think, to attract traders and travellers from the ends of the earth.

The amateur dragoman led me later to the roof of a ruined palace with a prospect of the glittering snow-clad Atlas mountains high in the sky above the 'rose-red' city. On the broken ramparts and crumbling towers- as so often on buildings in Morocco- black and white storks had made their untidy nests. Part of the ground floor of the palace had been used as a medersa; pigeon-holes in which the schoolboys left their sandals had been scooped out of the thick mud walls.

For my midday meal I selected soup and a sort of goulash (rather a horrid combination) and I drank mint tea. The Arab boy, Abdal Rasheed, appeared in the square and I beckoned him to come and have some tea. He came and sat close beside me on the wooden form and when it was obvious I was leaving much of the goulash he asked whether he might finish it, took over my spoon and ate every scrap.

Before visiting Marrakesh one should have read carefully its history from 1062 and know about the Almoravides, the Almohades and the Saadians, and something of the ferocious Moulay Ismail, the Ben Yussef University, the Koutoubia Mosque which is the Mosque of Libraries - so called because it was formerly surrounded by more than one hundred tiny shops in which manuscripts were sold - and much besides. I had neglected to prepare myself except with a few scraps of information. Once there, I was fascinated by the ordinary life of the city and spent most of my time gawking at and in it.

When the time came to leave I had not seen more than a tiny fraction of what the city had to offer. I left unseen the Saadian tombs, the Aguedal Garden, the Menara Garden, and almost all the palaces and mosques, and I didn't even glimpse the Mamounia Hotel.

Most long bus journeys in Morocco seem to start several hours before the crack of dawn. To catch the bus for Fez I had to be at the bus station at 4:00 a.m.. At 3:30 a.m. the night was almost silent under the moon. I put on my greatcoat - it was pleasantly cool - took my cases and groped down the half-lit staircases to the patio where the night-watchman lay across the heavy outer door with its stupendous bolts, and Wafi Lahoussein, fat with blankets, slept in two chairs. The watchman took my cases, Lahoussein woke up and surprisingly hugged me and kissed me on both cheeks, and I went to the bus station. There were still people in the Place Jemaa-el -Fna, food stalls were open, so was the restaurant where I ate, the barber shops were busy, and veiled and unveiled women, as well as men, passed to and fro. The bus was nearly full of passengers and the engine already running when I took my second class seat.

At 4:30 a.m. we set out - but only across the square. With the stars bright overhead I tried to accept, sleepily, that the old green bus had superseded Flecker's splendid camel:

The camels sniff the evening and are glad ..

Yet the bus also 'sniffed the *morning*', in its own metallic way and at least it had no inconvenient and hazardous hump.

At 5:00 a.m. an old beggar entered the bus, croaked a few stanzas to the accompaniment of his three-string fiddle, collected a few small coins. Then we set out. It was still night but we had 500 kilometres (312 miles) to go.

Moyen Atlas

The route was Tamelelt el Djedid, Beni Mellal, Kasba Tadla, Ouaoumana, El Herri, Khenifra, Hamman, Tiouririne, Azrou, Ifrane, Fez.

We were alternately on plains and among the beautiful hills and valleys of the Moyen Atlas. At Beni Mellal a huge area of flat land - I believe 10,000 square kilometres - was under irrigation. This was the Fkih ben Salah irrigation project, the water coming from the Bin el Ouidane dam somewhere in the blue hills above the town. Concrete channels, raised on trestlework above the surface of the plots, conveyed the sparkling water. Khenifa is sometimes called the pearl of the Middle Atlas; in prosaic words it lies - like an earthly gem - on the river Oum er Rebia at the foot of mountains in rich farming country, perfumed by its numerous gardens of roses, sweet peas and other flowers. Azrou is another flowery and delightful place surrounded by dark cypresses and apple and cherry orchards. Higher up among forests of oak and cedar is Ifrane, full of wooden chalets and pleasant villas that might have been lifted bodily from parts of Europe; there are many Europeans and many small hotels to accommodate a heavy tourist population.

Fez

We entered Fez through the new town. There are three Fezes, or perhaps one should say that Fez is in three parts: the old medina, Fez el Bali, with the Karaouine University as its heart and centre; the Fez Djedid which was built by the Merinides in 1276; and the Ville Nouvelle which was built by the French after 1912.

The bus terminal was next to the Boujeloud Gate leading to the old medina. As soon as I had recovered my baggage from the roof of the bus, I asked one of the youths who was waiting to carry luggage to take me to a cheap hotel costing about six dirhams a night. I followed him round a few corners, through a small arch, to the Hotel Shrabbelein. There was a mosque backing on to the lane and a public drinking fountain near the arch.

At the hotel an Arab receptionist, blind in one eye, took me to a room which I could have for seven and a half dirhams a night. It had a double bed with clean sheets, a wash basin, a wardrobe, table and chair; the heavily grilled window looked down on to the Kasbah de Boujeloud. The communal toilet was squat type with a tiled floor. I saw no bathroom.

Although families with children occupied some of the rooms, the place was a fairly small and simple fondouk; and the receptionist reminded me of Horatio

Nelson applying the telescope to his blind eye when he chose to avoid seeing what was obvious. Bringing in my luggage I had to brush off about six cherubic small boys in a hundred yards; around nightfall there were loiterers from the age of eight upwards in the outside lane; and when I came in for the night a yashmakked female - I suspect laid on for my benefit as a special treat - waited at the foot of the staircase.

The hotel 'thrower-out', a brawny young Berber with brown eyes and a thick mop of hair - his name was Haroon Harazam - enrolled himself as my guide and protector. That evening when I went out to eat he led me only a short distance through the onion-shaped arch of the Bab de Boujeloud before we turned downhill into the medina.

A narrow doorway led past tureens of steaming food into a restaurant open patio-wise in the centre with tables in alcoves and a tiny staircase leading to alcoves upstairs. I persuaded Haroon to eat with me and we had a delicious salad, followed by chicken-with-almonds and bread, with black coffee to drink. Aromas from the kitchen below wafted over the low cusped balustrade of the balcony.

In one of the alcoves downstairs someone who was presumably also a stranger had three small boys stroking his legs, licking his ears and attempting further intimacies - he flung them all off with a laugh when the waiter brought his food.

Although it was Friday next day and all the small shops of the souk were closed - some only in the morning, others all day - Haroon conducted me for miles through and around the medina. The houses and shops are built very close together, a mass of grey and white cubes of all sizes and at all angles with here and there a green tiled roof, the whole city filling a saucer-shaped hollow in the hills. The streets are a puzzling labyrinth of short twisting alleys and culs-de-sac in which the sun does not penetrate; steep, cobbled, sometimes barred with shallow steps, infinitely mediaeval.

We walked in alleys like deep canyons that encompass the Karaouine Mosque; this can accommodate 22,000 worshippers and it has nineteen doors. Some of the great knobbed and decorated doors were open, allowing a glimpse of brightly coloured courtyards and pavilions and long, rather austere naves with rows of horse-shoe arches. One of the visible courtyards had a fountain; elsewhere, in a stone pool, worshippers in white *djellabahs* washed their feet before going to pray. Alas, only Muslims and sparrows were allowed to pass the nineteen holy portals.

The people crowding in the alleys all moved at different speeds, strolling, loitering, threading quickly and purposively into and out of sight. The women moved in clusters, less conspicuous in their dark *haiks* than the men. I imagined that the sprinkling of pale-faced youths might be Karaouine students.

At one point on the way steeply downhill to the heart of the city there was an unmistakable odour of decaying mutton but it mingled with the frail perfumes of sandalwood, rose and jasmine, drifting from dignified and portly male passers-by.

In one of the leatherware shops I bought a briefcase to replace my battered and lockless 1949 model; it cost only £3.30. And in the big *tapis* emporia that were

MALAŴI

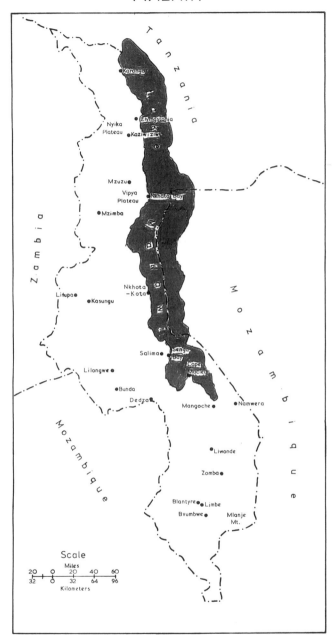

Map of Malawi.

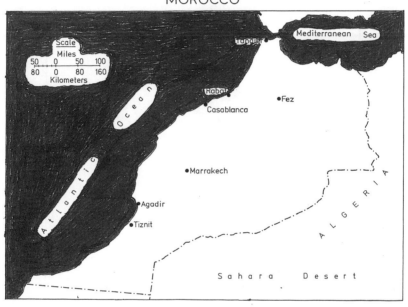

Map of Morocco.

A basket full of fish and women with head loads.

The 'bar' at Fort Johnston, 1916. Loading ships for Karonga.

Rodrick S Mabomba.

Clemence R Namponya.

The historic 'Cowbarn' - built 1968/69 - which was used as a temporary University library from 1969 to 1973. In 1988 it had been fenced and used as the International Development Agency Implementation Unit of the Ministry of Education.

Left to right: Ahmadi Tambala, Musa Malenga and Chief Malenga.

Interior of the 'Cowbarn', 1969, while still a library.

Terminus for fishing dug-outs, Lake Chilwa.

Fred Johnson and early Malawi national library Service staff.

O Ambali in 1992

**The 'Centipede' towing three badges on Zambezi river
in 1916 transporting troops to Nyasaland (World War I)**

Overnight accommodation at Lifupa Game reserve near Kasungu.

Food stores (*nkhokwe*), Senga Bay.

Preliminary work on the University Library, Chirunga, 1972.

Phase One of the University of Malawi Library.

Phase Two of the University of Malawi Library.

**President Banda looks critically at books on Malawi
in Chancellor College Library.**

University of Malawi main Library, Chancellor College.

Catalogues on Roneo stripdex, University of Malawi
main Library, Chancellor College, Zomba.

A Lake Chilwa dweller facing Zomba

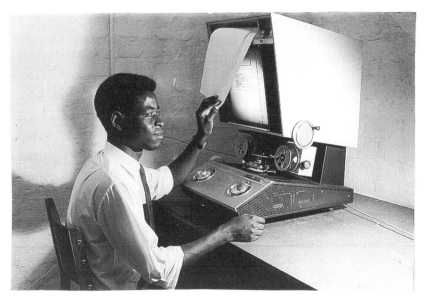

Dick Najira using the microfilm reader-printer at Chancellor College Library.

Malawi National Library Service HQ up to 1979, Limbe.

Malawi National Library Service HQ since 1979, Lilongwe.

Malawi National Library Service, Lilongwe Branch.

From right to left: N Chiwere (Soche Hill College Library,
Joseph Nduna (Chancellor College) and O Ambali (Chancellor
College Library).

Malawi National Library Service HQ, Lending Library.

Examining the catch of fish, Lake Chilwa.

open, Friday or not, I compared, coveted and caressed a dozen or more soft and sumptuous carpets.

Later in the afternoon we went, by petit-taxi, to the Ville Nouvelle where an agricultural fair and exhibition of *artisanat* was being held.

Again there were carpets; and leather pouffes in white and blue and gold and many other colours; and embroidered cloths and carved tables and basketry; and dazzling displays of silver, brass and copper trays; and goblets and ewers and bowls and long-necked silver containers shaped like pilgrim bottles from which rose or orange blossom water is sprinkled over the hands into a silver urn before a meal is begun.

I was particularly interested in the stall operated by the Co-operative Society of the Patrons of Tanners. Here were perfectly cured and dyed whole goat-skins in colours of exciting clarity - cobalt, scarlet, gamboge, as well as fawn, white and jet black, almost a whole spectrum of colours. Prices ranged from 24 dirhams for a dull brown skin to 32 dirhams for the azure blue. This organization is under the technical control of the Ministry of Tourism, Artisanat and Fine Arts.

I had hoped to visit the Karaouine University which is the oldest in the western world but the University was on vacation, the university office was closed and no staff or students were apparent. The only building to which visitors could gain access was a dining-room - to which we were led by a cheerful young man who climbed down from a roof - but this was monastically bare and chill. The garden outside was littered with torn paper.

Continuing our carpet prowl, I chose eventually a gorgeous carpet in Rabat style in sixteen colours at the Palais Mnebi which is the shop of Abdesslam Essentissi at 15, Souikte Ben Safi. It would be sent by air freight at my expense and the *proprietaire* assured me that I would receive it in England in a month's time. (I did.)

The Palais Mnebhi was as interesting as a museum. The 'shop' occupied three of the four alcoves around a tiled patio with a small extinct fountain in the centre. One assumes that shops of this opulent kind have been family palaces or homes in the past. They are utterly bare and blank on the outside walls, which may rise from a slum-like narrow alley, but inside they are full of light; the tiled columns and graceful arches and the rich geometry of the ceramic walls are at least temporarily pleasing.

The shop operated a restaurant for customers, very expensive it seemed, but as it was my last day in Fez and I'd had only a piece of bread for breakfast, I decided that Haroon and I should eat there. While preparations were made we went up on the flat roof from which there was a panoramic view of the city. Pink and red roses bloomed in the small roof garden around the parapet, the grey, buff and white rectangles and cubes of the buildings of Fez, with the green tiled roof of the Zaouia Moulay Idris, lay below and around, and the slopes of the Merinide Hills formed a background at the far side of the townscape.

Sitting among cushions on low divans, our meal began with ceremony: the waiter brought the tall-necked silver sprinkler, poured the perfumed rose water over our hands, allowing the water to trickle away in a large urn perhaps itself of silver, and gave each of us a small towel. We had a delicious salad, followed by a heavenly *bstila* - the meat of pigeons combined in some secret way with pastry and sugar - and we finished with fresh oranges and coffee.

Each day Haroon asked me to buy him cigarettes which I was glad to do; each time I noticed that he bought those which contained hashish; he said that it was very good for him. I tried to ask him what effect it had but we got into linguistic difficulties and he waved his hand around his head to indicate a sense of euphoria and I had to leave it at that. His wages at the hotel were five dirhams a day - enough to buy food although not as much as he could eat, and enough for his hashish. He slept at the hotel except for one night a week when he visited his father in a village outside the city.

The Slave Market

That afternoon - Haroon having gone to the cinema with some money I had given him - I was walking alone through the open space outside the medina where the buses and petit-taxis scoop up passengers for the Ville Nouvelle. It was the site of the old slave market and the time of day when slaves had formerly been sold. Many of the great walls and buildings within sight were said to have been built by Christian slaves from Europe, captured by the Barbary corsairs and sold in Fez. A group of people sat gossiping on a wall and I was surprised when one of them beckoned and called to me.

'Come!' he commanded. This was a man who reminded me of Van Gogh's postman, hairy and alive, brown - skinned, thirty-five or so, wearing rather frayed European clothes. Four youths were with him.

After shaking hands all round and declining a seat on the wall, I answered as best I could the expected and entirely friendly questions about my nationality, country, length of my stay in Morocco, profession, age, destination, and, finally, marital status. Then one of the boys said:

'You have only one wife,' and - referring to the older man - 'He has *four* wives.'

'Oh yes,' said the older man in English. 'I am too *hot*. Twenty - six childrens. Every year two more childrens. Very good, huh?'

I congratulated him.

Then he continued, 'you want boy? Here I have four good boys. I sell them to you? You buy them and take them to England. Or you buy one. They cheap. I not charge you much.'

Obviously, one needed a knowledge of the current price of slaves, grade one. Or perhaps I was not meant to take the offer seriously. Perhaps visitors were given this treatment as part of the normal chit-chat. I thanked Van Gogh for his offer but said that the inconvenient laws made it too difficult to get boys into my country at present. As I moved away a pleasant looking youth in a green T -shirt rose and accompanied me. He insisted that he wanted to be taken to England. He would be my servant. I need not pay him any wages. He followed me to a cafe and we drank mint tea. Apparently, he was twenty, his father (not the gentleman who was *hot*) had sent him to some sort of technical school where he learned the trade of welding.

But in Fez there was no work for him, no future, nothing to do day after day but wander round the streets and meet his friends, all of whom were equally jobless.

'Hundreds of us are without work', he said.

He wanted to study pharmacy but he would work as my house servant, do any work I wanted him to do, sleep with me if required, if only I would take him to England. His home was somewhere nearby and he dashed away for a few minutes to bring his younger brother, another intelligent boy still at school, to meet me. We all drank mint tea, and I tried to explain the real immigration laws of Britain and exactly why I could not put him in my suitcase and take him with me. In the end, after struggling with my feeble French and apocopic Arabic, he accepted the verdict - almost in tears - and escorted me politely back to the fondouk.

Fez was an enigma. Was Fez el Bali one huge slum? Was the famous Karaouine University, controlled by its *ulema,* still teaching mainly such subjects as the *Shra* (laws), theology, rhetoric, Islamic jurisprudence, panegyric of the Prophet? I had not yet discovered and for all I knew it might offer courses in modern management, tropospheric scatter aerial technology and systems analysis; in my ignorance I was not allowed to doubt or utter a depreciatory word. But what about unemployment and under - employment? The four boys who were for sale? What about the still smaller boys, who looked so angelic, who seemed to be part of *la vie de Fez*?

Yet against my doubts, I was conscious of the city's unique reputation, its wealth, its history stretching back more than a thousand years. Had not Leo Africanus and Ibn Khaldun both studied at the Karaouine? What of the opinion of a friend of mine who had lived in old Fez and enjoyed the cultural and intellectual life for thirty years? What about the medersas, the three hundred mosques, the 126 guilds of craftsmen producing some of the most exquisite *artisanat* in the world?

I knew I had caught only glimpses and echoes and quarter - truths that I could neither correlate nor evaluate.

Tangier

My journey to Tamgier began next day at 5:00 a.m. Even at 4:30 a.m., when I left the hotel, the one - eyed receptionist was already on duty in the reception recess; his final smirk was no doubt intended as a cordial *au revoir* and *bon voyage* but it was not up to Wafi Lahoussein standard.

The Kasbah de Boujeloud was deserted and still dark as I carried my cases quickly the short distance to the Bab from which the buses started.

The day's route was: Moulay Bou Chta, Mjara, Karrouba, Ouezzane, I think Laraiche although I am not sure of this, Arcila and Tangier. Again the country was very fertile, great stretches of land were bright with pimpernel, cornflowers, ox-eye daisies, larkspur, vetch, harebells, lupins, irises, buttercups and other wild flowers,and at one point there was a plain covered with red poppies.

I had not had a chance to drink even water before setting out and I was very glad when we came to a village where a whole ram, evidently skinned that morning, hung on a gibbet at the side of the road and the local butcher stood by with a long knife ready to execute orders from the passengers. About half a dozen men selected joints, brought them back inadequately wrapped and stowed them on the roof rack in the bus. Their activities gave me an opportunity to satisfy my thirst with Turkish coffee at a nearby stall.

I was very tired when we reached Tangier about midday, not having slept the previous night, and I really did not appreciate the town which, superficially, seemed rather like Brighton or Blackpool. I trudged from the sea - front up to the boulevard and the airline office which, as it was Sunday, was closed. From the janitor I managed to discover that a plane was leaving that afternoon for Gibraltar; there was nowhere to wait so I returned to the sea-front.

In the Espagnol Restaurant I had fish and chips and partially revived and fortified myself with Moroccan beer. A trinket seller was pestering a group of English North country lads and lasses; when he offered me some trumpery 'amber' necklaces that were obviously made of plastic I growled at him in my fiercest pidgin Arabic and he retreated abashed, asking, *'You are Marocain?'* Later, I watched him go to the back of the restaurant, hide in a corner, bring out his green hashish pipe and take a few puffs before coming out again and continuing his chore. I felt entirely sympathetic with him and he probably sensed this as he waved the pipe in my direction but it was too late to see whether hashish would revive me, too. We grinned across the remains of my fish and chips.

Later in the day I went on to England.

* * * * * * * * * *

MALAWI

In mid - December 1970 the seven Malawians returned to Blantyre from the College of Librarianship Wales, and after a short holiday they started work in the various libraries. We gave a 'welcome home' party for them and Gladys managed to cook for thirty - two people.

The university administration only grudgingly conceded that they were senior staff and even more reluctantly conceded that the Part II examination of the British Library Association should be equated, for salary purposes, with a Malawian degree. It was obvious they would have to prove their merit by hard work before they were accepted.

From my diary 1971

11 January
Gladys has sewing - machined eighty - five feet of curtains for the lakeshore cottage; she is now making covers for the mattresses.

I have been buying galvanized piping so that at the Cottage, by using a T - joint, we can take water into the outside kitchen which, so far, has had none. I have also bought electrical fittings by means of which I hope to get electricity into the kitchen. Also more cornices for the last of the ceilings. At Abegg's, the hardware shop in Limbe, I am now granted contractor's prices, less 20%.

The internal decoration of the Cottage is now finished. It was delayed because the railway had been washed away and a consignment of timber I sent from Limbe was consequently late in reaching Senga Bay.

Antony arrived from Dar es Salaam on 3 January, looking very tired and thin, so I took a few days local leave and we went to the Lake. There had been a freak storm and the strong stone wall in front of the Cottage had been undermined by water from the roof and had fallen on to the beach. The walls of the garage had also collapsed so I have hired a builder to come and re-build them.

The evening before we arrived a hippo wandered into the garden and Dalamkwanda who was concerned to protect the crops of the villagers shot at it - ineffectually - with his gun.

In the lagoon we saw two crocodiles: they will have to be destroyed before it is safe to swim in the Lake.

18 January

In Blantyre last week the rain scarcely stopped. We planned to have a party for the Old Lady on Thursday but she was unable to come as she was ill in bed. On Friday we went to see her and found her seriously ill with malaria. On Sunday, however, when we called again, she was up with her hair dressed, her make-up on, receiving visitors and wearing her floral dressing gown with a Chinese collar. She is to have a companion to live with her, a Mrs Dann.

26 January

I have been allowed to see a government file on the 'Salima Lakeshore Tourism Project'. After I described the proposals as best I could to the Old Lady, her comments were castigatory:

'An absolute pipe dream! People will never live on the lakeshore because it's too hot! Motel! *Conference centre! Golf course!* People will only go there to swim!'

But I think that most of the Project is feasible and that the lakeshore can easily become a holiday place for expatriates from Zambia and Rhodesia as well as Malawi. As for people coming out from the future Capital City of Lilongwe - the road to the Lake could be thick with cars every week-end (which makes it sound horrible).

My only adverse comments relate to the way local ordinary Malawians may be affected.

For instance, Dalamkwanda came to me, very upset, because he had been ordered by government to go back into the forest from which he had been removed some years ago. He does not know why. No one has ever told him about the Project. If he goes, it means, presumably, that his village of 79 households will also have to move. This could include semi-skilled artisans who have worked on the Technical Institute project or who work for Walter Stansfield at the Grand Beach Hotel. These people could usefully remain near the future cottages where there would be plenty of work for them. Is it necessary to herd the local population into a kind of ghetto where they will not contaminate the cottage dwellers?

And what will become of Kandulu? How could he build boats - modern boats, not dug-outs - far from the beach?

And what of Heston Tandaza who keeps a herd of cattle in the area scheduled for development? Most of the present lakeshore cottages buy their milk from him, and I believe that the Grand Beach Hotel and the Germans of the Central Region Lakeshore Development Project, who are our neighbours, also buy his milk.

If fishing is not to be permitted in Senga Bay, the tourists will not see the fishermen haul in their nets in the early morning and at sunset - itself a great tourist attraction.

And I wonder whether the European old-stagers in Senga Bay - Stansfield (29) and Mrs Smith - have been consulted by the planners? Stansfield's advice could be most valuable.

I would like to see the fishermen retained; Kandulu and other artisans allowed to stay where they are; Heston and his cattle and poultry allowed to remain; market gardening developed; the beach kept clear of weeds; the crocodiles shot. I would be quite willing for tourists to use the Cottage when we are not staying there ourselves but I would like to retain the right to say 'No!' to wreckers and riff-raff.

On the whole, I think the scheme is workable and sensible - in fact exciting.

Conference in Addis Ababa

The Conference of the Standing Committee on African University Libraries (SCAUL) was held at the Haile Sellassie I University in Addis Ababa 10-13 February, 1971.

I flew first to Dar es Salaam where Antony clattered me around the city and out to the coast in a disreputable car which he called 'Tinkerbell'. The Bureau of Resource Assessment & Land Use Planning for which he is working is based in the University and when he is not 'in the field' he inhabits a small room in one of the multi-storey concrete blocks that embellish an impressive campus.

The next leg of the journey was to Nairobi where I stayed overnight at the New Avenue Hotel. At the airport next morning there was half an hour's kefuffle as Ethiopian Airlines had over-booked the flight by about twenty people, many of them librarians en route to the Conference. The outcome was that they had to fill empty seats in the first class cabin with a disreputable rabble of university librarians with economy tickets.

Once on the ground in Ethiopia, the arrangements made for us were impeccable. The wife of the University President who is on the Library staff greeted us at the airport, arranged for visas to be issued to us, and we were wafted through Customs and Immigration with no attempt made to look at our cases. I was booked in at the Ethiopia Hotel which was very modern and pleasant in every way. Four guards armed with lathis, at the main doors of the hotel, ensured that thieves could not slink into the building after dark.

Over lunch, Tucker Lwanga of Makerere University gave us a first-hand account of the coup d'etat in Uganda. He lives only nine houses away from Amin's house on the same hill. He and his family stayed indoors while there was spasmodic shooting and then, when it stopped, they began to go through the garden hedges at the back of their houses to visit each other and find out what had happened. They heard on the radio that Amin had taken over. Tucker said that after the announcement he had never seen such scenes of jubilation. The Baganda rushed into the streets, climbed aboard the tanks and other military vehicles and sang and cheered all over Kampala. Milton Obote had been unpopular since he seized power; although originally voted into office, he had given himself authority over Government, on one occasion when the Constitution was changed telling his Ministers they could find copies of the new Constitution in their pigeon-holes as they left the Parliament building.

That first afternoon there was an official opening ceremony by Dr Aklilu Habte, the President of Haile Sellassie I University. Later, we elected Tucker as Conference chairman and discussed 'The development the National Bibliographic Apparatus in Eastern Africa'.

In the evening Richard and Rita Pankhurst (30) invited delegates to a buffet supper at their home which stands on a hill in Addis Ababa city; a heavy iron gate guarded the entrance to the compound. Richard dispensed drinks which, after a quantity of local wine, included coffee tea, mimosa tea and jasmine tea. I think it must have been the last I had; it was as red as wine. The lounge where we congregated was full of beautiful carvings, ceramics, paintings and unusual objects.

On 11 February we had four sessions, concerned with 'Eastern Area Exchanges', 'Acquisition of African Government Publications', 'Cataloguing and Classification of Africana' (with which I had to deal) and 'Education for Librarianship in Eastern Africa'.

That evening some of us attended a meeting of the Society of Friends of the Institute of Ethiopian Studies and heard a lecture by Ato Solomon Deressa of the Broadcasting Corporation, followed by readings of stories and poems by contemporary writers some of whom we met as they were present in the audience. Solomon was bearded and looked like a younger version of the Emperor Haile Sellasie. The readers were Solomon's wife, a young playwright and his wife, and Rita: the language was English except for an initial poem in Amharic.

Next day we had sessions on ' An Organization of SCAUL Eastern Area and a 'Proposed Constitution and Future Activities of SCAUL Eastern Area' and 'Relationships with Library International Organizations', and a final session in which finance and the *Newsletter* were discussed.

That evening there was a sumptuous reception by the University President at Addis Ababa Restaurant. The bus rattled up another stony approach lane and we were ushered into a large circular room, panelled in red cloth, with shields, spears, drums and carvings pendent on the walls. Divans covered by rugs had been placed around the room as seats, and some of us sat on small concave-topped stools covered with animal skins. In the centre of each cluster of stools and divans was a table with a huge basket woven of decorative rushes.

In one arc of this extraordinary room two rows of eight musicians, dressed in white and wearing white *shammas* around their shoulders, played the *kabaro* drum, a one-stringed fiddle called a *masank'o* similar to those I had seen in Marrakesh, the *kerar* (a lyre), the *begenna* (a harp), the *washint* (a fife with four holes in it), an *embilta* (flute) and a *malaket,* a trumpet with which sheperds call their sheep. From time to time the musicians danced as they played, mainly the *esketa* shoulder clicking dance.

It was suprising what attractive and plaintive music could be wrung out of such a weird collection of wire, wood, animal gut and goat-skin, and the dancing, first with the shoulders and head only with the lower part of the body motionless, and later with the feet only, in a peculiar scampering and scuttling amazingly fast, was also exciting.

To begin with, we were all given a welcoming glass of gin and vermouth. Then the serious business of an Ethiopian meal began. Girls in white cotton dresses came and removed the covers on the large baskets, revealing in each basket an enamel bowl covered with a great pancake that looked like foam rubber - called *injera*--limp and slightly sour but very light and tasty. One had to eat the *injera* (like eating the tablecloth as well as the food), using it to pick up the delicacies which the girls came and placed in little heaps in front of each guest. The food consisted mainly of meats, including *berando,* raw minced beef, and cheese, all of it - except the *berando* which I could not stomach - delicious. There were no knives or forks.

With the food we drank carafes of *t'ej,* a fermented beverage made of honey, water and malt, which was very agreeable, and one's carafe was filled up the moment it passed from under one's eye. Some people claimed later they drank fifteen carafes of this honey beer: I drank only two as I was not sure what the after effects might be.

At one stage after I had eaten about two square feet of *injera* and sampled about eight heaps of delicious but unidentifiable meats and gravies, some spiced, some not, the wife of Dr. Aklilu Habte thought some of us were being too reticent and came and fed us with her own hands.

After all this, we were expected to dance, and the whole room was quickly whirling with wild librarians clicking their shoulders like mad in the *esketa* and performing everything from High Life to Apollo 12. The band were also dancing - no longer like Ethiopian shepherds - and I hope the photographer got some of the interesting sights on to film as they would greatly add to the interest of official journals of librarianship.

From my diary 1971

26 February

Louis Frewer, Keeper of Rhodes House Library, Oxford, came to visit us in Malawi after the conference in Addis.

On Thursday I took him to Zomba to visit the Government Printer and the Government Archives. We had lunch with Marion and Jeff, then drove up Zomba mountain for Louis to see the view, but there was heavy rain so we came down again and visited instead the site of the future University at Chirunga. Most of the grass and bushes have been scraped off the site and it is flatter now than it formerly was. The architects plan to use Chirunga House as their office while construction of the University takes place, so Jeffrey's bookbinding staff will have to vacate the rooms in which they are squatters.

On Friday Gladys took charge of Louis in the morning and took him to Phekani's and I took him to Mulanje in the afternoon. Friday evening we were all out at Fred Johnson's to dinner.

Louis was willing to face the possible hazards of a drive to the Lake in the wet season so early on Saturday morning we set off for Senga Bay and arrived there about 2:00 p.m. The Salima/Grand Beach road was worse than I have ever known it - pot-holed, corrugated, eroded and slippery; the best way to get along it was to drive at the extreme edge of the road.

The beach wall in front of the Cottage, although crudely rebuilt, now appears to be strong again, and there is a buttress at one side of the front steps. The walls of the garage fell down again after the builder, half-wittedly built them up with mud instead of waiting for more cement. As soon as we'd had a meal I had to drive back to Salima to buy six more bags of cement and replenish the supplies of petrol and paraffin.

On Saturday the water pump was not working and in the course of the evening the Honda generator 'died'. On Sunday morning Member repaired them both, completely dissecting the water pump and adjusting a tappet; and in the Honda generator he substituted a piece of wire for a sparking plug. On Sunday, as a result, we had both water and light.

During Saturday/Sunday night two hippos came into the garden. We didn't see them but Louis heard them burping and in the morning we found their spoor between the cottage and the servants' quarters. The local people say that the crocodiles in the lagoon have now been killed. An eight-foot python, dead, was floating in the lagoon and we had it fished out so that Louis could photograph it. Several other snakes have been killed in the garage. The government has removed part of the great heap of debris that the day labourers I engaged (Esau Pirabuta, Kachiri Pikis & Co.) had taken from the Lake. The garden looked neglected and Aisa said Stephen had been drunk every night for the past month - he certainly looked thin and I shall probably have to find another gardener.

On Monday morning as we were having breakfast a large floating island of sudd drifted slowly across the Lake from the direction of Cape Maclear and came to rest twenty yards beyond Plot 7, between us and the lagoon. It was eighty yards long, forty feet across and it consisted of matted papyrus and bulrushes eight feet high. We hope that a storm or the government - whichever is the more efficient - will dispose of it.

On the way back on Monday we had a delicious late lunch at Joan and Richard's at Domasi.

Louis departed on Tuesday's V.C.10 - a very easy guest to entertain.

9 March

On Saturday we had Bridglal Pachai, Professor of History, Leela his wife and the Old Lady to lunch. The purpose of bringing them together was to give Bridglal a chance of meeting the Old Lady and eliciting reminiscences from her. She can recall uncomfortable travelling conditions coming up the Zambezi River before World War I and she remembers vividly (and has photographs of) the arrival of troops in 1916 when the 'Centipede' steam vessel towed three barges upstream from Quelimane. I warned Bridglal beforehand that she would undoubtedly refer to Indians as 'Banians'.

He asked her about her early life in Malawi (then Nyasaland), about the places in which she had lived, her experiences at the time of the Chilembwe 'Rising' in 1915, about her life at Fort Johnston during the First World War, about Mr Hynde who gave Blantyre its first electricity and piped water and organized, at Fort Johnston, the first cinema in the country, and about people who held posts of responsibility when she first came to the country. The Old Lady co-operated splendidly and recalled the past vividly and systematically and even when she forgot herself and denounced the 'Banians' I think Bridglal was merely amused.

The following day (Sunday) Joan and Richard came from Domasi and we made another excursion into history, taking a picnic lunch to Chikwawa, down the still terrible escarpment with hairpin bends strewn with loose stones and rocky snags sticking up through the surface of the road. Half-way down, a Peace Corps girl hailed us and asked for a lift to Chikwawa where she was a teacher at the Day Secondary School. She had four white rats in a little wooden cage and she deposited these in the back of the car next to our food for the picnic.

We crossed the splendid Kamuzu Bridge, failed to find a satisfactory picnic site near the river which was full and smooth and shining in the sun, so we took a road labelled 'Chibisa's Traditional Court', parked the car under a locust bean tree and ate in only moderate discomfort.

We probably had the same view of the Shire River that Chief Chibisa had of Livingstone's party when they came up the river in 1859. It was near here that the first Christian church in Malawi was built in five days of wooden posts and reeds by Richard Martin Clark, a tanner and shoemaker who wrote about his pioneer creation:

> I must tell you that we have no church bell,
> and that the substitute for one is a native drum.

To-day Chikwawa is mainly an administrative centre: a large and impressive Boma building, modern mosquito-proofed houses for the administrators, the District Comissioner's house with a view of a bend in the river, a few shops including several evidently owned by 'Banians', and African thatched huts among the trees. From the escarpment there was a magnificent prospect of green ridges and blue mountains and the Shire Valley; the sky was crystal clear and one could see a hundred miles. (31

Smart has had news that his house in Namwera (between Mangoche and the border of Mozambique) has been burned to the ground, so he had to go off this week, leaving his wife Aswan and the two children here.

A piece of coralita from the Lake garden has taken root in the Blantyre garden; the cannas are flames seven feet high; there are thickets of chrysanthemums; and the oranges are almost ripe.

Smart cut the lawn with his langa langa before departing for Namwera which was thoughtful of him.

15 March

Last week I arranged to get my ears syringed which is a great relief as I was deaf for three days. I went to Byl, the Dutch doctor who lives in Chirimba, but he had no surgery that day, so in desperation I went to the first other doctor whose nameplate I saw. This turned out to be a Sikh so rotund that only his enormous waistcoat prevented him from bursting. He had once been employed by the Shire Highlands Railway but was long retired although still 'practicing'.

On one wall of his surgery was his framed certificate allowing him to practice, plus various framed press cuttings; on another wall were astrological charts from which, presumably, he obtained guidance. After muttering an incantation in Punjabi, he shone an ordinary electric torch into my ear, muttered, 'Yes' as if he'd seen something horrible, then tried to syringe my ears with a huge syringe like a vaginal spray. This had no effect at all, but I said it made me feel more comfortable and, after paying his modest fee of 5/-, I made my escape.

Next day I went to Byl. He was very efficient and quickly cleared both ears without any fuss but with proper instruments, and I can now hear again - in fact, my hearing is so good that this typewriter sounds like a traction engine going along a metalled road.

23 March

Having a day's holiday due to me, we set off for the Lake on Friday morning at 6:00 am, waited three-quarters of an hour to go down the Kasupe Escarpment where road repairs were taking place, and another fifteen minutes in Lilongwe where the Ngwazi was visiting the first completed factory on the Capital City site, and arrived at Senga Bay about 1.30 p.m.. The road through the Angoni Highlands has been scraped by a grader so that the Ngwazi who travelled by road should not get concussion; the road from Salima to the Lake was still very corrugated but less dangerous than a month ago. It was a hot day for driving.

At the Cottage all was well. Both faithful retainers were present and correct. Aisa looked very tired; Stephen not too exhausted. There had been more hippos in the garden, right up to the stone terraces. While we were there the garden was visited by a pair of red-billed hornbills (or perhaps Von der Decken's hornbills) which came to the Afzelia tree at the front of the Cottage. At night there was some small creature, probably a galago, in the roof.

On Saturday I seemed to be active all day. First I found a labourer (Mseni Aka) and set him to work burning the dried lake weed that is still spread out on the beach. Then I showed Stephen the gardener how to excavate and level the road up to the Cottage. I also had Madi and Chintambo II (builders) constructing a drain alongside the garage and I had to show them by demonstration that water would not run up-hill. I arranged with painters to come the next day and paint the wooden wardrobe. I asked the fishermen to keep some fish for our household when the dug-outs came in. I asked Member to service the Honda. Late in the afternoon Kandulu and I removed the old sitting-room suite (a settee and four chairs), now cleansed of fleas, plus the moth-eaten lion skin, a pair of buffalo horns and the wreckage of a record player, from the small store to Kandulu's thatched hut, in three car loads: he said he would like them as momentos of Mrs Snowden.

In between times there was the routine trip to Salima. I had bought three extra five-gallon oil tins and I had to clean these out with petrol, then drive to Salima, buy some fattening groundnuts for Stephen, buy six bags of cement from Bharucha, buy twenty gallons of petrol and four gallons of paraffin - and I managed to get Gladys a bunch of green grapes.

At 6:00 p.m. I couldn't get the generator to work, so we had to manage with the Aladdin lamp and the Tilley lamp which Kandulu demonstrated to Aisa.

Sunday was more restful. I paid the two builders; they charged £23.00 for building the garage wall and it is not well done; I encouraged Member who was dissecting the Honda so that later it went very well; started the painters painting the wardrobe; turned out junk from the paint store, started Kandulu repairing mosquito screens and fitting springs on doors; got Member to re-adjust the lavatory cistern so that it did not overflow; asked Aisa to engage somebody to remove stone, bricks and timber from the old pigsties to the back of the servants' quarters where - when we have the money - they will be used to build a new kitchen for the servants; showed Stephen how and where to plant out forty tomato plants brought from Blantyre; paid the painters and Aisa; helped Kandulu take measurements for glass for broken windows and curtain rails and pelmets and compiled a list of items that must be bought for other odd jobs.

In between times, we collected the local gossip from Kandulu and Member. The Grand Beach Hotel will be taken over by Government from 5 April. Stansfield has removed all alcohol from it and much besides. In Salima, Bharucha's shop has been burgled; the thieves cut the throat of the night-watchman and strangled his wife who had come to sleep with him, then broke in and stole the money. Bharucha has bought another cottage farther along the Lakeshore, next to that owned by John 'Kaka' Msonthi, Minister of Transport and Communications.

Yesterday, coming back to Blantyre, I ran into a cow twenty miles out of Lilongwe. The car bonnet was dented and the cow was knocked down and probably dented, too, but she quickly scrambled to her feet and ran off to the side of the road where she was pursued and severely beaten by the cowherd who had allowed her to step out from the herd smack in front of the car.

We called in at Domasi to see Richard and Joan.

Within half an hour of going to work I was asked to do a radio broadcast on the Library.

Today I've checked through forty letters applying for vacant library assistant posts and have drawn up a short list.

25 March

We are experiencing the chaotic aftermath of the British postal strike. *The Times* arrives the day after it is published, but little surface mail is coming through, and airmail dated March, February, January and even December is dribbling in erratically. The official examination results of our 'returned Malawians' have arrived via the diplomatic pouch, Rodrick's landlady, the British Council and the Library Association but two of the seven results have not arrived at all. Correspondence about Msiska's scholarship seems to have been lost; it should have been conveyed in the diplomatic pouch.

We are in a period of rapid staff change and some consolidation. Gordon Hazeldine, sub-librarian, is to be Librarian of the Technical Institute in Bandung, Indonesia, in September this year. Ann Yarr, chief cataloguer, is now working exclusively at Soche Hill College, re-classifying the stock in preparation for total re-cataloguing. Brian is at Chancellor College as acting chief cataloguer. Moira Woods, our VSO, completed her assignment in February but we have offered her a contract position for two years and she will be in charge of acquisitions for that period. Rodrick is understudying Brian and will take over cataloguing when he leaves in July. The postal strike has given us a lull in some of the work and we are taking advantage of it by bringing out arrears of accession lists.

Our Blantyre garden has been bright with dahlias, petunias, chrysanthemums, balsams and flowering bushes. We are having a flush of guavas, avocado pears, oranges and lemons. But it has been raining on and off since last October which is phenomenal and many small plants have been drowned. We have recently experienced the tail-end of a cyclone - Felice - when it rained non-stop for four days and two miles of railway was swept away.

27 March

Driving back to Blantyre from Zomba on 19 March I met the Ngwazi's motorcade. It shrieked round a tight bend in the road at about 70 mph, siren blaring, a machine-gun visible in the first vehicle, armed Police and Young Pioneers in the jeeps and the Ngwazi behind the closed windows of the armour-plated car in which he travels. It is a serious offence, punishable by imprisonment and perhaps death, to stay on any Malawian road when the President and his motorcade use it. I therefore tore the Volvo off the tarmac road into the roadside grasses and rocks, braking fiercely so that I would be stationary by the time the motorcade swept past. Perhaps I was not quite quick enough but I was certain that the Volvo was stationary and the engine turned off by the time the car containing the Ngwazi approached and streaked past with the rest. Apparently as part of the official adulation that is expected, it is customary for motorists to stand beside their cars and *clap* as the car containing the Ngwazi speeds past. I did not know this.

I have since been served a summons to attend a local court in connection with my 'offence' of not pulling off the road and stopping for the President's car to pass. Fortunately for me - as I don't wish to be slammed into jail for an indefinite period - I had as passenger on 19 March a young policeman who had asked me to give him a lift back to Blantyre. At the time of the incident he told me I should use his name as a 'witness for the defence' if the Police brought a case against me. Of course I took the summons immediately to the local police station from which it had emanated, claimed that I had not committed the offence and asked that reference should be made to the young policeman who had been my passenger and given me his name and number. He was found at once somewhere in the rooms at the rear of the police station, he corroborated my version of the story, and the summons was withdrawn.

30 March

About half the seventy oranges on the tree by the bathroom wall have now ripened. We are planting orange and grape-fruit pips in pots to see whether we can secure seedlings in this way. The petrea has a splendid new spike on it and Smart has built a little arbour against which the shrub can climb and proliferate its flowers.

There is a six-inch spider, with a crimson middle segment to its legs, in a huge web near the nests of the weaver birds.

13 April

In the garden we have a fat little toad like a puffball. Margaret Kalk says it is a *Braviceps*, so I think we shall call him 'Braviceps'. The spider's web by the nests of the weaver birds was broken during one of the recent downpours of rain but the arachnid owner has repaired the damage. Gladys has persuaded Million's and Smart's children to pick - and pick up - the guavas; they must have had nearly a thousand this past week, carrying them indoors in anything from Alice's clean skirt to the far from clean dustbin lid. The peach trees are in bloom.

We visited the Old Lady one evening, taking her some of our oranges and lemons. In return we came away loaded with yellow and red bananas, red peppers and tree tomatoes.

Our friends Fred and Irene Johnson have been at the Lake cottage this last week-end. They seem to have enjoyed it and want to book it for a whole week in July. (32) Others are due to be there next week: we think five adults and three children. I have notified a friend at each of the Colleges that the cottage is available for rent when we are not using it and I hope they will tell other people.

30 April

Dorothy Thora Merry and her sister Eleanor Jeanette arrived on 14 April. 'Dolly' is a very experienced teacher of English in secondary schools. She taught at Ashton-in-Makerfield Grammar School, the Queen Mary High School, Anfield, Liverpool, and Mirfield Grammar School in Yorkshire before coming to the Royal Latin School, Buckingham, in 1926 (where she attempted to teach me English 1926-1931). After leaving Buckingham in 1945 she lived in London and taught at the Lauriston Secondary School in Hackney and the Battersea Secondary School until 1955 when she retired in order to look after an elderly aunt. All her Buckingham pupils regard her with esteem and affection. Jeanette, for the seven years before she retired in 1958, had been General Superintendent of the Queen's Institute of District Nursing and had held other important positions and travelled widely, advising on health services and systems of state nursing.

Dolly is now 75, Jeanette 73.

They have arrived here as part of a trip round the world on the cruise liner 'Chusan' to the Bahamas, Cristobal, Acapulco, Los Angeles, San Francisco, Vancouver, Honolulu, Suva, Auckland, Sydney, Darwin, Hong Kong, Singapore, Penang, Colombo and Durban; then up here by air. Of course, both are very lively and pleasant companions with a wide range of interests.

In the first week I took them to Mulanje and Zomba and Grace Snowden's and from 20-28 April we were up at the Lake. It was very enjoyable at Senga Bay, and I tried not to get too involved with chores. The Lake was rough at night but calm in the afternoons, there was a pleasant breeze and everything was green and colourful. Dolly and Jeanette were thrilled by the fishermen hauling in their catch on to the beach late at night, by the white and purple lotuses in the lagoon, the black Afzelia beans capped in red sealing wax, and by the bright clothes of the women everywhere. The fish eagles soared and dived spectacularly over the *naphini* trees, and on a steep hill overlooking the Grand Beach Hotel we found their nest completely filling the top of a large tree.

Gladys was able to take a good rest, for once, sitting chatting on the *khonde* in the mornings. We made several small trips - up the Kuluundu road past the Rice Scheme; to Leopard's Bay where dhows come in from across the Lake; and for lunch to the Grand Beach Hotel and the Fish Eagle Inn.

In between times I cleared the site near the former hen house for a future vegetable garden; my latest labourers - Johnnie Lashidi, Johnnie Mhango, Moffat Mairi and *Pink* Charlie (not to be confused with *Green* Charlie) placed stones around the edge of the plot, the surface was levelled and compost and ash and chicken manure were scattered over it. The tomato plants brought up from Blantyre are all flourishing and yielding well. I had to adjust the lavatory cistern and get Member to repair the Honda and put several washers on taps, and I asked Kandulu to put new glass into half a dozen of the windows - but I found it more restful and relaxing than previous trips to the Lake have been.

Unfortunately, the Volvo gave trouble on the journey up to the Lake. The propellor shaft mounting was, apparently, worn out and the gears constantly jammed, so we decided not to go farther north but to return to Blantyre, have the car repaired and spend longer in Rhodesia. So, on Wednesday we came back here to Blantyre - much more slowly than usual. Today DM Motors have put in two new universal joints and mountings and overhauled the hydraulics of the clutch.

Yesterday and to-day I have arranged car insurance for Rhodesia and Mozambique and obtained travellers' cheques, currency and visas for Mozambique. The last gave the most trouble. I paid the extortionate amounts demanded for visas yesterday and was asked to collect them to-day. At 3:00 p.m. they were not ready so I went again to the Portuguese Embassy office at 3:45 p.m., only to find that they were still not ready - the official responsible had been out all night crocodile hunting and had been 'too tired' to come to the office. As they were closing at 4:00 p.m. until 9:00 am on Monday, there was nothing for it but to be unpleasant, so I said if I did not get the visas that afternoon I would complain to the Ambassador and that if the official concerned was asleep somebody should wake him and call him to carry out his duties. Two Dutch women, a Pakistani, two Portuguese and a Scotsman were also restive, and as several of us said we intended to stay in the office until we received attention, the official eventually came to work (some people had waited all day for him) and we got our visas. Our plan was to visit Victoria Falls, Zimbabwe and the Gorongosa Game Reserve in Mozambique.

We left on Sunday 2 May, travelling to Salisbury the first day. The road to Mwanza was rough and there were fearful road corrugations both sides of Tete. We ate lunch under a baobab tree; then pounded along non-stop to Mtoko where the tarmac begins. After fourteen hours on the road we reached Salisbury about 8:00 p.m. and stayed at the Selous Hotel which was comfortable and reasonably cheap.

Next day was shorter and all on Rhodesian tarmac: 275 miles instead of 385. We spent the night at the Carlton Hotel in Bulawayo - again, not too expensive but quite unlike the old Carlton at which I often used to stay in my Air Force days which was then less modern but more friendly and with better food.

The next day we reached Victoria Falls and managed to rent a chalet in the Rest Camp which proved very comfortable and convenient. The Falls were a few weeks past their peak but the Zambezi was still spectacular and there were fleecy white cataracts thundering into the gorge across the whole expanse of the river which is a mile and a quarter wide. We went on a river launch trip up to Kandahar Island, fed the monkeys and watched two elephants on the return journey. Of course, we visited the Big Tree (a baobab), the Game park (where we saw only a single waterbuck), and the curio den which was selling 'airport' art.

On Thursday we returned to Bulawayo and spent the night at the Glass Castle Hotel -built as a house by a Mr Rendell Glass but converted into a rather vulgar and shabby motel.

Then on Friday we went on to Fort Victoria and Zimbabwe, explored the ruins, stayed at the posh and expensive Sheppards Hotel and revelled in luxury for a night. It was at Zimbabwe that the car silencer broke for the first time; I had it mended the following morning in Fort Victoria.

We went on to Umtali and the Vumba by the Birchenough Bridge route. The rich ochres and purples of the rocks in the valleys around Moodie's Pass surprised and impressed us. We spent the night over 5,000 feet up in the Vumba at the Rippling Streams Guest Cottages, run by a Mrs Peacocke, a tall craggy sort of woman, probably in her seventies but very active and alive. One of Mrs Peacocke's sisters had trained with Jeanette. The garden under the windows of our rooms included a bed of primroses and innumerable English flowers and flowering creepers. At dusk we were taken to visit a large untidy garden in the heart of the high hills that was said to contain an example of every flower grown in southern Africa.

From the Vumba we drove into Mozambique down the Beira road and eventually turned away from the main road for thirty-three miles to Gorongosa Game Reserve where that same evening - at unmentionable cost - we hired a Volkswagen mini-bus and drove close to elephant, hippo, waterbuck, wildebeest, oribi, impala, bushbuck, black buffalo, baboons, wart-hogs and lions, the last lying in heaps on the track. In and beside the ponds were clusters of pelicans and storks and ducks. Dolly and Jeanette were fascinated. In fact, none of us had previously encountered so many wild animals. In the ponds or lakes were hundreds of hippo, young and old, and when one of them trotted off across the swampy grassland, our driver used the Volkswagen to head it back to the main herd.

Back at the Game Reserve Camp where we stayed overnight Gladys spotted an *mvumbi* (33) in our bedroom as she was getting into bed. Neither of us wanted to share the room with an unpredictable snake so we got one of the guards to evict it with a forked stick before we settled down for the night.

Next day we started on the return journey - tarmac to Guro but fearful corrugations thereafter to Changara. A Portuguese Army helicopter came over the hills at one point and buzzed us. We were thankful not to be machine-gunned. Later the car silencer broke again and in order to remove it completely I had to take off one of the car wheels.

That night we reached Changara and stayed at an odd little Portuguese hotel where all the plumbing was defective but grapes grew in ripe bunches on wires outside the bedrooms and government soldiers filled the bar and four Alsation dogs barked most of the night to guard us from the Frelimo. A dusky non-maiden lurked in the shadows and small ragged boys infested the environs of the bar, drained customers' bottles and begged for centavos. During the night one unidentifiable person entered the hotel and the dogs didn't bark at him and it was not clear what was going on. The soldiers were there to guard the bridges, we were told.

When, eventually, I managed to get to sleep I had a vivid nightmare about the Frelimo. Finally, we limped home to Blantyre, still without a silencer and with the windows wide open to blow out the carbon monoxide fumes sucked into the car: we were one day late but safe and uninjured and the seventy-year-olds not too exhausted.

Social life: On 1 May we had lunch with Robin Haydon (34) and his wife in Zomba -he is the British High Commissioner and a family friend of the Merrys - quite pleasant and very informal. Yesterday we had Grace to lunch and Gladys gave us prawn cocktails, marinaded chickens, apple crumble and some wine brought in from Mozambique.

Dolly and Jeanette departed to-day and we saw them off at Chileka airport on the afternoon VC.10. (35)

23 May

Immediately the Merrys departed southern Africa began to have freak weather. Snow in South Africa, four inches of hailstones on the Bulawayo-Gwelo road, and piercingly cold in Malawi so that we have hot-water bottles at night.

Esnath, wife of Million the cook, whom he left staying with relations in Limbe last week-end, apparently escaped from the relations, got drunk as fast as possible and was picked up by the Police as drunk and disorderly so that she has to go to Court on Tuesday.

30 May

I have interviewed potential secretaries and have persuaded the Administration to appoint Mrs Susan Chibambo, daughter-in-law of Qabaniso Yesaya Chibambo, Minister for the Northern Region.

Gordon Hazeldine tells me he will be leaving by air on 26 July. Ann and Brian Yarr and family are going earlier - on 16 July, alas! Once these departures have taken place I hope I can settle the Malawian staff into the jobs they may well occupy for the next few years.

8 June

Last week-end the new Blantyre traffic lights began to operate. As a result there was intense chaos and a large number of minor accidents. I heard several imprecations about 'new-fangled obstructions' as indignant motorists crunched into each other. Yesterday the robots came into use at the end of Mahatma Ghandi road and Ginnery Corner and there were long traffic jams of puzzled and honking motorists.

I have bought for £3.00 a 50" x 36" aerial photograph of Senga Bay with the Cottage in the middle of it. It is so clear that the circles of soil around the citrus trees look like ringworms and dug-out canoes on the beach look like chocolate eclairs. I have also framed a couple of Chinese scrolls painted by Chuah Thean Teng, two of his batiks, a water colour by Lim Cheng Hoe, and a variety of coloured Christmas cards by Teng and C. Uche Okeke. All these will brighten up the Cottage the next time we go there - which I hope will be 18 June.

Ruth Partridge was at the Cottage a week ago and she has brought back news that the Shaws (friends of the OL) have replaced a baffle in the refrigerator so that it now manufactures snow as well as ice. Apparently there are beans and tomatoes in the garden - and cockroaches in the sideboard.

In Blantyre we have started having a log fire in the evenings and the house is full of the odour of pine, eucalyptus and mahogany. Some of the Malawians wear tea cosies and Balaclava helmets in the mornings.

13 June

Yesterday Gladys and I attended the Queen's Birthday Celebration ('the Annual Orgy') at the British High Commission in Zomba. There were supposed to be 900 guests, we were told, but I believe only about 700 turned up. Robin Haydon did us proud: the gardens of his Residency lent themselves perfectly to the occasion, and there were two enormous marquees accommodating the bars, and unlimited alcohol including, I was amused to note, contraband Mellowood brandy from Rhodesia - perhaps old stock being used up.

The High Commissioner proposed a toast to His Excellency the President (who was not present), his Ministers and the People of Malawi; John 'Kaka' Msonthi proposed a toast to the Queen of England, mentioning, inter alia, that many people in Malawi held the view that the *chiperoni* mists of which we have had so many were thought to be attributable to Scottish missionaries who, many years ago, smuggled them into the country from Scotland. Both of them made short, apt and sincere speeches. Haydon has a beautiful microphone voice and could easily make a living as a top BBC broadcaster.

The Army played light music suitable for the occasion and, of course, the two National anthems. The gardens were colourful with pretty frocks as well as flowers and the narrow roads of Zomba mountainside were choked with cars. The crowd included every possible caricature of diplomats, civil servants and settlers, and would have delighted Somerset Maugham or anybody with an interest in psychiatry. G. and I wore roses. Altogether a pleasant occasion in flowery gardens on the slopes of Zomba mountain with a blue sky overhead and clumps of golden and green bamboo to remind us it was the tropics.

Today we have been out again, to Grace's. The other guests were Ruth Partridge and Eileen and 'Tuppence' Spicer. 'Tuppence', well past seventy, does a job connected with the sale of maize; his wife has a poultry farm of 5,000 birds, she is Irish, gesticulates a lot, clinks her false teeth like castanets when she talks, and small feathers float from her person when she flaps her hands in the heat of conversation.

It was a delicious lunch - pate de foie gras on thin toast, followed by chicken cooked in wine and cream, marmalade pudding, fresh Camembert cheese, served with a light wine. These old dears seem a bit odd at times but they are very kind to one another, most of them have great courage and they have had to live extremely 'rough' in the past.

Chintambo, the Old Lady's faithful retainer, was today wearing his new set of false teeth and looking very distinguished, handsome and ten years younger - not a day more than sixty.

24 June

Chancellor College has had auditors examining its financial records. After we have had to take so much flak from the accountants I found it gratifying that the auditors had to refer to the library's records to correct mistakes in the records of the accounts office.

On 22 June Robin Haydon and his wife visited the Library. When we had lunch with them in Zomba on 8 May, he said he would be delighted to visit the Library as soon as he received an invitation to do so. Not wishing to 'tread on any toes', I asked the Principal of Chancellor College if I might invite him informally or whether he should be invited officially; the Principal didn't know, so rang up Freeman the university registrar; he didn't know either so he contacted the Vice-Chancellor who asked Freeman to 'phone me and find out the circumstances of my receiving the request; the outcome was that the Vice-Chancellor must have sent him a formal invitation as he and the Provost and the Principal all arrived escorting Robin Haydon who seemed rather amused at the overwhelming propriety and protocol. Yesterday I had a meeting of Chancellor College Library Committee: three hours of faff and incoherence. But I got most of what I wanted, mainly because the Chairman could not make up his mind.

This morning Smart and I visited Bvumbwe Agricultural Research Station along the Thyolo road. It was their Open Day and they had an exhibition of fruit and vegetables. In the experimental plots were panoramas of gigantic cabbages and cauliflowers, and carrots and tomatoes by the ton. I bought a granadilla - the giant kind we used to have in Nigeria - and ordered more orange and grape-fruit trees for the Blantyre garden.

30 June

Antony is in the 'field' at present in Tanzania. Recently, on his motor-bike, he forced his way for seven miles along a grassy track through elephant infested forest, emerging in a battered state in southern Kisarawa.

8 July

There has been an Independence holiday 2-7 July. I was quite happy to be on duty at the Library for three of these days as I can take time off and go to the Lake when it suits us better later in the month.

At the Blantyre Stadium at least four people were killed during the celebrations of Independence. A child was trampled to death - seen by one of the library staff; two people in the stands fought each other and were tossed over the stands by other spectators - seen by another member of library staff; I think the fourth person was the mother of the trampled child. All this is denied by the *Blantyre Times.*

10 July

At Newlands Home for Elderly Europeans is a character named Etty Smith, now in her sixties, whose parents came out to Nyasaland as missionaries before 1890 to a place near Ntcheu. Funds for supporting the Mission 'at Home' failed and her father had to buy land and live on it at much the same level as the Malawians. It was possible in those days to buy 'sixteen acres of land for a few bags of salt'.

She and her sister grew up with Malawians and spoke fluent Chichewa but with Independence in 1964, when the parents were dead and one daughter was a welfare worker and the other a nurse, the local people turned against them and the two women had to go back to Scotland, taking with them two African children they had adopted. Etty Smith (I think her father may have been the Rev E Bucknall L Smith who joined the Universities' Mission to Central Africa in 1884 and retired in 1906) came back to Malawi for a month to visit old friends and she decided to stay on, in a working capacity, at Newlands.

As a baby still at the breast, Etty's parents were trekking somewhere round the back of Ndirande mountain (where, at Chirimba, we lived for three-and-a-half years) when, in the night, they suddenly encountered a lion. The shock caused her mother's milk to dry up and thereafter, at every village they visited, she had to be fed on goats' milk to keep her alive.

20 July

Ann and Brian left yesterday. They did not want any sort of send-off, official or personal, as they preferred to avoid scenes of emotion: they encouraged us to go to the Lake which we did. They will be sorely missed.

24 July

On our trip we found that the road through the Angoni Highlands had been completed so that there is now blacktop from Liwonde to Salima.

In addition to clothes and food we carried a baby's cot for those visitors who need one, two framed scrolls, my framed aerial photograph of Senga Bay and three boxes of tomato plants ready for setting out.

The various visitors since we were last at the Cottage have somewhat tarnished the cleanliness of the place, leaving children's finger marks on the white walls, marks of scraping shoes under the windows and stains on two of the blankets. Gladys gave the place a general clean-up including the washing of two sets of bedroom curtains.

I was hoping to take a day's rest, but not much had been done in the garden in the previous four weeks, so I had to water the dying lemons, revive the grass lawns, organize the removal of dead beans and dying tomatoes and re-plant the vegetable garden after it had been enriched with a heap of excellent pig manure remaining from the Da Costas' pigs.

The second and third days it was necessary to procure bamboo, *tsekera* grass and the outer layer of grass for re-thatching of the kitchen, to find a thatcher, and visit Salima to bring in stores of paraffin, petrol and oil.

To locate the bamboo and *tsekera* grass I had to take Kandulu and then the second day Aisa the cook, along the Kuluundu road where bundles of grass of the required species can be bought for 2/- a bundle and bamboo is available for 3/- a bundle. The long-suffering Volvo was again grossly over-laden.

I had to make two journeys on Sunday, buying twelve bundles of *tsekera*, and one journey on Monday buying four bundles of bamboo and five bundles of *tsekera*.

Sunday happened to be the day the young boys returned from the circumcision camp, and nineteen of the homes had flags flying to denote they were rejoicing to celebrate the boys' safe return. The initiates themselves were probably only 10 or 11 years old; they were dressed in bright clothes - red and blue jackets, small white *kanzus* and shoes - and they carried wands of reeds. Their mothers had smeared their own faces with white *ufa* to indicate their happiness. All this activity made it difficult to find the owners of the cone-shaped bundles of grass that were displayed for sale, and even after they were found there was a problem over small change as there was none in Kachulu village and none in Kuluundu. Not everyone has money in these villages.

The Kuluundu road is an interesting area: it is purely Muslim, the houses are square or rectangular, some with windows, some without, many with verandahs; and the compounds are surrounded by grass or reed fences. The paramount chief is a woman, Bisi Kuluundu, descended from Chief Mwase, and a sister of President Banda.

On Monday afternoon Aisa took me, in the opposite direction, to Nkuti village, farther south in Senga Bay, showing me where I could manoeuvre the car along narrow tracks, around the rubbish pits and through compounds, until we came to the home of Mdalamdoka Nkuti who had just returned from the 'Bapitisti' Mission where he had been to buy some cough medicine.

I walked round the village which is surprisingly large. A small stream runs through it to the Lake. The beach is of black sand, glistening with silicate. There is a newly built mosque, and each household exists within its own grass fence. The people looked well fed. I have promised Mdalamdoka some 'Histalix' for his cough; he looks really ill.

Outside the village, in a crook of the Lake, is the district's initiation camp for boys, and about fifteen boys are still in it. It is not hidden away but has been constructed on the edge of the reeds, only a fenced enclosure with a fine grain bin to hold mealie cobs donated by family and neighbours, standing conspicuously in front of it.

From the Nkuti villagers I ordered 80 bundles of ordinary thatching grass at 6d. a bundle, plus another 3d. a bundle for head transportation to the Cottage, a distance of two miles.

Late in the afternoon a thatcher turned up and said he wanted £8 for thatching the kitchen. I would willingly have paid him but my advisers Aisa and Kandulu, who were present, said it was too much and that £3 would be fair. He accepted the reduced amount within ten minutes which greatly surprised me as local people generally enjoy an ingenious and inveterate haggle.

The canoes were out fishing. Agiga's canoe brought in four bags of big fish and four bags of small fish on Saturday night - a very big haul.

Birds are returning to the lagoon. We saw hammerkops, darters, pied kingfishers, turquoise and pink kingfishers with red bills, a white crane, a paradise flycatcher, lake gulls, a lilac-breasted roller and an unidentifiable red collared bird.

There has been a wedding in the Kandulu family. The sixteen-year-old daughter has married Sanudi, who was formerly Kandulu's apprentice but now has a job at £9 a month as electrician at the Technical Institute. It was a Muslim wedding with nearly two hundred guests. Kandulu told us that as the Cadi read the marriage vows - which are binding - some of the young men at the back of the crowd muttered uneasily among themselves that 'this marriage business' was 'very dangerous' for any young man and should be avoided if at all possible.

28 July

Last week in Blantyre the wife of one of the library assistants was attacked by the wife of another library assistant. She defended herself by biting a piece out of the ear of the second lady, so there is a Court case pending and a somewhat chilly relationship now exists between the two husbands who work in the same room.

Smart has chopped down the last of the *Dombea* wild pear trees at the corner of the Blantyre house while Million and I pulled on a long rope to ensure that the tree fell into the drive. At the time of the felling the wind was gusty and unpredictable and we had to pull with all our strength when the tree came crashing down. Since then Smart has dug out most of the tree stump; the roots led away like tentacles of an octopus and when they were trimmed level with the ground the embedded stump looked like the footprint of an enormous elephant, with scars from the axe as toe-nails.

3 August

At last the Independence decorations have been taken down. The poles that were painted white have been stripped of bunting and lie in disorderly heaps, each pole brown at one end after being buried for a month in the soil: they look like cork-tipped cigarettes, now discarded.

Interviewing potential library assistants, I asked one young man if he ever did any reading and he confessed, as if to a secret vice, that he 'didn't do it often'.

7 August

On Thursday I had to visit the Bindery in Zomba so I took the opportunity of taking Rodrick, Dick and Augustine to see the new site of the University. The concrete platform for the Library has been constructed and the first bricks should be laid by the end of the month.

I am again having car trouble. One morning when I drove from Mahatma Gandhi road across the Kamuzu Highway the car brakes failed totally and a young traffic policeman on duty had to leap aside like an impala in a game reserve so that I did not annihilate him. I thought he would 'book' me for dangerous driving but when I managed to stop at the side of the road and we both discovered that the brake fluid had leaked away he only grinned amiably as if he enjoyed the hazards of the highway. So, after having managed to keep the car out of the hands of DM Motors for two months I am again at their mercy. They have fitted a new 'servo-mechanism' which I hope will stop the brake fluid leaking away and tomorrow they have to find out what causes a sinister clanking noise - their driver says it is the 'diff', and I fear the worst.

13 August

On Monday we collected the Old Lady and went to Senga Bay. We had a picnic lunch thirty-five miles beyond Lilongwe, sitting in a disused quarry where the excavated banks glistened with quartzes. We shared our roast chicken and strawberries and cream with Chintambo; I am not sure the Old Lady approved - she tends to launch into disparagement of African intelligence if we pay too much attention to Chintambo.

At the Lake the vegetable garden had been ravaged by goats which had eaten off the tops of 100 tomato plants and maybe more beans; but there are still nine rows of beans growing luxuriantly at the other end of the garden. The goats invaded the garden at 11:00 o'clock one morning while Stephen the gardener was in his room, the alarm being raised by Aisa's wife. Four goats were captured and impounded in the sheep house and the matter reported to Dalamkwanda and Kandulu; but before I got there the goats had been restored to their owners who, apparently, are Indians. A swift and invisible greasing of African palms by Indian palms had evidently taken place before my arrival.

Stephen had spilt scalding cooking oil or porridge on his leg (the versions of the story varied) and had been so badly injured he had to go to the hospital in Salima. Gladys re-dressed his leg with Burnol.

Soon after we arrived the water pump ceased to work and for a day we had no running water. Then Member and George - 'George' is Walter Stansfield's driver - re-ground a valve and miraculously made it function again. The pump has to have a new sparking plug, a new piston ring and new inlet and outlet valves.

Member had been in hospital with a boil, into which a worm had burrowed, in the hollow between two of his fingers. The medical assistant at the Salima hospital carved a deep and painful groove between the fingers after first giving him an injection presumably to prevent lock-jaw. Gladys dressed the wound with Germolene.

On Wednesday afternoon we went to Ntimbasonja village to meet Mkwinda the mat maker. He is a tall, smooth-skinned smiling man, Muslim, in a long black coat, with something soft and cat-like about him. He was obviously delighted to have the small tins of dyes I had brought from Blantyre; these will give him an 'edge' over other local mat makers. I have asked him to make me circular mats of scarlet and gold and also rectangular mats. Mats somewhat larger than those Mkwinda makes, but less brightly coloured, sell for 35/- at the Ivory Carver's hut near the Grand Beach Hotel and the Ivory Carver can get up to 50/- for them from rich Zambian tourists; but these are imported from Nkhota-Kota.

On my earlier visit to Nkuti village I had promised Mdalamdoka I would bring him some *muti* for his cough, so on Wednesday afternoon I took along a bottle of 'Histalix' I had bought for him. He was not expecting visitors and he appeared in a dirty vest, looking rather grubby and ill. He must be well into his eighties, perhaps over 90. I hope the 'Histalix' will cure his cough; but apparently he has a hernia as well, which is painful, and all I could do for that was to tell him to go to the nearby Baptist Mission.

There were the usual chores. I managed to cut the citrus hedge with the secateurs so that it will bush out and produce lemons; I cut the hanging twigs of a tree near the small detached store so that they will no longer slash passers-by; I staked peas and persuaded Stephen to stake the rest; I caused another box of tomato seedlings to be planted to fill about forty of the gaps created by the goats; and started James Chindambo - who is really a builder's mate - building a new fence to replace one that had blown away; and I supervised a new thatcher who succeeded the earlier thatcher who failed to thatch the kitchen; I bought *chambo* for our lunch; and James and I moved wooden trestles into the small store under the water tower; but there wasn't time for anything else although many other odd jobs ought also to have been done.

Around the lagoon there were red-billed hornbills, pied kingfishers, a hammerkop, paradise flycatchers, jacanas, and fish eagles in the sky. The lagoon had sunk by at least a foot and the Lake itself had receded except during the night when it thundered on the beach and breakers fanned up the sands to the same level as a month ago.

26 August

Tony Loveday, University librarian of the University of Zambia, has paid us a quick visit. In Blantyre we gave a small party for him, the guests being Fred Johnson, director of the Malawi National Library Service, Blodwen Binns, Ernie and Mrs Rowe (Ernie is the Chief Technician at Chancellor College), Rodrick Mabomba and Beston Mphundi and his wife. After our meal Rodrick played African folk music and pop tunes on his guitar, singing his own accompaniment. We paid a brief visit to the Lake, staying there only two nights. At Ntimbasonja village Mkwinda was out - but we met him at one of the other villages, just wiping the rice off his right hand after having his lunch. Tony bought a few mats. Then we had to dash back to Blantyre for him to catch his plane to Kenya and Lamu Island where he has a holiday house.

1 September

Here in Blantyre James Kamponde is scraping grime from the corrugated iron roof of the house and the servants' quarters. We plan to paint the roofs cobalt blue which will cost £35.00; then there are the walls to be snowcemmed; then the interior to be re-painted. At some stage we want to carry out a small conversion that will result in another bedroom and another bathroom - plus a bathroom and new toilet for the servants' quarters.

Stamford Kacisa, a messenger at the Library, while 'flying fish' (his own words), splashed the chilli and Indian pepper juice into his eyes and was blind for two days. Million - like Chintambo - now has false teeth. He takes them out to eat.

14 September

On 8 September we went to the Agnews for dinner in the evening. Both Fulque and Swanzie seemed better for their holiday. Swanzie has a new cook named 'Damson'. We had smoked salmon, followed by a chicken dish, followed by raspberry tart. When I enquired at one point, 'How much of this is Damson and how much is Agnew?' Swanzie replied, 'What you are eating, dear Wilfred, is Fortnum and Mason!' Crispin, their son, who was about to lead an expedition to the mountains of Patagonia, had sent his parents an expensive parcel from F & M to help sustain them in their domestic difficulties.

On 9 September we set off at 6:00 am for the Lake, collected Joan and Richard at Domasi, and reached Senga Bay at 1:00 p.m.. It was pleasantly cool at the Lake; at night there was a strong wind and waves pounded on the beach as if they were coming in from an ocean; curtains in the front bedroom billowed out into the room like sails filled by the monsoon.

The new thatcher, Sainid Makomula, was in the last stages of thatching the kitchen. All the *tsekera* was in position and the first layer of brown ordinary grass had been pegged around the lower edge of the roof so that strands of grass formed a ragged arcade all around the building.

Stephen has left and Member Matora has appointed a new gardener for us, James Ndici Hamisi, aged thirty, father of five, a refugee from Mozambique who now lives in Dalamkwanda's village. He is very strong and seems to work unflaggingly - without my approval - from six in the morning till after seven at night.

Stephen is now selling hats and mats of woven grass.

One day I took Joan and Richard to Kuluundu and at Ntimbasonja we met Mkwinda the mat maker.

Another day we went to Leopard's Bay, leaving the Volvo where the track becomes impassable and walking half a mile downhill through grey granite rocks into the cove. A dhow was anchored and the crew men had hung their sail over a scaffolding of poles so that it became a tent in which they could lie in the shade and rest. The dhow was due to sail for the other side of the Lake at 1:00 p.m. after the men finished their meal of coarse *nsima* and *matemba*. Three dug-out canoes, one of them very straight and fine, had their prows nosing into the reeds. Monkeys leapt in the bare trees on the cliff-side.

One morning I bought firewood from Asmani Ndembo who has a garden behind the Kalulu Bar. I bought seven 'heaps' (possibly three tons) for 35/-. It was scaly *Nchenga*, striated *Ntomoni*, grey smooth *Ntoto*, and grey blotchy *Sombuti* with long cracks like claw marks from a leopard in the bark. This I transported in seven journeys in the ill-treated Volvo.

I also discovered from Asmani the names of the trees near the Cottage. The tallest trees are *Naphini* (*Terminalia sericea*); the Afzelia is *Ng'kongomo*; the tree at the top of the terrace near the back door (it has small round fruit) is *Mukangaza*; and the tree with sharp galls is *Mtonga* (*Strychnos spinosa*); the tree with edible fruit, just off our plot, is *Mbula* (*Sclerocarya caffra*); and the mushroom shaped tree is *Mbawa* which I think is *Zizyphus abyssinica.*

We all enjoyed our stay.

Back in Blantyre Gladys picked five and three-quarter pounds of strawberries this morning.

20 September

On Tuesday I had an hour with the Vice-Chancellor, Henry Colbert the new development officer and John Banda the registrar, about the implications of receiving a big influx of books following a promise of £36,000 from the British Government. The Vice-Chancellor agreed that the Buildings Committee should consider the second phase of the library building - the first phase is only just appearing out of the ground at Chirunga - and I asked that the Inter-University Council should be requested to send a Visitor to make recommendations about staffing of the Library and the training of library staff.

The wife of the library assistant I mentioned on 28 July has been fined K60 for biting a piece out of the ear of the other library assistant's wife.

Stamford Kacisa's common law wife has given birth to a son. They had nothing to wrap the baby in, not even a cloth, so some of us clubbed together to buy the first batch of napkins.

A new library attendant, Richard Chilombo, was absent one day in order to donate blood for an uncle who had been in a car crash, but at the hospital they had only just started to draw blood out of Chilombo when his uncle died.

Million is on his annual leave, apparently feeling rather miserable with his new false teeth and no daily tit-bits.

The flower garden is brilliant with dianthus, phlox drummondi, antirrhinums and petunias.

Yesterday at least twenty minute seed-eaters were bathing together in the bird bath. Today two wagtails are making a nest in the top of the bungalow chimney. This morning a black drongo became entangled in the nylon fishing net stretched over the strawberries to protect them; James the painter cut the net to set the drongo free and it screeched piteously while two black and white crows circled overhead, hoping no doubt to peck out its eyes. Once freed, it darted up to a leafy refuge - and its mate - in one of the big trees.

24 September

On the first day of term we found that one of the students had left behind in the reading room a matchbox containing Indian hemp.

Up to the lake again last week-end, taking with us Rodrick who is now in charge of cataloguing and Dick who is the senior catalogue assistant. There is tar all the way from Blantyre to Salima and it is possible to do the 293 mile journey to Senga Bay in 5½ hours.

We swam every day. The Lake was dead calm for the first two days, varying in colour from cornflower blue to jade green, but there were waves and winds for the other two days which, however, were not rough enough to prevent fishermen going out in their dug-out canoes and bringing in suppers of *chambo* and another similar fish with black scales and another which had a bright black nose.

We walked to Leopard's Bay but found the dhows had put in at a smaller cove (perhaps for shelter); so we strolled over the hilltop, blackened by grass fires, to this deep little cove between high rocks. Several hundred people were assembled there - in bright blues, pinks, greens, reds - squatting with their head-loads and bundles of blankets, cloth, packets of sugar, plastic bowls, palm-bark for weaving into mats, plus a good many sacks of maize, on the steep sandy shore, waiting in turn for their loads to be put into the two dhows, 'Kalulu Ng'ombo' and 'Mr Tandayo', by men who had to wade hip-deep in the water to hoist the loads over the gunwales. This was a Sunday morning, and later the same day the 'Chauncy Maples' put in near to this cove so perhaps some of the congregated people were travelling to the North on the steamer.

I have been searching the beach in front of the Cottage for coloured stones and pebbles. We have been told that garnets and zircons can be picked up from the beach; and it is amazing what a variety of stones there is, varying in colour from jet black and charcoal to clear white and colourless quartz, with a great range of pinks, reds, browns, and yellows. My haul will need to be examined by a geologist before I know whether it includes any semi-precious stones. I have put the whole collection into a Kilner jar with a screw top and my specimens look like an assortment of toffees and boiled sweets, with a few chunks of granite and mica among them.

Gladys has been manufacturing clowns made of rag for the Christmas 'Fayre' which is held each year to raise money for charities. She is now the representative of the Council of Women ('The Naggers') on the Save the Children Fund and, she says, for the first time in her life she has to write a report.

5 December

I felt rather odd for a fortnight after what I think was a double strength vaccination against smallpox, the serum being from USSR. The pus and inflammation have now dispersed, however, and my arm is again almost normal.

We have had several good rains; 4½ inches one night and smaller downpours on other occasions. The strawberries have stopped fruiting; the granadilla vine grows several inches a day; dahlias and cannas are sprouting madly; the petrea has been smothered with brilliant blue spikes. Thunderstorms roll round the sky each afternoon but most of the rain has fallen at Zomba, Mulanje and farther afield.

Early one afternoon there were four hoopoes on the lawn - the two parents showing off their offspring? Today I saw a splendid purple-crested loerie, blue, green and purple, in the jacaranda tree. A few sunbirds like tiny brilliant jewels have appeared in the front flower garden.

On Friday Grace Snowden and Ruth Partridge came to lunch. Some interesting cannibalism stories:

A Mrs Trataris had a brick and concrete grave prepared for her husband near Port Herald; after he had been bricked inside she sat on the grave each night for a fortnight with a loaded gun in her hand.

In Limbe, when babies are buried in the Catholic cemetery they are put into cardboard cartons for burial but when the nuns go to the grave the following morning it is alleged that they find the corpses have been dug up in the night and only the cartons left behind in the graveyard.

17 December

The University has received a letter from the government Censorship Board (of which an elderly Malawian clergyman is the chairman) asking us to treat all books on Physiology as reference books and not to stock them if they deal with Sex. Schapera's 'Married life in an African tribe' - a standard work for many years - has also been banned. (36)

Yesterday, at the house, we discovered an invasion of termites in the cupboard in the bathroom. I had to climb into the roof to find out if they had penetrated there but mercifully they had not done so. The personal and sanitary habits of our hoopoes, which breed up there without the inconvenience of a nest, are evidently appalling: I wonder if the City Health Department is aware of them?

Term ended today: it has been a shocking rush.

26 December

I have agreed to employ Aufi Kananji at the Lake in place of Aisa who, recently, has not been cleaning the Cottage properly and seems to have lost interest in work of any kind. He is at least 76 so he may be prepared to retire. Later we shall also have to find another gardener.

Kananji is 52 years old, four feet eleven inches tall. While they were here he worked for Ann and Brian Yarr, and before that for JG Pike, the geographer; his collection of employers also includes two British High Commissioners - CG Harper and HA Payne. He looks like one of the Seven Dwarfs and is an excellent cook.

At the Library we have received a development report in English on the Central Region Lakeshore Project, and it is evident that the government has almost handed over development of this area of Malawi to the German government: they are resettling farmers, building houses, building roads, boring boreholes, carrying out a large programme of irrigation and earth movement, and have spent half a million pounds.

The garden at Blantyre is being visited by a Zambezi Red Mongoose. (Actually I don't know whether it is *Herpestes sanguineus* or *Herpestes melanurus Zombae*. Million the cook who is properly suspicious of Latin names calls it a *likongwe*.) It has a long tail tipped with black which it holds permanently upright.

I have applied to the University for a three year extension of contract w.e.f. 1 August 1972.

From my diary 1972

9 January

On Wednesday Raphael Masanjika arrived here to be interviewed for an assistant librarian post. He is 28, Malawian, has a Zambian diploma in library studies, and is at present on the staff of the Library of the University of Zambia. He was interviewed at 10:00 am and he addressed the Selection Committee for forty-five minutes non-stop so that at the end of it they looked dazed and hypnotized - his English is very good. It may be June before he is able to come to us.

At work we have had two minor thefts this past week - an electric torch and a hurricane lamp, both kept in the loans desk to cope with electricity failures. The value of the items is not great but it is annoying to know that we have a petty thief in our midst.

There has been a good deal of rain, as one must expect in mid-January. Soche Hill was invisible in low cloud at tea-time. There were two fat little *Braviceps* in the water at the bottom of one of the holes Smart has dug for orange trees.

23 January

The electric torch that was stolen has been returned after I ordered its return by Saturday, after which, I said, other measures would be taken to secure its return. It was found among the Physics books with a note twined round it:

'Borred by one of the night staffs.'

In the garden we now have a tree tomato thicket. I bought six young trees of the large New Zealand variety from Bvumbwe and have planted them near the others. We now have four grape-fruit trees, four Orlando orange, one Jaffa orange, one navel orange, one naartjie (tangerine), one lime, two peaches, three avocado pears, one granadilla, three guavas, one paw-paw and a dozen tree tomatoes. In March I hope to buy Red Gauntlet strawberries from Bvumbwe to replace some of the other varieties we have now. We still lack mangoes and pineapples but if we can add those and if everything grows and produces we shall have a reasonably well stocked garden as far as fruit is concerned.

30 January

I had to go to Bunda on Thursday to discuss with the acting Principal of the College the arrangements I have proposed for reorganization of the library there. We then went on to Senga Bay and came back on Saturday. To the Lake we took a new gardener, Simon Moses, and his wife. Seeman Mosses (as he pronounces his name) has been in the Young Pioneers for two years, teaching them how to run and how to climb trees, and he has been a garden-boy for five years. In Blantyre he worked for a week with Smart, among other jobs felling the tree at the back of the servants' quarters; and on his first working day at the Lake by six o'clock in the morning he was in the top of a tree overhanging and menacing the servants' quarters there. He speaks fluent English and seems to be a hard worker so I hope he will be a worthy addition to our extended family. He is an excellent representative of the Young Pioneers at their best.

It was very pleasant indeed at the Lake; although warm there was a breeze night and day, and the lake water was calm so that we could swim. At night in the moonlight the surface of the lake sparkled in a thousand silver ripples.

The night we arrived there was an *ngoma* in Dalamkwanda's village and another drum beating in Nkuti village at the far end of the bay. About 11:00 p.m. when the moon was full and high there was a howling noise like wild dogs or coyotes down on the beach, and when I went to investigate I discovered a group of youths stark naked clustering in a small circle, then all straining towards the centre so that their bellies were pressed together in intimate contact, then shaking loose and hurling themselves into the Lake, then re-forming the circle and howling again, their faces turned to the moon. It may have been some kind of sexual moon-rite or maybe only the effect of too much *chibuku*.

On an earlier visit (unrecorded here) I had been up to the Cottage to deal with the problem of Aisa and to install Kananji. Aisa seemed thankful that he was not any longer expected to work and the severance was amicable on both sides. He, his wife, his mother and the little boy went back in Heston's pick-up to Kuluundu and the other six or so women who lived with them packed up in a single day and melted away, with head-loads, into the mealie gardens.

Kananji has transformed the Cottage; the floors shine and one doesn't get one's feet dusty walking on them in the evening. Kandulu and the builder have fixed new doors and windows in two of the servants' quarters and soon they will be decent little cottages.

Mkwinda has left three mats with Kananji, one of them a masterpiece, but I have promised them all to Tony Loveday. I am urging Mkwinda to increase his output as I could easily sell twenty mats for him at £ 2.00 a time.

Kananji is living in the laundry room; after occupation by Aisa and his harem there are bed-bugs in the rooms they occupied - they must have brought them in as I fumigated the servants' quarters when we had the plague of fleas. I can easily get rid of the bugs, but not until our next visit when I can see that safety precautions are observed.

The Senga Bay Cottage

Now that the Cottage is habitable, and Kananji is in charge of it in our absence, many friends and acquaintances are asking us if they may stay there, and as this might provide a modest income to help recover the £ 1,500 I have spent on its improvement, we have compiled an informative brochure, with a title page as follows:

HOLIDAY COTTAGE

ON

LAKE MALAWI

Plot 7
Senga Bay
For reservations please
contact Mrs G J Plumbe,
P O Box 5200, Limbe.
(T N Blantyre 31956)

The text tries to be fully descriptive, viz.

Location. The Cottage is 78 miles from Lilongwe, 12.2 from Salima, 3 from Salima airstrip. The road between Lilongwe and Salima is winding and narrow but tarred. Beyond Salima the road is laterite. The turning to the Cottage, rather inconspicuous, is on the *right* at 11.6 miles from Salima on the Grand Beach road, about 150 yards beyond the sign for the Central Region Lakeshore Development Project Centre, and it is marked by a name board: 'Plumbe'. It is advisable to drive up the hill in the lane at not less than 15 mph and in a low gear. The Salima/Grand Beach road is regarded as an all-weather road; at present it has a few rough patches but it is negotiable by car even after heavy rain.

The Cottage. Once at the Cottage, cars may be left under the trees. There is a lockable garage for one car which may be used if desired; the key is with the cook. The Cottage stands on a small knoll at the top of a sandy beach and looks out over Senga Bay towards the hills of Cape Maclear on the right. On a clear day the Namwera escarpment and mountains at the far side of the Lake are visible.

The Cottage, which is generally airy and cool, is brick-built, cement floored, with roof of asbestos sheets and ceilings of softboard. The three bedrooms are 22' x 18', 22' x 14'.6" and 20' x 14'.6". There are two bathrooms, each with bath, wash basin and W C. The lounge is 21' x 17'.6" and the dining room 22' x 12'. There is a small pantry containing an elderly refrigerator and fly-proofed food cupboards. A verandah 7' wide runs most of the way round the house. A kitchen and laundry room are in a separate building. The engine house is separate again and has its own petrol store. The servants' quarters are about 100 yards distant and consist of three rooms. The Cottage plot is of 3 acres, it has many shady trees, and the house itself stands at 1,569 feet above sea level, 12 feet above the highest recorded level of the Lake.

On one side of the plot is 'The Lagoon', uncompromisingly described on government maps as 'Marsh'. In it grow blue lotus flowers, papyrus and a great many reeds and weeds; it and its surroundings provide a home for a variety of birds including from time to time, herons, kingfishers, lilytrotters, hammerkops, coucals, black craiks, ibises, weaver birds, cattle egrets, lilac-breasted rollers and paradise flycatchers. Two fish eagles are regular visitors.

Water supply. Water for the Cottage is pumped from the Lake by means of an Atalanta water pump on the beach which the gardener can operate. There is a 'Rhodesian boiler' and cold and hot water are available in the bathrooms. Drinking water should be boiled and filtered (there are two filters in the pantry) and it is wise to use drinking water for brushing one's teeth. In a plumbing emergency the water could be turned off at the 'main' by turning the handle on the pipe leading up to the water tank.

Lighting. Electricity for lighting purposes is generated by a Honda 1500 generator in the engine-house; it takes a gallon of petrol at a time and for each gallon it will provide 4 hours' electric light for 20 lights. The generator needs to be turned off at night (3 switches on the machine) and the engine-house locked. The gardener will fill the Honda's tank each day and start the generator at dusk but he normally goes off duty immediately afterwards. Naked lights should not be used in the engine-house (there was a fire in the past); an electric torch is the safest source of light when turning off the generator and locking up before going to bed. In case the Honda should become unserviceable there is a small Zeus Arcon generator which will provide rather dim light for 12 lights, and in the house a Tilley lamp, an Aladdin lamp and 3 small night-lights. The cook and gardener know how to obtain a mechanic quickly if the generators (or the water pump) need attention.

Refrigerator. The paraffin refrigerator is old and of battered appearance but it will produce ice and preserve food that requires refrigeration. The cook has a stock of paraffin and he will light and service the refrigerator and turn it off when visitors depart.

Furniture and fittings. The Cottage is equipped with beds, mattresses, mattress covers, blankets (6), curtains, furniture, etc. for six adults. There is also a dropside cot and mattress for a baby, and a studio couch in the lounge which could be used as a (rather hard) seventh bed. The 4 iron and 2 wooden bedsteads have foam rubber and spring interior mattresses, respectively; all pillows are foam rubber. Bed-boards are available for one bed in case a hard bed is needed. There are three large wardrobes. The dining room has an Ercolion dining suite, with older sideboard and dumb waiter. In the lounge is a settee and two easy chairs, a studio couch (aforementioned), and 6 tubular chairs suitable for the verandah or beach; also a writing desk, book cases and books, and various small tables. In the kitchen there's a Dover stove, a two-burner paraffin stove, a table, two cupboards and various buckets. The kitchen is fly-proofed and has piped water and electric light. In the laundry there's an ironing table, ironing board, charcoal, charcoal iron and ironing blanket.

Cooking utensils. Pots and pans (including five saucepans) sufficient to cope with the needs of six people. Dishes, plates, dinner service, tea service, tumblers, wine glasses, cutlery, etc. for six persons. Plenty of empty bottles for storage of drinking water.

Servants. Aufi Kananji is the servant in charge of the Cottage and he keeps the keys. If lamps should have to be used he would provide them and provide the necessary fuel. He is an experienced cook and is willing to cook for visitors but it is advisable to allow him plenty of time to prepare meals. He may be able to procure fish, eggs, chickens and perhaps ducks, if given a day's notice. The gardener, Simon Moses, will operate the water pump and the Honda generator and be responsible for the stock of Regular petrol and paraffin; he will light the 'Rhodesian boiler' and, if required, will fetch milk at 5:00 p.m. and obtain change from various sources. Both servants understand and speak English.

Food locally available. Chambo (1/- each) and other fish can be bought on the beach in season when the fishing dug-outs return at 6.30 am and sometimes in the late evening. If not available from the beach near the Cottage fish is generally available from fishermen at the north end of the beach beyond the Trade School. Chickens cost about 4/- each. Ducks 8/- to 12/-. Fresh milk is available from Mr Heston Tandaza (across the lagoon) at 9t. a pint: send any kind of bottle and boil the milk before drinking. Heston also has a useful shop on the main road. Vegetables (mainly beans and tomatoes) if available in the Cottage garden can be had from the gardener upon request. White and brown bread can be bought at Bharucha's in Salima. Fresh vegetables and fruit are some times available in Salima market. Food produced locally is generally cheaper than it would be in Blantyre or Lilongwe. There is a small market on the main road where local meat is sold on Monday, Wednesday and Saturday.

Pests. The house is completely screened against mosquitoes and almost all insects can be kept out if doors are kept closed and window screens carefully fastened.

Swimming and water sports. The temperature of the water varies between 69 degrees Fahrenheit and 86 degrees Fahrenheit, according to the season. Depth of the water varies at different points along the beach and children need to be under observation. Sailing rights exist and anyone who brings a boat can tie it, when not in use, to a tree on the beach.

Local people. Mr Kandulu Chintambo, a carpenter, is very helpful if small difficulties crop up. Mr Member Matora, a plumber/ electrician/ mechanic, services the Atalanta and the generators and is familiar with the plumbing. Kananji knows how to contact these two after their working hours. In any case of loss, theft or difficulty with local people the village headman, Mr Dalamkwanda, would probably be helpful. The local sub-chief under Chief Maganga is Mr Mdalamdoka Nkuti. Both Mr D. and Mr MN turn up from time to time to receive their tribute of Coca-Cola.

What to bring with you. Please include: Sheets. Pillowcases. Towels. Extra blankets in cold season. Rubber sheets, please, if small children are not yet 'dry'. Food, especially tinned food which are dearer in Salima than in Blantyre. Fresh fruit which is not always available in Salima market. Toilet paper. Maybe a transistor radio. Binoculars if you have them. An electric torch for use at night. *Please* - no dogs or other pets.

Losses and injuries. Although the servants are believed to be honest and the local people appear to be honest, visitors must please accept responsibility for any personal losses or injuries which might occur while they are staying at the Cottage. The Cottage and contents are insured but the insurance does not cover visitors or their possessions and we do not feel that we could accept liability for anything unexpected which might happen while they are at the Cottage.

Suggested payment for use of the Cottage.

14 days for up to 8 persons---K80. (£ 40).
7 days " " " " " " " " "   K40. (£ 20).
6 days or less: per night per person,
adults and children--------K1. (10/-).

The following are covered by the payment:
Petrol for generator and water pump
Paraffin for refrigerator and oil stove
Firewood for kitchen and 'Rhodesian boiler'

If the servants prove useful we should be pleased if visitors care to give them something for their help.

From my diary 1972

2 February

Last week I had a meeting of the University Library Committee on Wednesday and a meeting of the Publications Committee on Thursday. At the former, the Principal of Bunda College of Agriculture launched a fierce attack on me personally, claiming that I was not carrying out Senate's policy of centralization of library technical services. The truth is that Bunda College has refused to co-operate as I can easily prove from my files. My offer to make the files available to anyone who cared to see them has not been taken up.

After the cement famine in recent months I was able, yesterday, to buy twenty bags from Portland Cement Company in Blantyre. This involved three car visits to collect it, and later two visits to the Railway Station to send off fourteen bags to Salima for me to collect there on Saturday (insh'Allah). At Portland Cement Company it was 12/1 a bag as compared with 16/4 in Salima. Carriage by rail for the fourteen bags was 27/6.

11 February

Kananji had written to us:

'I can be very glad if you come with mother. Come and see your house both of you. I used to sleep on londly because the cottage is not good. I pass warm greetings to mother who is the madam.
Yours fellow Aufi Kananji.'

When we went to the Lake last week-end 'our fellow' was at the side of the car almost as soon as we stopped under the frangipani; within two minutes the Cottage lights were switched on (it was 6:35 p.m.) and the luggage was quickly whipped into the house. Everything was very clean and Kananji was very quick in service - one could hear his chubby feet pounding along the *khonde* as he ran to fetch the forgotten gravy at lunch time, and he seemed to run most of the time.

The gardener had also been working; the surrounds of the Cottage were clean. Member had connected hot water pipes from the 'Rhodesian boiler' in the garden to the bathroom but, owing to the absence of cement, the builder had been unable to construct the base for the boiler so Simon Moses still had to bring in buckets of hot smoky water laced with dead leaves and insect wings - the mixture as before, in fact.

For the first time we have seen it, the lagerstroemia near the garage was in full froth of delicate lilac coloured bloom.

On Saturday I made three journeys to Salima: the first to fetch petrol, paraffin and oil, and see whether the cement had arrived at the railway station. It had, and the other two journeys were to bring it up to the Cottage, seven bags at a time.

Saturday night a hippo crossed the garden, entering it near the heaps of discarded and rotten thatch by the paint store and ambling straight across to the lagoon; the spoor was very clear in the morning.

On Sunday, from 6:00 am till breakfast time, I pruned fruit trees, then drove to Ntimbasonja. Kananji wore his Jordanian headdress, given to him by Mr Pike, for this trip and the locals were suitably impressed. The new road, built by the Germans, ends at the Nyungwe River (37) and the plank bridge crossing it is as rickety as ever, except that some of the planks may have been nailed down instead of being left half-loose.

Kananji and his wife have named their last child 'Anne' - which he pronounces 'Annie' - after Ann Yarr who was our cataloguer.

The reason Kananji's 'cottage' was not good was that it still contained bed bugs. I have now re-fumigated all three of the servants' rooms.

5 March

I have spent the past week having a severe attack of malaria. G. probably saved my life on Sunday night by getting my temperature down with ice packed on my forehead; she has waited on me hand and foot, washed me, fed me for two days, held me up when I would otherwise have fallen down, and gradually got me back to something like normality.

The attack started on Saturday afternoon, 26 February, although it was coming on while I was still at work in the morning. I went to bed in the afternoon and soon had a protracted fit of shivering and teeth-chattering, so I took my temperature and found it was 103 degrees Fahrenheit. My pulse was fluctuating from 56 to 160. Gladys tried to get a doctor but four telephone calls failed to locate Dr Byl. I took Phensic to try to control the headache and the ache in all my bones. On Sunday morning G. went to the chemists' as soon as they opened at 9:30 a.m. and obtained some chloroquine phosphate. I took forty milligrams at once and six hours later another twenty. Unfortunately we had nothing to control the uraemia which accompanied the fever and which necessitated visiting the toilet every half an hour.

Sunday night was grim: I was intensely hot, my head felt as if it might burst, I had a rheumatic pain in all my bones. G. says I became delirious but I have no recollection of that.

Dr Byl, contacted early on Monday morning, came at 1:20 p.m. and injected about half a tumblerful of something into my buttock; I felt like a stuck pig with two inches of syringe forced into me, but the pain went off at once, and I think it was the injection which brought me out of danger. My temperature began to fall, the aches became bearable, I began to sweat all over again and the bedclothes and mattress were soon sodden. I had not been able to sleep and had been having hallucinations with a 'work' basis, but on Monday-Tuesday night I slept briefly before dawn and had a surrealist technicolour dream which, because of the colours and the wonderful luminous light, was perhaps a glimpse of the same world some people enter under the influence of mescalin. (I had three lots of drugs in action inside me: the chloroquine phosphate, the antibiotic for the uraemia, and whatever the doctor injected into me - probably penicillin). Since then I have sweated out the fever. We have had three mattresses in use and many changes of sweat-soaked pillow-cases and sheets. Yesterday I got up and walked about. Today I have been out in the garden for twenty minutes. Tomorrow I hope to get back to work.

26 March

I had to be at Bunda College on Tuesday, 21 March, to try to get agreement to their participation in centralization of library technical services and to general re-organization of the library there, so we went to the Lake on 18 March, taking Rodrick to give me moral and technical support at Bunda.

Somewhere south of Lilongwe the car accelerator jammed. I was driving at 75 mph and the car suddenly started going faster and faster. I caught a glimpse of the speedometer when it showed 92 mph; fortunately, immediately afterwards I was able to bring it to a stop but there was a frightful screech from the gears, smoke poured out of the exhaust pipe and the radiator boiled over. G., Rodrick and I all jumped out quickly and we waited half an hour until the various parts of the car were cool enough to touch. Then Rodrick and I fiddled with the various rods linked with the accelerator and it suddenly became unjammed. My nerves were so badly shaken that for the rest of the trip I dared not drive at more than 55 mph.

At the Cottage, the telegram to Kananji that I had sent three days earlier to announce we were coming was delivered five hours after our arrival. The refrigerator wasn't cold, the generator lay in pieces all over the engine room floor, and at least 1,000 bats had got into the roof. There were even a few bats inside the bedrooms and bathrooms - one of them flopped down into the water while I was having my bath; it started swimming towards my face but I scuffed water on it and hastily scrambled out of the bath.

On Tuesday, Rodrick and I went back up the road to Bunda. We had lunch at the Pinneys: slices of Bunda beef and slices of cheese, with hot rolls, followed by tinned peaches. In the afternoon we had our meetings with the Heads of Departments. It is evident that the College's library problems cannot be overcome internally. I must therefore assume my role as professional beggar and try to secure more funds for book stock from some source outside the University, arrange for a clean up of the classification and cataloguing, and try to obtain a cataloguer for six months from the Overseas Development Administration.

Before it was dark we got within twenty miles of Salima, but the rest of the journey was horrible - people streaming about the road, clouds of dust, and not enough light from the headlamps to make it possible to avoid some of the potholes. We arrived safely, however, and hours before Gladys expected us.

Two Germans from the Lakeshore Development Project have been drowned - presumed drowned - in the lake . The boat in which they had gone out on was found undamaged on rocks near Cape Maclear.

27 March

This afternoon has been the most exciting in the history of Chancellor College. During the lunch hour the building that accommodates the College Hall, the Senior Common Room, the Junior Common Room, the Extension Studies Centre, the Geography department and various offices, was seen - suddenly - to be on fire. It is not known how the fire began but evidently it started in the maintenance stores - full of paint, blankets and furniture - at the rear end of the hall. Although it was disastrous for the College, there were moments during the three hour blaze that were like a comic film.

The local fire brigade was summoned but, accustomed as it was to its principal duty of putting out grass fires with wet hessian sacks, it arrived without ladders. The firemen assembled on the tarmac, were fallen in, in a straight line, and only after they had saluted their leader (or was it Ngwazi?) were they allowed to tackle the fire.

With the nozzles of their hoses they smashed glass in the windows, creating a strong through-draught; they dragged their hoses over jagged pieces of glass left in the window-sills, puncturing them in many places so that fountains of water sprayed into the air from the holes; from time to time hoses whipped themselves out of the hands of the firemen and pelted water into the crowd of spectators; one intrepid fireman mistook twenty four square feet of plate glass for an open door and charged in head down - like James Bond he emerged unscathed from an explosion of broken glass and to the cheers and clapping of appreciative spectators.

As the fire roared along the building, students and junior staff cleared minor offices of their equipment, eviscerated the senior common room and the Extension Studies Centre, and someone trying to be 'useful' ripped the College telephone exchange out of the wall. Upstairs, from seven small rooms that were formerly used as the Library, which later became the Department of Geography, a cascade of desks , chairs, files, maps, stationery and books were thrown from the balcony to the flower beds fifteen feet below.

While her own department was burning fiercely behind her, Kathy Myambo the psychologist, very sensibly snatched all the mail in the pigeon-holes in the Porters' Lodge into a mailbag and carried it out to the tarmac, and we later received it for safety at the library.

The Civil Aviation Department at Chileka Airport sent their fire engine but the firemen got their hose into such a hopeless tangle it couldn't be used.

Thirty Police arrived to maintain order and brushed several hundred spectators out of the way of firemen so that they would not be trampled underfoot.

At the height of the chaos Namate, the maintenance officer, appeared in dense smoke with singed eyebrows and his shirt hanging out of his trousers; he should have had duplicate keys that would have opened some of the locked doors.

I noticed all Swanzie's aerial photographs of Malawi blowing around on a grassy bank so I scooped them up along with a few heaps of maps that were in danger of being soaked by unpredictable jets of water from the fire hoses. Earlier on, mercifully before the telephone exchange was wrecked, I had 'phoned Swanzie at her house to let her know that the Geography department was in danger of being incinerated, but she had gone to Zomba and Fulque, who remained in the house, had no car - all he could do was telephone her in Zomba.

When the fire was out we carried the heaps of debris into unburnt classrooms for the night.

2 April

Following the spectacular fire at the College on 27 March, we have had a case of attempted arson in the Library.

On 28 March Jeff Stickley had to go to England and he and Marion had early tea with us before we went to Chileka airport to see him off on the plane. After watching the VC. 10 take off and disappear into the sky Marion drove straight back to Zomba and Gladys and I came back up Makata Road so that I could call in at the office and see whether there was any personal mail.

As soon as I unlocked the side door of the 'Cow Barn' I could smell fire. As there is always a risk of someone tossing a forbidden cigarette into a waste paper basket, I rushed into the reading room and inspected the waste paper baskets. There was nothing amiss with them so I quickly unlocked all the doors in the passage outside my office.

In the small store-room next to the back door - where the messengers change their clothes and keep cleaning materials, and where we kept masses of publications that we exchange with other libraries - I found a small heap of burnt paper in the middle of the floor. This had burned to ash except for two fragments that had failed to burn. The paper had been placed on the cement floor in such a way that it was evidently intended to burn first and then set light to a heap of the President's printed speeches six inches away from it; after that a whole lot of pamphlets and publications would have caught fire. Mercifully, only a corner of the heap of speeches had ignited and then the fire must have gone out.

The door of the store room had been locked until I unlocked it. When I saw what had been attempted, I called in Gladys who was sitting waiting for me in the car outside, and I also called in the night-watchman who was guarding the Library. I did a quick security check of the rest of the building. There was one complicating factor. On the enquiry desk in the reading room I found a note from a student who had been shut into the microfilm reading room when the reading room was shut at four o'clock; at five o'clock he scribbled on the note that he had been shut in for an hour but had found a key and was letting himself out. I checked that he had locked the front door - I assumed that was the door for which he had found the key - and that he had taken the key to the Porters' Lodge and handed it in. He had; and only a few minutes before I got there myself.

I saw the Head Night-Watchman and asked him to ensure that nobody entered the Library during the night.

We were due out to a birthday party at the Old Lady's at 6:00 p.m. (she was 86 on Tuesday) so - somewhat late - we then went out for the evening. Much to my surprise I had a good night's sleep.

Next day I arrived at work at 7:00 am, before the other staff. I wanted to get hold of the two messengers who were supposed to arrive at 7:00 am, confront them with the small pile of ash, and see what their reactions were. Stamford Kacisa arrived first; his exclamation of surprise seemed genuine enough. And Arnold Kabazali, a few minutes later, was obviously astonished. I told them not to use the room and not to tell anybody what they had seen. Later on, I was able to determine the order in which the staff had left work around four o'clock the previous day.

The CID have now been called in but I doubt if they will be able to solve the mystery as it requires a knowledge of the personalities of the people involved and, perhaps, of events behind the scenes in the Library, including the various jealousies that exist. The evidence suggests that an assistant librarian was responsible. This particular individual knew I had gone to the airport and that I was expected back at 5:30 p.m. By that time the store- room, my office and the work room, including the acquisitions section and the cataloguing section, could have been on fire. I don't think the CID will be able to work this out but it is not too difficult for senior staff of the Library - and perhaps the messengers - to deduce which member of staff was responsible.

17 April

A consignment of new steel shelving arrived on 7 April and was erected over the week-end.

We have been able to secure the £36000 worth of books under the British Government's (O.D.A) Books Presentation Programme, but I am still trying to find more aid. Thirty cartons of books have arrived and the work room is overwhelmed with the spate of new books, at least a thousand of which I was able to choose myself without reference to cost.

As Jeffrey is away in England I visited the Bindery on 10 April and again today. On the Chirunga site I had a session with the Development Officer and the

Quantity Surveyor about various bits of equipment, such as stripdex stands, caliphones and my swing-fog machine which have not yet been ordered.

20 April

I seem to be having a worrying time. The CID investigation continued spasmodically all last week. Six members of staff were called to the Police station for interrogation and the two messengers and an assistant librarian had to appear twice.

I suspect that two of the assistant librarians have gone outside the University - to the President's Office or the Malawi Congress Party - to try to effect my removal. One of them has accused me in writing, of 'racial discrimination' and I have made an official request that this should be withdrawn. One of them, also, has been seen leaving the house of *a local witch doctor* so possibly no stone is being left unturned in the effort to get rid of me.

7 May

Today we had Marion and the children to lunch and tea. Jeffrey is still in Southend where he has had his appendix cut out, followed by unknown complications.

In the afternoon I drove as far up Ndirande mountain as one can get by road - surprisingly far along a good road and forest track. The mountain is much more impressive with its startling precipices and huge rocks and ravines dense with vegetation than it appears to be from below, and the views were superb: Zomba and Mulanje both in the same picture and very clear, and on the other side a tremendous panorama extending to Zobue and a ridge beyond it in Mozambique, and also most of the Kirk Range. It was more impressive than Zomba mountain because one's outlook was not obscured by trees, although vast carpets of young conifers have been planted on the lower slopes. In the grass bright red and blue and orange flowers were like sparks of fire.

18 May

To the Lake on Saturday morning, starting out at 5:45 am when there was still cloud over the Shire Highlands. Frank and Elizabeth Warren stayed with us, coming in from Bunda College where Frank - who is Finance Officer - had been trying to sort out the College's finances.

On Sunday at the Ivory Carver's shack Elizabeth bought three grass mats, one of them a work of art in green and yellow, made in a village farther up the lakeshore towards Nkhota-Kota. Although the lake was rough throughout the week-end, with an *Mwera* blowing and white horses sweeping landwards before the wind, Matora's dug-out had a big catch of fish and I bought ten *chambo* to feed ourselves, Kananji, Simon Moses, his wife Nachitechi, Kandulu and Member.

Simon had worked hard in the garden and everywhere is clean and tidy. He has even caused beans to grow at the sandy end of the vegetable garden; to achieve this surprising result I think he mixes an equal amount of sand and sulphate of ammonia.

If people don't cancel their requests for the Lake Cottage, we have over £250.00 worth of bookings up to the end of September and we have already taken £70.00 this year.

We came back early on Tuesday morning, reaching Blantyre at 11:45 am. I had to be at work at 1:00 p.m.

1 June

Yesterday the Attorney General and the Chief Justice came to see the 'Cow Barn' which they think might be suitable for use as a Court after Chancellor College moves to Zomba next year. I think it more suitable for a supermarket or a skating rink.

14 June

On 9 June we had an earth tremor at 2:25 a.m. I woke up to find the bed vibrating and a mild roar quickly dwindling. Gladys pays no attention to earthquakes and slept through it.

Up at Senga Bay at the week-end, I found that Simon Moses had been involved in an incident with Heston Tandaza's milkman and that his right arm was in a sling. His story was that he had been going to one of the canteens for sugar when Heston's milkman, high on dagga, rushed at him with a panga. Simon had to disarm him, which he did, but in doing so the milkman's thumb was cut by the panga. Simon brought the panga back to his room, intending to show it to Kandulu and Dalamkwanda, but before he could do that the milkman and five other men arrived at his room and attacked him, breaking his collar-bone with the butt of a gun with which the milkman aspired to shoot him, and beating him till he was unconscious - which was how the Police found him.

The milkman brought a case against him for 'injury with a sharp weapon' (or some such wording) on account of his snicked thumb, and Simon was taken away to the Police station in Salima where it was found he was in a very bruised state with his clavicle broken. The Police, on the evidence of the broken clavicle, and the damaged state of the door of his room, and his general condition, have been collecting evidence against the milkman and have taken away his gun for which he had no licence, and several people have had to make statements.

A detective from the CID came to see me, and I went to see the Police in Salima on Simon's behalf to see if he was likely to be jailed. The case was to be heard this morning but we couldn't wait to know the outcome. I have left K10 with Simon which the 'Chief of Crime' said would be enough to pay his fine *if* he was convicted. There is a tribal angle to all this: the 'Chief of Crime' is an Mlomwe, as is Simon, and the detective looked like a Mang'anja, whereas all the rest of the crowd - the beaters-up - are Yao.

The attack on Simon has evidently scared Kananji. While we were at the Cottage he brought another cook to see me and said he wanted to go back to Liwonde. I said I wanted a month's notice, that I would not engage the man he was offering but would bring a new cook from Blantyre on the occasion of our expected visit in July, and Kananji, if he still wanted to, could leave then.

Not only the human situation is getting complicated: so is the animal situation. The vegetable garden has been trampled on by hippos who stamped their way into it and ate five rows of beans, leaving spoor more than a foot across. I have put up a protective fence and I hope that any hippo who reappears will impale his (or her) tender nose on a sisal spike or a two-inch acacia thorn.

Afzelia, Erythrina and tamarind beans are now ripe; with the first two I can make attractive hippie necklaces.

Back this morning to the cold air of Blantyre.

Gladys is due to go to UK on 15 July. I should be there myself on 19 August after completing six and half years' work at the University. But I shall go for one month only and spend the rest of the vacation here in Malawi, partly at the Lake, re-roofing the garage at the Cottage and the small store and maybe the servants' quarters, in between swimming and eating large quantities of *chambo*; and partly in Blantyre where I need to be present while an extension to this house is built.

26 June

I have been subjected to increasing nervous strain in the past week or so. With my leave approaching and Raphael Masanjika, our new assistant librarian, due to arrive from Zambia in two days' time, I have had two wring from the Vice-Chancellor a statement in writing that I am responsible for the deployment of library staff, and then obtain the agreement of three Principals to various postings, and then discuss the work situation with senior staff and invite their co-operation in the postings that are necessary. At the same time I have had to reiterate to the administration that I want Rodrick to be acting librarian while I am away.

All this has evoked a convulsion of jealousy and suspicion among some of the assistant librarians, and one of them has written a long letter of complaint, accusing me of dishonesty, favouritism and misuse of university funds - statements which I regard as libellous - and sent a copy of it to all senior officials in the University. This man and one other of the assistant librarians have accused me of having a 'negative attitude towards Africans', the result of which has been that Albert Muwalo, the Minister of State, has asked the Vice-Chancellor to investigate. (38)

Since Friday I have been expecting to be deported at short notice but today the situation has eased again, and I have gained a temporary reprieve. I have had a long meeting this afternoon with the Vice-Chancellor, the university Registrar and the Principal of Chancellor College. I have made it clear that unless they are willing to take action against the assistant librarian who accused me of dishonesty I will resign; and that the letters from another assistant librarian involved must also stop. I have pointed out to the Principal that he failed to take action when I reported to him that I had been accused of 'racial discrimination'. I have said that if I am to stay here I expect my views to receive consideration; that I have had to dilute my professional standards for six years to take account of interference by ill-informed and junior members of the academic staff; and that the University Library Committee must be strengthened as it has become too juvenile to enable it to function. A number of home truths came out but I was suitably tranquillized, kept my temper and managed to speak in a quiet voice, even when I announced that, with the solitary exception of the University of Zambia, the University of Malawi Library has added books faster than any library on the Africa continent since the time of Callimachus.

In the past week I have had to try to secure fair play for one of the library messengers. The last time we went to the Lake he was absent from work for four hours, was reported absent after one and a three-quarter hours, three senior staff went to his house after three hours, and a long report on his absence was made by the assistant librarian left in charge, so that the registrar at Chancellor College wrote saying he had no alternative but to dismiss him. The assistant librarian concerned has burst into a shower of inaccurate accusations and innuendoes, possibly to hide his own complicity in some of the small incidents mentioned, including the arson case. But the messenger has become confused - the enquiry was conducted in English not in his own language - and he seems to have told lies on two counts so I am having to allow him to be dismissed. It is a straightforward instance of victimization but because I insisted on a full investigation of the case I am accused of favouritism.

At the same time I am attacked for not having defended another member of library staff - a library assistant - who was caught red-handed eating in the students' dining hall without paying for his meal and whom the registrar wanted to dismiss peremptorily: I had no real objection but I knew his home circumstances and was able to secure for him the statutory two months' notice.

This kind of harsh treatment for junior staff is obviously the result of administrative inexperience. When a student steals fourteen books, worth perhaps more than £50.00, he is fined 10/-, patted on the shoulder and told not do it again. When a defenceless messenger is absent for half a day he is dismissed and deprived of his livelihood.

Yesterday evening we had dinner at the Old Lady's. Ruth Partridge was also there. She is being prosecuted for a motoring offence - so it seemed possible that neither of us would be in Malawi in a week's time. Grace decided to celebrate in case there was no future opportunity and she took a bottle of champagne off the ice and we had that along with our chicken au lemon and chocolate ice-cream.

9 July

We are back at Senga Bay. It is always a relief to get here, even if one has many chores to accomplish while here. Vera Dunn is with us.

Simon Moses was fined K20 which I have paid to keep him out of the notorious Dzeleka Detention Centre at Dowa. (39)

One of the largest trees in the grounds of the Cottage has been fired and felled. Apparently a large cobra was seen to enter a hole in its base and Simon thought he would smoke it out and kill it. The tree was hollow, it burned internally and then crashed to the ground. I suspect that the servants wanted firewood. Anyhow, I shall plant another tree. I assume that the cobra escaped.

I have collected more beans from the trees in the garden. The red *Erythrina caffra* Thun. (*Kaffirboom*) has seeds that are said to yield an alkaloid with a curare-like action but which are 'practically non-toxic' if taken by the mouth. I am not sure which Afzelia it is we have. If it is *Afzelia cuanzesis Sm.*, the red aril like sealing wax over one end of the beans is regarded as edible in Senegal, and the bark is used as an aphrodisiac. If it is the *Afzelia cuanzensis* Welw., this has a poisonous root, but in Zambia the bark is used to cure toothache. Whatever the species may be the timber is used locally to make dug-out canoes. The beans are sometimes called 'mahogany beans' or 'lucky beans' ('*mkongomwa*' in Chichewa).

Once again, hippos have eaten all sixteen rows of french beans but they stopped short at the tomatoes which I hope they will leave well alone.

We brought the new cook, Henderson Mateya, up to the Lake and he has installed himself quite well, being fed initially by Nachitechi the wife of Simon Moses. He has very knobbly knees and I think he should be given long trousers to hide them. He looks as if his wife beats him but he has left her in Domasi so he should enjoy a spell of domestic peace up here.

One of my journeys to Salima was to convey Kananji and his family to the station. We are most sorry to lose him but the parting was amicable. I think he was too scared after the attack on Simon to remain at the Lake, even although he is a Yao.

I have received my gratuity (K3,796) and five months salary (K2,425) so even after paying the final instalment for the Cottage and allowing for various deductions I have about K2,780 left for living expenses and alterations to the Blantyre house - which I must now see about. There is still money to come from ODA.

15 July

Gladys left on this afternoon's plane. For the next month I shall live alone, then go to England for a month's leave, then come back here to deal with the extension of this house.

Today we have had a meeting of the Appointments Committee to decide who should be acting university librarian in my absence on leave. I recommended Rodrick who is the only suitable candidate, but the Committee decided to ignore my recommendation and have appointed the oldest of the assistant librarians. There is no point in struggling on if the administrators are not prepared to co-operate, so from today I shall be looking for another job, hopefully in Central Africa.

22 July

Tuesday morning the Vice-Chancellor came to see me: I had written him a note telling him I felt I must seek another post and enquiring whether he would act as referee. He wants me to stay but at present I feel I can't stomach any more of this University.

3 August

Yesterday I went to Zomba to see what progress had been made with the new Library building and to visit the Geological Survey.

The builders are now at work completing the top floor of the Library and I think it will be a fine functional building. From the top floor one can look out over the rest of the campus: the blue wall of Zomba mountain six thousand feet high is to the left, and Lake Chilwa is a few miles away in the opposite direction beyond undulating terrain scattered with small villages of thatched huts. All the main buildings are supposed to be finished by next May and we are due to move from Blantyre in July 1973.

At the Geological Survey I wanted to see specimens of the rocks one sees everywhere in the mountains of Malawi; some of these are three thousand million years old, among the oldest rocks in the world. I also wanted to see some of the economic minerals and semi-precious stones - copper and manganese and graphite and monazite and bauxite; and garnets, beryls, chalcedony, rose and smoky quartz and ilmenite and many more. So much seems to lie under our feet and on every side of which we - or at least I - know practically nothing. On the sands of Lake Malawi, including the sands in front of our Cottage, fragments of these rocks wash up in form of gravel and the sand is sometimes glistening with mica and biotite.

5 August

My vacation leave started Tuesday. Kenneth Chitika of Norman and Dawbarn, the architects, has made sketch plans of the alterations we want to make to this house in Blantyre, and this afternoon I took him to R J Grover's and we had twenty prints made of his drawings, after which we went to the Town Planning Office and submitted the plans along with the forms I have had to complete.

12 August

Senga Bay. I came up here with Dick last Sunday.

Not far from the second turning to Bunda a large llama-shaped mask was cavorting in the road. I thought it must be Nyau but apparently it was Chewa. Its head was seven or eight feet high and its body five to six feet long. It had a little fibrous beard and a narrow fibre fringe around the base of the body which was raised only an inch or two above the tarmacked road. The head, neck and flanks were painted with black and red scrawls of paint, probably to suggest hair, and it was constructed of plastic with two 'eyes' or windows of clear plastic in the bottom of the neck so that the person inside, who provided the locomotion, could see out. The man leading the mask said they were going to a funeral where the mask would take part in the Gule Wamkulu dance; according to Dick he was embarrassed to be stopped and questioned in the public highway but was slightly mollified when I gave him a shilling.

The Cottage was very clean, and Henderson evidently plans his work methodically. While we were there he roasted two plump chickens (50t. each) and some local steak which was tough when roasted but very good in a pie; yesterday we had fried *chambo*, in which he forgot to put any salt; and today for lunch we had a three and three-quarter pound *mpasa* which is regarded as the Lake's no. 1 fish and looks like a salmon - this cost 35t.

Until yesterday the Lake was too rough for dug-outs to go fishing but yesterday morning Matora had a very big haul, probably over a hundred *chambo*, and there was great excitement on the beach as his canoe was the first to come in after the rough weather.

Kandulu and his helper have been working every day on construction of the garage roof. He has at last obtained a supply of *mitengo migwalangwa* (palm poles), forty poles costing £ 4.00. Today I hope he will begin to nail on the corrugated iron sheets.

It has been too rough and cold to swim but Dick and I have made two pleasant excursions. On Thursday we took a guide, Justin Aisa, a leper (and no relation to Aisa the cook) who has built a hut outside plot 7 near the lagoon. I drove to the gravel pits and we then climbed Senga Hill. It is 2,786 feet high and it took seventy minutes to reach the beacon on the topmost rock. From the top there is one of the most startling and unexpected views I have ever seen - right round the compass. When we arrived back at the Cottage Kandulu and the gardener were uneasy about us as they feared we might have been attacked by "the Chongwe" which is evidently a kind of big cobra alleged to live on the mountain.

Yesterday we went to Nyungwi, a beach of white sand we had seen from the top of Senga Hill. Nyungwi is a very lovely beach, with Senga Hills and a marsh to the south and Rifu (accent on the "fu") with ancient baobabs and great dark rocks to the north.

Simon says that Nachitechi is three months pregnant and has to go back to Penga-Penga to have the baby at home.

Tomorrow we return to Blantyre, using the Lakeshore road which everyone says is good.

I am due to go on leave to U.K. on Friday 18 August, and I expect to return to Malawi on 18 September.

* * * * * * * * * *

In 1972 I tried to summarize impressions of Senga Bay. The 'essay' (if that is what it should be called) has never been published, but as it may have historical interest now that so much has changed I include it here.

After the Akafula

At Lilongwe giant yellow excavators and tippers have scraped soil and bushes back from the narrow tarmac road north of the town and a broad avenue of crumbled sepia loam, destined to be a future highway, flanks the tarmac on either side and leads away to the east. South and north of the road Malawi's new capital city is being built: government buildings, residential and commercial areas on one side, heterogeneous light industries on the other.

Twenty miles to the east the atmosphere of the countryside begins to change. The plateau is left behind. The 'petrol lorry road', jagged at its edges, eroded on its shoulders, up and down which tankers grind all the way from railhead in Salima to Lilongwe and on to the Zambia border, begins its descent across green spurs that lead always to new descents where villages and their gardens hide amid luxuriant banana clumps in pockets of the valleys.

To our right, a prospect of grey and lavender mountains is wreathed in frail cloud and farther east the escarpment and the heights that menace Golomoti drown in shadow from advancing cumulus, while later still, glimpsed from a forested hill-top, sparkles the magnesium line of Lake Malawi.

In the high villages there is no tsetse fly and small boys tend straggling herds of cattle. Tribes of goats, black, white and chestnut brown cross and re-cross the road, and pigs, hens and ducks forage securely in the shade of trees.

People of the villages offer for roadside sale new maize and millet bins of neatly woven wicker, hats and sleeping mats of woven grass and palm leaf sometimes dyed green and yellow, faggots of firewood, pyramids of charcoal, golden bamboos for lining roofs, baskets and clay pots and decorated wooden spoons and - in season -paw-paws, pumpkins, plantains, maize and cassava.

Women and girls, bare-footed but attired in cotton dresses of indigo, marigold, cinnabar and pink, comatose babies on their backs, gossip and saunter to and fro with head loads. Some of the old men sit in the shade and fashion hoe handles while they wait for the daily local beer to ferment.

The lake breeze blowing from the Rift Valley forty miles ahead brings a promise of heat.

It seems possible in the hills that 'the old Africa' begins with the silence only a hundred yards from the modern tarmac. A witch-doctor has strung an assortment of antelope horns, medicinal roots, pangolin tails, bicycle chains and bird skulls at the mouth of a footpath leading to his sanctum, which is a thatched hut in need of repair.

Two men in face masks of tree bark with eye slits, and wearing nothing else but modesty pouches made of monkey skin, are trekking to the Lake; they carry spears and one of them has a Nyau drum slung from his shoulder.

Beyond the hills the fertile lakeshore plain with areas of experimental cotton, groundnuts and rice begins. Pandanus palms, topped with serrated fins of leaf, and prehistoric baobabs, their elephantine trunks swollen with arboreal varicose veins, remain as vestiges of the past among the plots. The villages and homesteads thicken and a multitude of men, women, children and goats walk in rising dust along the verges of the road.

Quite suddenly, among the enormous flame trees, we reach Salima: Police lines and busy market on the right, secondary school and avenues labelled Second Street, First Street, leading to the mosque, the post office, the District Commissioner's office, the offices of the Town Council, the Lakeshore Development Project, the Police headquarters and streets of gaudy cloth shops on the left.

At the far end of the small town, sixty-three miles from Lilongwe, is the railway goods station, railhead of the line that comes from Beira. Here is the arrival point for petrol, and some perhaps is stored in the painted glittering tanks adjacent to the station but most is rushed by road to fuel-thirsty Zambia.

In return for the largesse of modern development - cement and enormous concrete pipes for culverts and fertilizer and corrugated iron sheets and machines of unknown function and wagons of "Super Shell" - *down* the line goes lucrative copper from Zambia, groundnuts, sun-dried fish, tobacco, cotton, and all the produce of the Central Region and the north. Salima is in fact, for all its modest size, one of the important distribution points of southern central Africa.

From the town it is twelve miles to the Lake, a pleasant but dusty drive in dry weather along the broad laterite road, preserved by government 'grader' which in this part of the world consists of a tractor pulling behind it an immense and heavy faggot of battered sticks which scrapes the corrugations and packs the pot-holes full of soil.

After heavy rain parts of this road in years gone by became notoriously impassable with mud and even in recent times at the beginning of the rains it demands dexterity to force the family car, skidding and yawing, through the churned up slush, especially across the dambo where the Mpatsanjoka stream passes beneath a narrow earthen and timber causeway slippery and hazardous to cars.

The dambo area is open grassland where in April lotus flowers star the muddy pools and wicker fish traps for a few weeks of the year yield a harvest of fat fish. Once there were lions and herds of antelopes and buffalo but now there is, at most, only a passing kudu or a family of wart-hogs, and small boys peacefully herding cows.

Homesteads standing back among the roadside trees are mostly mud and thatch affairs with loofahs growing on the roof and granaries under paw-paw trees but many, too, express the relative prosperity of the owner-occupier by their white-washed walls, glazed windows and brightly painted doors, often with a bicycle propped in shadow under ragged eaves.

Beyond Salima air-field - usable by light aircraft flying in from Blantyre, Lilongwe and Mzimba - rise, on the left, the Senga Hills, forested to the top and even to-day reputedly the haunt of lions and leopards, certainly little climbed, part of the Northern Forest Reserve. On the left, appear, therefore, no more thatched huts and compounds but only women carrying loads of firewood on their heads, threading in single file through tall grass to Dalamkwanda's village.

Our destination is near.

A hundred yards beyond a side road pounded smooth by vehicles of the Central Region Lakeshore Development Project we slither cautiously - on account of the car's silencer - off the camber of the laterite road and, on the right, enter a narrow track. Between maize gardens we climb a sandy ridge; there is a sudden vision of the vast and splendid Lake, blue and glittering under the sky; a few more yards and we are in a tiny patch of parkland, breathing the fragrance of the frangipani, poinciana, tamarind and *ng'kongomo* trees that shade the garden and the cottage.

Lake Malawi (formerly Nyasa), lying at the southernmost end of the Great Rift Valley, is 365 miles long and varies in width from fifteen to more than fifty miles. The cottage - a large and solid bungalow - looks out over Senga Bay and faces the open Lake which at this point is forty miles wide: its white roof, framed in trees, is treated as a beacon on which to paddle home by fishermen in canoes far out in the Lake.

To the left of the Cottage, three miles from the land, is Namilenji Island around which in the early morning lake birds whirl in dense black skeins, in the great rocks of which giant monitor lizards live like saurians of a prehistoric age. Behind the island on the Lake's far side, across its 'narrow waist' - fifteen miles - is Makanjira's village to which in Livingstone's day dhow masters ferried many thousands of slaves.

Round to the right, twenty-nine miles across the water, is the rounded headland of Cape Maclear where, a hundred years ago, missionaries died in quick succession, and in the last World War Sunderland flying boats maintained an anchorage.

Far to the right again within the Lake's south-western bight are several uninhabited islands, Maleri, Mamkoma, Natenga, where tiny tropical fish of brilliant colours are caught and subsequently sent by VC.10 to Europe; from one of these islands fishermen bring specimens of curious stone, jet black and quartzy white.

On a clear day mountains across the Lake can readily be seen: Namwera escarpment purple in the south; Chilapula and Mikonga mountains lilac in Mozambique, and a long faint ragged range leading to the north.

The Senga Hills forming the background to Senga Bay are said to be three thousand million years old. Malawi's earliest known human inhabitants, apart from Stone Age men, were the Akafula, a people so small of stature as sometimes to be called 'dwarfs' who lived along the Lakeshore three thousand years ago, before the Bantu came. Some of the pottery fragments that wash up from the Lake could be Akafula artifacts.

The beach above which the Cottage stands curves gently from a rocky headland in the north, behind which flourishes the Grand Beach Hotel within its own small bay, round to Kambiri Point, another headland four miles to the south. The sands are wide and clean and vary in colour from hour glass white to biotite blue-black; storm beaches form and reform again throughout the year. At the beach top, straggling over half a mile of shore, are bungalows owned by Malawians, Asians and Europeans.

A few steps inland from the Lake are two small villages, Dalamkwanda's on the northern ridge and Mdalamdoka Nkuti's on the site of a stream and near a marsh towards the southern end of the beach.

During recent years the government of the German Federal Republic, on behalf of the Malawi government, has established the Central Region Lakeshore Development Project, responsible for agricultural development in the widest sense, over a large area inland from the Lake. Its office headquarters is in Salima but the residential headquarters for the scientific and administrative staff has been built at Senga Bay.

What used to be an area of sandy dunes has become a settlement of well-built houses, each standing on concrete pillars so that its rooms may catch the breeze, surrounded by gardens and lawns of trim and succulent green turf, planted with bougainvillea, perfumed with frangipani, the complex self-sufficient with its own electricity plant and unlimited water from the Lake. The contrast to Dalamkwanda's village with its mud-walled, grass-roofed houses and grass compounds, mostly very brown and dry and dusty, just over the wire fence, could not be more marked.

Farther up the beach the Germans have taken over buildings of the Senga Bay Hotel, added enormously to them and created a trade school where youths are taught carpentry, plumbing, bricklaying and electrical work; discipline is very strict but tradesmen are urgently needed in the Development Project and the whole area.

On the beach, beside the Lake, local fishermen dry their nets in the sun and squat amongst them, dexterously and rapidly repairing holes in the nylon mesh and re-knotting weakened links in the grass pull-ropes by which the nets are played out from canoes. The dug-outs, which need to be dried on the beach by day, put out for fish in the late afternoon and very early morning, so that all repair work must be done in hot sun on sand which sometimes rises in temperature to 160 degrees Fahrenheit.

In the afternoons the fishermen and youths and men from the village soap and scrape themselves at the water's edge and bathe and swim for pleasure. Except at weekends, when there are visitors on the beach, they bathe naked but they turn their backs or flop into the water on the approach of strangers.

Women and girls, by custom, have their separate sections of the beach where they abrade the family pots and pans with sand, batter thin blankets and miscellaneous clothes and bathe for the most part decorously half-drowned in cotton frocks.

There are always people passing up and down the beach with strings of fish for sale, or carrying home bottles of paraffin from the canteen, or firewood or sun-dried laundry or newly-woven sleeping mats; and occasionally a cyclist speeds along the hard wet sand at the edge of the water.

The Lake is infinitely varied in its moods, colours and textures; it has a presence of its own which alters not only through the seasons but also from day to day and hour by hour. So far no one has been able to do justice to it in any of the books in which it is described. It awaits a painter of genius or a poet with perfect words.

At the first light of dawn there is at once a pathway of molten gold linking Makanjira's village in Mozambique and Senga beach in Malawi; the eastern sky irradiates marvellous changing tints of red, orange and yellow and the hills of Mozambique are mistily silhouetted against the sunrise. In the stillness of the night in blazing moonlight the surface of the Lake becomes a vast expanse of sequins and silver ripples and Cape Maclear stands bold and well-defined under the moon, and even the outline of Namwera fifty miles distant can be seen. In October before the coming of the rains there is sometimes a dead calm, the Lake no longer seems to breathe, and its colours vary from pure and brilliant cornflower blue to turquoise and pale jade.

But it is unpredictable and infamous for its storms. In July 1946 the lake streamer 'Vipya', caught in enormous waves, capsized and sank and 150 people were drowned. Almost every year fisherman from Senga beach and Nyungwe beach are caught in sudden storms, their dug-outs are swamped and they too are drowned. When the south-east wind known as the *Mwera* blows the Lake is like an angry sea with powerful waves and white horses sweeping landwards before the wind. The breakers surge and fan far up the sands; new storm beaches are formed; the fishermen remain at home.

Many of the fishermen lead a harsh and uncomfortable life. Some of them sleep on the beach in flimsy straw structures that are little better than fences giving shelter from the wind. Others are transitory trekkers who have no money, no work, and only the clothes they are wearing; they sleep on the sand with no shelter of any kind and rely on village fishermen to give them food in an exchange for labour in pulling in the nets. A few of the local fishermen are well-known outside their main occupation. One of them is famous as the leader in Nyau dances. Another, as a sideline, is a seller of Indian hemp. Several are prosperous and own their nylon nets; two of the dug-outs are owned by families. Occasionally, especially after wild weather which brings fish nearer the shore, there is a heavy catch with plenty of *chambo* and *mpasa* and cat-fish for everyone to grill on the beach or split open and kipper in the sun, and even the 'jobless' are happy for a while.

There is no bilharzia in the Lake at Senga Bay and normally no crocodiles or hippo.

Hippos, however, do occasionally invade the vegetable garden of the Cottage at night, coming from the lagoon. It is a female and her calf who have acquired a taste for beans.

The Lake has one strange phenomenon that occurs at the beginning of the rainy season. Somewhere towards Makanjira's village what appears to be smoke from a steamer rises from the surface of the Lake and blows down-wind in the direction of Cape Maclear and the southern bights of the Lake. This is the annual swarming of the *kungu* fly which are, in fact, chironimid midges that hatch by the trillion, rise in the air and blow before the breeze in dense columns and clouds which from a distance exactly resemble smoke. There may be several columns advancing down the Lake at the same time. The local people claim that the *kungu* are blown or vomited into the air by a colossal fish living in the Lake - a kind of Lake Malawi monster. If you get caught in a swarm and do not cover your face you breathe *kungu* instead of air and die of suffocation.

WP Johnson, in his 'Nyasa, the great water', 1992, writes of them as follows:

These midge clouds are conspicuous out on the Lake, sometimes in columns forty feet high; they take almost any fantastic shape. When the wind carries them over the land they make it dark, as if there were a fog, and the natives come out with baskets in which they catch them deftly in order that they may make them into a cake, which is not wholly disagreeable to European taste and has a shrimpy flavour.

Although the terminus of the regular dhow service is farther north at Leopard's Bay, a dhow from Makanjira's village occasionally crosses to Senga Bay Beach, off-loading passengers and goods opposite one of the small gullies that lead to Dalamkwanda's village. The dhow is a sturdy craft, built of thick unpainted planks; the deck consists of heavy planks that are removable; the mast is a blue gum pole, not quite straight; there is a lateen yard to take the great square sail; and a curiously shaped wooden rudder at the stern. The crew of ten tough Yao men and boys might be pirates from a film; they wear bright shirts over their faded jeans and tie pieces of coloured rag around their heads; their features indicate that all of them have Arab blood.

The dhows are always overloaded with at least forty passengers jammed together on the deck, yet they rarely overturn. The baggage department - the space into which in the past manacled slaves were put - is below the planks of the deck, and it is surprising what an assortment of bundles of banana leaf, sacking and ancient cloth containing tobacco, charcoal, rolls of matting and strongly smelling fish, emerges from this 'hold'.

On the return trip to Makanjira's village passengers carry more sophisticated loads -transistor radios, hurricane lamps, brightly decorated enamel bowls, two gallon tins of paraffin, and bicycles, besides indispensable bales of cotton cloth and bulging bags of rice from the shops and market in Salima.

Of course, a dhow cannot glide close up to the beach like a fisherman's canoe. It has to moor in waist-deep water ten yards from the edge, and women and girls are carried ashore astride the bare shoulders of eager youths; ribaldry among spectators arises from the fact that the girls do not wear pants. One leathery old grandmother, however - for whom there is no competition - scorns the politely proffered help of several sturdy youths willing to do their duty, splashes down into the water and strides ashore in the spirit of "Women's Lib" - true man-hater style.

Formerly there were twelve dhows sailing on this part of the lake but nowadays there are only two. Their owner's names are crudely painted on the sun-scorched prows: 'Mr Tandayo' and 'Kalulu Ng'ombe'.

Near the Cottage is the 'Lagoon', described on government maps as 'Marsh'. It is, in fact a stream named the Nguwu which rises in the Senga hills and is frustrated for most of the year from reaching the lake by a large sand dune which blocks its mouth. As a result it has expanded and formed a terminal lagoon, or lake with swampy edges.

From time to time crocodiles appear in the lagoon but these are shot as soon as possible after being sighted. Hippos are present in the breeding season but they emerge only at night.

In the dry season the lagoon almost dries up. But during the rains it sometimes manages to breach the dune and pour its water into the Lake. On the night of 4-5 December 1970 the worst cyclone in living memory - when twelve inches of rain fell in three hours - changed the Nguwu to a tossing torrent which swept away culverts and hens and turkeys, sheared through the sand dune so that it became, instead, a creek sixty feet wide with banks of sand eight feet high, and precipitated a tangled mass of tree trunks, branches, banana trees - and a large and battered python - plus a mass of papyrus and reeds and rushes scoured from the lagoon, into the Lake.

In the course of that night and the following day much of the debris drifting in the bay was flung up onto the beach in front of the cottage so that it took a gang of labourers a week to clear the decaying stems and vegetation from the sands, drag them to a point above the storm beach, dry them in the sun, then burn them all in a line of acrid bonfires.

The lagoon is not the only spot attractive to birds. The dignified and gracious trees that shade the cottage grounds with their enormous spread of leaf also form a sanctuary for them.

The largest and most splendid visitors are a pair of fish eagles - white with black wings and chestnut abdomen and a wing span of five and a half feet - whose wild screams ring from the topmost branches of a *naphini* tree where they alight. Most of the time they patrol the bay but between aerobatic show-offs - soaring on undetectable 'risers', sliding, gliding, gyrating with every feather outstretched - one or other of the, birds sometimes swoops to catch a fish from the surface of the lake and carries it, in powerful talons, to tear to pieces in the *naphini* tree. The eagles have their nest near the top of a rocky hill inland from Namikombe Point: an impregnable structure of sticks and twigs in the crown of a large tree which must command a view of the whole of Senga Bay from nearby Senga Hills to Kambiri Point five miles to the south and of the coastline and crags round to Rifu Hill in the north. (40)

Less aristocratic and distinctly smaller birds who are occasional visitors and (we hope) nesters in the grounds are Layard's bulbuls, black-headed orioles, fire finches, exquisite small sunbirds like daintily feathered jewels, glossy black drongos, common grey hornbills and a pair of brilliant red-billed hornbills - perhaps Von der Decken's hornbills - which once spent fifteen minutes inspecting the trunk of the *ng'kongomo* tree on the front lawn, presumably with a view to excavating and nesting and then, alas, took fright and flew away to look for something much more private.

The trees in the vicinity of the Cottage are a delight. A favourite with children is a giant tamarind, now lying on its corrugated elbow at a corner of the Cottage, which must have fallen in some storm, impaling itself in the soil of the terrace, many years ago. It has tassels of sweet-scented flowers, squirrels come and bark with excitement if they think some interloper is going to pick the beans, visiting children swing on its craggy limbs. At one time its hollow trunk provided a den for a python but this visitor had to be smoked out and shot after it began, one by one, to eat the domestic ducks. It is well-known that the tamarind is the 'Tree of Life'; perhaps less well-known that a pleasant aphrodisiac cool drink can be concocted from its beans.

The flowers of the *ng'kongomo* which stand on three sides of the garden have a pervasive and delicious scent. When ripe and dry the big grey heavy pods enclose beans that are black and glossy, each capped with a scarlet aril exactly resembling sealing wax. The beans make attractive black and red necklaces and can be found as 'lucky beans' in curio shops. The thick straight trunks rising fifteen feet to a wide umbrella crown can be axed and chiselled into small dug-out canoes, and in the past the timber was favoured for the building of dhows.

Two strange trees are the *mtonga* and the *nkobe*.

The first, the Kaffirboom of South Africa, is an immigrant from that country; its trunk and branches are covered with prickly galls and anyone aspiring to climb the tree would need protective clothing including leather gloves; the beans which are said to yield an alkaloid with an action as deadly as curare, and which grow at the very top of the tree, fall to the ground when ripe and explode from their globular pods like small red beads.

The *nkobe* is a sinister tree which grows - or begins - on the beach near the water pump; its skin flakes off to reveal a malicious purple and green interior; its branches become creepers and coil inexorably from tree to tree along the beach.

Any tree or shrub the roots of which can penetrate the water-table seems to grow to more than normal size.

Near the stone steps at the bottom of the terraces the frangipani are as tall as oaks and have a wider spread; after the sap rises, red claws on their stiff grey fingers uncurl into tiny leaves, and large star-shaped cream and coral pink flowers cover the candelabra of branches; the heavy perfume attracts the sunbirds and the bees.

The neighbouring poinciania explodes in showers of flame even higher up among the grey striated *ntomoni* trees; later its long dark heavy pods lunge earthward like an armoury of scimitars.

The lagerstroemia, in comparison a mere weed, masses its mauve and lilac froth twenty feet above the ground; and even the hedge of caesalpinia - which to some people is 'Pride of Barbados' and to others 'Peacock flower' - aspires to grow into a line of trees and has to be cut back.

In the vegetable garden the paw-paw trees produce their litters of golden fruit and we have sweet paw-paw and the juice of green lemons for breakfast.

One morning in the feathery twigs of new young caesalpinia there are *eighteen* baby chameleons, each like a tiny green sea-urchin with curling tail, precious, immaculate, defenceless - no mother chameleon around. Will the bulbuls eat the lot? And in the roof of the Cottage there is a bush baby which a scientist friend calls a *galago*; the gardener who is Mlomwe calls it a *kadzidzi*; and the cook who is Yao says it is *lamani* - 'one who walks with witchcraft'. Whatever its name and whoever it 'walks with', it is rather a noisy beast at night, scampering about the roof above the softboard ceilings but, for all that, a charming fluffy little creature with enormous apprehensive eyes.

Dalamkwanda, the headman, suffers from a cough and is anxious about his liver: he opens his shirt to exhibit a well-nourished and shining torso. We can probably cure his cough but to protect his liver we suggest he should be careful not to drink *kachasu* or too much fermented beer of which there is an ever-flowing fountain in his village.

When we investigate *kachasu*, the locally distilled illegal gin - to consume half a bottle of which is said to be fatal - we find it is a drink with many names. At the lakeshore it is called *jang'ala*; the Chewa people call it *madzi oyera* which means 'pure water'; but the Zulu word brought up from the south, raising a picture of imminent danger and police truncheons raised against illegal drinkers, is a laconic *gijima*! - 'run!'

Medical fame spreads rapidly and within days of Cough Cure no.1 a message comes from Mdalamdoka Nkuti, sub-chief under Maganga and headman of the other village. Not to be outdone by Dalamkwanda, he too has a cough and asks that we will also cure his hernia.

His village is purely Muslim, and he spends most of his time inside his compound, sitting in a rickety deck chair the fabric of which is a hessian sack that, long ago, held maize. A tottery old man, perhaps ninety years of age, he responds quickly to the simple cough medicine, part of the merit of which is that it cannot be bought locally. But for the hernia he will have to go to the 'Bapitisti Mission', conveniently near his village - the snag is, he will have to pay for treatment.

Member Matora, a boatman and mechanic known to us who wrestles almost weekly with our water pump and electric generator, produces his baby daughter who, he says, has been bitten by a *chigedegaji*. We do not know what this biter is but apparently it is a poisonous spider which preys upon young children at night while they lie asleep on the floor of the hut. Alas, we don't feel we can stretch our medical quackery to cope with a *chigedegaji* - although we are willing to deal with cuts, burns, fever and sore throats as long as the medicines and bandages last - and a note has to be written for Member to take to the properly qualified nurse, again at the 'Bapitisti' Mission'.

Aisa, the cook, who is at least seventy-five, demands that we take him in the car to collect his mother who is sixteen miles away at Kuluundu village. She, we decide, must be either ninety-two or ninety-three since she has another son who is older than the cook.

Aisa, himself, would be noticeable in any community. He is six feet tall and strong although he walks with a limp deriving from some injury received when he was an askari in World War I; he has visited most of the countries of East and southern Africa, and as a result he can speak twelve languages; he is non-committal about how many wives he has had.

The road to Kuluundu passes behind the Senga Hills winding among fallen rocks. Vervet monkeys scatter in roadside trees. Three years ago a cow grazing too near the hills was killed and carried off by a lion.

At the Nyungwe river a long harzadous plank bridge with no parapet, and at least one plank always loose or missing, tests the driver's nerves; as the car creeps - and sometimes skids - across the weatherworn and rattling planks it seems entirely credible that as local fishermen say, a large crocodile lurks under the bank, watching for the 'bridge' to crash into the river.

Beyond the Nyungwe on the left extend paddy fields of the Rice Experiment, like an enormous expanse of wall-to-wall green carpeting, and the road enters a purely Muslim area of small fishing villages - Mbere, Nawanga, Ntimbasonja, Mgwalu, Kachulu, Kuluundu - each village thick with mango trees, each house mud-walled and grass-thatched, with maize and cassava gardens at the back. Tall trunks of palm, dead as a result of tapping for palm wine, stand erect and charred outside the villages.

We find Aisa's mother sitting on a mud verandah in the shade. She is small and light, wrapped in faded cloth, guiding herself with a bamboo wand since she is blind. Aisa, quickly surrounded and cushioned in comely matrons, points out half a dozen daughters and grand-daughters, some of whom bring the old lady to the car.

At the last moment a little boy, aged perhaps five, with arms and legs like match sticks and eyes like big brown bumble-bees, pleads to come too. He is Aisa's youngest child, born more than fifty years after his first-born son; Grandma says he may join us - perhaps this is the first car ride he has known - and back we go, menage complete.

We come to know the Kuluundu road intimately since the kitchen at the Cottage has a grass roof which needs to be re-thatched, and it is from Kachulu and Ntimbasonja that we buy many bundles of bamboo and tall cones of *tsekera* grass - a species long and strong which forms the waterproof under-thatch of all the most respectable kitchens on the Lake. The final, outside, layers of common thatch we are able to buy in bundles from the women of Dalamkwanda's and Mdalamdoka Nkuti's villages and the children trot the new thatch to the Cottage on their heads and as soon as they receive their payment of small coins they sprint to the local market to buy gritty doughnuts as a special treat.

It is at Ntimbasonja that Mkwinda lives. Many of the men along the Kuluundu road are weavers of mats which they sell very cheaply at local hotels and in Salima market, and Mkwinda is the most famous of them since he employs several dyes to colour the strips of *kanchindwe* palm of which his mats are made.

The single room of his large square hut is divided by a pole from which a curtain hangs to hide his bed which is behind it. On the floor of the outer part of the single room is a single large plaited mat on which, perhaps, his children and family visitors sleep in a row. Within the grass fence enclosing the back yard are granaries for maize and rice, a small kitchen with a fire in the centre of the floor, a grass-walled bathroom tucked away under a paw-paw tree at a corner of the compound, and a raised platform on which he dries and dyes the *kanchindwe* palm. There are several gourds, calabashes and a white enamel basin.

I particularly want to see how he produces a very bright and pleasing blue dye unused by other mat-weavers. Mkwinda, therefore, fishes into a dark corner behind the curtain demarcating his bedroom and brings out a sheet of good quality - but used - carbon paper which, he says, he bought from traders in Salima for a few pence. To demonstrate the manufacture of the dye he pours water into a white enamel basin, tears off a corner of the sheet of carbon paper and places it in the basin, and immediately a blue stain spreads in the water, becoming an intense brilliant blue rather than purple; in this he soaks the palm leaf.

He has only recently discovered this method of dyeing but, using half a sheet of carbon paper, he has created one complete mat which he brings out from behind the curtain and unrolls on the floor of the hut for our inspection. It has a magnificent blue bull's-eye centre and several brilliant blue encircling rings, rather like a target for archery practice. He is willing to sell and so we buy it to brighten the polished grey floor of the dining room at the Cottage, and we promise to bring him dyes of other colours which he can use for future mats.

From that time onward we purchase his entire output. He produces beautiful mats of scarlet and green and yellow as well as blue; an entrepreneur trader from Tunduma brings him Tanzanian dyes; our friends see examples of his work and covet his mats so that before long all his mats are 'ordered' for a year ahead.

Mkwinda suffers intermittently from lumbago and claims that he has been bewitched by someone in the village. We take him a tube of 'Fibrosil' and tell him to get his wife to rub it well into a lumbar region of his back. We have to emphasize to all the solemn faces watching that the this is a very strong 'medicine', stronger by far than the spells of any village sorcerer. By the time of the next visit the lumbago has disappeared; and we receive a bowl of rice as a present.

On one occasion near Ntimbasonja we overtake a wedding party walking from one village to the next under the mango trees. The women are in their brightest clothes, dancing and chanting, wiggling their buttocks and hissing like snakes.

Inevitably, visiting villages along these sandy tracks one becomes a kind of human vacuum cleaner and at the end of each journey I have to spit dust from my lungs and snort it out of my sinuses.

One Tuesday morning in August we have to take Aisa and his wife and his mother to Kuluundu village where the mother's brother is reported to be dying. One message is that he has, in fact, died already at 11:00 am the previous day but that later on, at 4:00 p.m., according to Aisa, he wakened up again and announced that he wanted to see his young sister - Aisa's mother, a mere ninety-three - before he died.

We find him propped against a wall on the rear veranda of a little house, sitting on a black goat-skin. Like Aisa's mother he has a light complexion but he is fairly dirty so that in comparison she looks golden-brown and smooth and brimming with good health and food. His feet have swollen and the lids of his right eye are puffed into bags like purses of brown skin; the flies walk on them.

He appears to be definitely alive, not yet glazed by death, and even ready to talk. When I ask him how old he is he says he cannot remember but he was born 'in the year the Portuguese came.'(41) He says that the previous night someone - Death, maybe? - came into the hut and seized him by the neck and tried to strangle him.

Soon he is relaxed and sleepy again and perhaps even content and happy to have reached the end. We leave him propped there, oblivious of the silent crescent of womenfolk squatting in attendance, yet evidently conscious of his favourite sister clasping his dusty hand to comfort him through the last loneliness.

Musa Chiwele lives at a village inland from the Lake but is well-known in all these coastal villages. We sometimes run across him in the towns but his working headquarters is here. He is a small strong man with a loud voice; his hands are squat and small; his eyes surrounded by dark wrinkles; he smiles and laughs readily.

He is a trader in animal skins, musical instruments, drums, masks, bows and arrows, spears and carvings which he sells to tourists. He must know all the hunters in the bush between Nkhota-Kota and the Dzalanyama mountains far inland. He says he can buy hippo teeth, crocodile skins and python skins around the Senga Hills. Recently he saw two kudu near Chief Maganga's, only a few miles out of Salima, and he has no difficulty in obtaining big spiral kudu horns, zebra hides, leopard pelts and elephant tusks and elephant tails, possession of the last of which is supposed to bring good luck. He knows hunters who can peel the skin off antelopes and leopards without leaving a hole or mark to deface the pelt. Recently he sold the skin of a crocodile fourteen feet long, and he cured and sold the pelt of a leopard for £35.00.

At his hut he pegs the skins on the ground to dry in the sun, rubs plenty of salt into them, cuts out the small pieces of 'meat' that have been left behind, brushing out fragments with a small brush, and then when there is no longer any 'smell of stink' he rubs in alum to make the skin soft, continuing to brush it many times a day until it is completely soft and 'warm'.

If he cannot sell skins he cuts them up and turns them into handbags. If anyone wants a crocodile handbag he can provide it.

Once, when we call at his house we find a very pretty young girl there who might be his sister or his wife. All the young nymph can tell us of his whereabouts is that he is *uko*, and she points vaguely to the hills where he has gone to collect elephant tails from a hunter.

There have been no reports of dangerous animals on Senga Hills for a long time and so, one day, we decide to climb the highest hill, Nyungwe Hill - a mere pimple by African standards - which rises 2,786 feet above sea level. The local villagers do not encourage exploration of the hills: their orientation is towards the Lake.

They have their reasons, we discover, to make them shun the hills, one of which is a fearsome creature known as the *Chongwe* which is said to have the body of a giant serpent and upon its head a cockerel's comb; it is supposed to sleep most of the time in the hills but it has recently killed several cattle. In addition, or perhaps associated with the *Chongwe*, there exists according to Kandulu, a mysterious small pool 'from which no bird can drink'; we can glean no further information except that it is a 'very bad place'. No one local will agree to lead us to the pool and the only guide we can find to take us up the hill is a cheerful leper from Makunula village across the Lake who now lives in isolation outside Dalamkwanda's village but is not excluded from society in any other way.

Our guide leads us up baboon trails, scrabbling and scrambling among bushes, grass and rocks, for seventy minutes. As we pass rock shelters he says apprehensively, that there may be hyenas or leopards in them, although he has not seen fresh tracks, but mercifully we encounter nothing more ferocious than an Agama lizard.

The top is astonishing beyond anything we have imagined.

There is a startling cycloramic view all round the compass: to the south-east, the southern bights of the Lake with Maleri, Mamkoma and Nakatenga islands - which the local people call *Misala* - looking like small rocks beyond Kambiri Point; then south-west, Ntundama mountain and the entire flank of the Rift; northward a marsh, a white beach south of Rifu Hill, the noble sweep of Domira Bay, Chitanda - where Livingstone was robbed while he slept in 1861, Mbenji island where Bishop Chauncy Maples drowned on 2 September 1895, the whole coastline up to and beyond Nkhota-Kota, with the Lake stretching endlessly north and spreading wide so that on the horizon there is nothing but blue water and blue sky. To the east is Losefa and beyond the Lake the Lisaninga and Mandimba Hills with the peaks of Chilapula and Mikonga; and in the Lake itself a small island, white with the excrement of birds, called Nangwazi.

The crumbling biotite-granite of the topmost boulders of Senga Hill (or Nyungwe Hill) is black and pink, and on the highest rock is a surveyor's black and white trig point painted 'June 1967 26NYP Senga'.

At the foot of the hill on the return journey we find small blue orchids growing like violets in the withered grass. (42)

Next day we explore the bay with the white sands seen from the beacon on the hill. A track runs from the familiar Kuluundu road towards the Lake, passing a small quiet Muslim graveyard in a grove of trees no one has attempted to burn, leading to a giant baobab but at the last moment twisting aside and winding through low bush towards the beach, diving finally into a tunnel of tall bulrushes and emerging at the fishermen's village officially named Bandawe although the local people call it Nyungwe.

Ahead is the blinding scintillation of the open Lake and a very lovely beach of pale beige sand stretching flat and wide between the baobabs and granite menhirs and monoliths of Rifu and a far-off marsh full of crocodiles and hippo. The fishermen's huts and compounds straggling between the white beach and the black fertile soil of the gardens are neatly walled and roofed with freshly cut *tsekera* which in the sunshine gleams like gold.

The Lake is calm and silvery in the late afternoon and the beach is a scene of purposeful activity. Several teams of men sit one behind the other, rhythmically pulling at their nets foot by foot, the farthest floats bobbing half a mile out in the Lake. Others push sun-bleached dug-outs into clear shallow water, dry nets heaped into the narrow belly of each of them; it will be several hours before the nets are cast and pulled ashore again.

When the catch is landed we see that most of it consists of *usipa* fish up to six inches in length, some with silver noses, some with blue, or else the larger *mbaba* which have blue or yellow noses. Tens of thousands of tiny fish are landed in each net; they are tipped unceremoniously into heaps on the sand and later are spread to dry on bamboo drying platforms at the top of the beach where they are sold to middlemen who carry them off in huge baskets, top-heavy on their bicycles, to Salima market.

On the sand near the grey rocks at the Rifu end of the beach small ragged boys - the fishermen of tomorrow - squat in a circle, gambling with a pile of lifeless sand-encrusted fish and a very worn-out pack of cards. Every now and again one of the boys throws a handful of fish in the air and cries 'Lizabet!'. The game is called 'Elizabeth' in honour of the Queen of England but we are unable to discover why, and it seems doubtful whether Her Majesty is aware of the anachronistic part she plays in the post-colonial lives of the children of this remote and timeless beach.

* * * * * * * * * *

Returning from the UK after leave in 1972 my plane landed at Nicosia, Entebbe and Nairobi.

At Entebbe, in Uganda, passengers in transit were not allowed to leave the aircraft, and I am sure nobody wanted to. Detectives who seemed to be Special Branch of the Police or CID came on board and inspected us. Their leader examined all the London newspapers that had been distributed to passengers; evidently he wanted to know what Britain was saying about Amin. As he read with his lips his perusal took 45 minutes.

At Entebbe airport parts of the tarmac were heaped high with crates, cartons and bundles. Some of the heaps were as big as our house in Mahatma Gandhi Road; whether the items had been confiscated from Indians or were being consigned outside Uganda we had no means of knowing.

We could not re-fuel, and I think it was for fuel we had to go on to Nairobi - as well as the need not to fly over Tanzanian territory in the region of recent military clashes. The plane was packed on all legs of the journey. About ten people for whom there were no seats came on board at Entebbe; some were diverted into first class; the cabin crew gave up their seats for the rest. There was nowhere left for them to sit except in lavatories but no one was turned away.

At Nairobi those who wanted to could visit the airport lounge for ten minutes only: very few people bothered.

We were two hours late arriving at Chileka. Rodrick met me and brought me up to Plot 479.

From my diary 1972

19 September

The plans for the alterations to our house on Mahatma Gandhi Road have been accepted by the Blantyre Town Planning Committee. Tomorrow I will try to get this work started.

Million and Smart had moved the house furniture back into position several days in advance of my return, and Million had every carving in its exact position and flowers placed in a couple of pots in the lounge. He had made scones, re-ordered the milk, and he produced a dish of strawberries for tea.

Smart has evidently failed to water the garden in my absence. The strawberry plants are stunted as are the vegetables. Vera Dunn and Ruth Partridge have contacted me, however, to let me know that they had a plentiful supply of tomatoes while I was on leave; I knew there should have been hundreds more than the servants would need. Strangely the flower beds are all doing fine: masses of petunias and antirrhinums and Barberton daisies, a few agapanthus, buds forming on the Amaryllis lilies and cup of gold in flower for the first time.

The President has offered to take 500 Asians evicted from Uganda.

The Police have been given power to arrest men with unduly long hair.

Today, two Indians were killed in a car accident along Mahatma Gandhi Road; they ran into the same electric power pole on which a doctor wiped himself out a few months ago. Million went to view the gore; I did not.

24 September

The electric cooker wasn't working when I came back and Million managed for three days with a small calor gas stove. On Friday Namate the maintenance officer installed a new cooker, a Belling compact three.

It is very hot at present; a sheet at night is more than adequate. The countryside is brown and parched. Our bird bath is well patronized; a bush robin with a white streak over his eye enjoyed a cool dip at 6.30 this morning.

I hope Progressive Builders will start on the alterations to the house on 2 October; they expect to finish the job in six weeks. The cost will be K2,600, which is more than I allowed.

6 October

Last Saturday I went to the Lake. At the Cottage I wasn't expected until the following day but Henderson soon had the bedrooms habitable and, as I'd had no lunch, he cooked market meat and vegetables for me in the evening that were delicious. It was very hot but most of the time there was a cool breeze through the dining-room. The generator had been unserviceable for two months, the Aladdin lamp had lacked a mantle for over a month, visitors had been without water in the house for two days, the gardener had gone off for a week without permission, there had been trouble between the cook and the gardener, the cook alleging that the gardener had sold the vegetables, refused to cut firewood and abused him, even threatening to assault him - and the gardener saying the cook had been selling the paraffin. Simon was in a sulky mood and did little work.

I came back to Blantyre on Tuesday, 3 October, bringing Henderson's wife - she followed him to the Lake - so that she could go to Ndirande to collect a radio.

Yesterday I had to appear in Court as first witness in the Kacisa case. Moira Woods, Namate the maintenance officer and a CID detective were the other witnesses. My secretary Susan Chibambo, Kabazali the second messenger, Kalimbika the library attendant in Moira's section, and one of the assistant librarians, were present as observers.

We had to wait two hours while another case was heard. The Magistrate was an Irishman and the Police were courteous. It was a very hot day. In my best suit I streamed with sweat as I stood in the witness box; the traffic roared outside; and from the corrugated iron roof of the Courthouse over our heads a groundsman swept flowers and leaves with an intermittent rasping and rustling sound so that it wasn't easy to hear, down below, everything that was said.

Kacisa was accused of stealing a whole list of items but he could be acquitted on at least part of the charge: all the stolen keys had been taken from Namate's office, none from the Library; he was not seen to take money from a desk in the library - that was an inference; and the Police admit they searched his house without a search warrant. But identification of magazines bearing the library ownership stamp, which I had to make, will probably be enough to convict him and I am full of nausea at the thought that it will be on my evidence he goes to jail.

If the University had not sacked him for a triviality that could have been dealt with administratively, he might well have remained honest - as I have always found him as far as the Library is concerned. The case is adjourned till 14 October.

The general situation in Malawi is one of tension. The Commissioner of Police and the Commander of the Army are said to be in detention. The Head of the special branch of the police has been given five days to leave the country. None of my European friends and acquaintances know why - but I have been told secretly by a Malawian friend that at the end of September in the grounds of State House, Zomba, an attempt was made to assassinate President Banda, the bullet passing through his hat instead of his head as intended. (43)

13 October

I have received £300 from G. of which I was in dire need, living on a very simple diet - mostly bread and vegetables - as the cost of the extension to the house proved greater than my estimate.

At the Lake I have parted company with Simon Moses who had almost ceased to work and seemed to be depressed; a pity, as he is a likeable man. I have learned that at all these lakeshore cottages owned by expatriates the servants are asked periodically by the Police if they have any complaints to make about the way they are treated by their employers; so I was careful to give Simon a month's pay in lieu of notice and to pay his and Nachitechi's train-fare back to Blantyre; and I obtained his signature to a statement that I had done this, Kandulu being a witness of the transaction. Henderson says he can find another garden-boy.

Here in Blantyre, alterations to the house have not pushed far ahead. The wall of the new kitchen is about two feet out of the ground but the rest of the backyard is like an area of bomb damage. The servants' washroom and toilet have taken shape but again the walls are only two feet high.

Amaryllis lilies, agapanthus and hydrangea brighten the garden and everywhere are masses of petunias. The bougainvillea hedge between this plot and the next has become bushy and is a bank of flame. The jacaranda is shedding blossoms the colour of bluebells.

20 October

The kitchen wall is now nearly built but window frames are not yet available. The servants' quarters are finished. I hope that the work of destruction and construction can be finished next week and the roofs put on.

Every time I look out of the windows I see workmen gulping water from the green garden hose that supplies water for concreting. At lunch time they use the metal bowl, shaped like a wok, in which they mix cement and they cook their *nsima* in that over a wood fire.

I had dinner with Grace today. I thought she would have someone else there but we were alone. We had a nutritious soup, followed by fillet of steak, ice-cream and black bread and cheese (the bread brought back from Holland). Grace thinks I am insufficiently nourished, which is not so at all, and when I came away she gave me a pot of Malawian pate de fois gras, a Kilner jar of mulberry jam, a bundle of rhubarb and a tin of shortcake. I am summoned to dinner again tomorrow along with Mrs Franca Sabatini, an ancient Italian lady, and I shall be pleased to go as Grace says there will be pork which is outside my budget at present. I shall take her a couple of lettuce which now have good hearts and are young and tender and a few onions which are beginning to plump out nicely.

The father of one of the assistant librarians has had to flee to Zambia, after being beaten up and having his house burned.

31 October

I was up at the Lake 23-29 October but I had to rest one whole day - the shade temperature on the verandah was 100 degrees Fahrenheit at midday and the humidity was high.

One day I walked down the beach to Nkuti village and on the return journey I was hailed by Bharucha who was at the new house he is building near the Baptist Mission. It is to have five bedrooms, each with a different coloured ceiling; there is every conceivable (and some inconceivable) species of glittering silver, gold and coloured glass light fitting, and the real *piece de resistance* is to be the bathroom which is to contain (all in one room) one long bath, one shower behind a plastic curtain, one European type toilet and two squat type toilets. Bhuracha is spending £6,000 on this palatial building.

Among yesterday's personal mail was an official letter from the Dulverton Trust announcing that, in response to a begging letter from me, they are giving £4,000 towards the build-up of stock at Bunda College library.

1 November

A Tanzanian newspaper claims that 10,000 Jehovah's Witnesses have entered Zambia from Malawi. The Voice of America has given the same figure on the radio. Other sources give the number of refugees as up to 19,000. The *Rhodesia Herald* has been banned. Last month I saw a good many people trekking hurriedly northward through the Angoni Highlands. Rumours of killings and atrocities are widespread. It is said - I believe reliably - that at a village near Zomba a group of Young Pioneers seized a Jehovah's Witness, tied him to a tree, lit a fire of dried grass between his legs and then asked him whether he was prepared to buy a Malawi Congress Party card; when the fire reached his genitals he was asked again, but he still shouted 'No!' - and they laughed as he burned to death. In Kasungu area, when gangs of youths began raiding the villages, a group of Witnesses fled into the bush. One girl of 17 has made a sworn statement that ten Young Pioneers caught her, carried her away from her friends and while some held her arms and legs the others raped her one after the other.

Ngwira, the new deputy registrar and Susan Chibambo's brother, appointed to the University in August, has been carted off to detention. So has the husband of Frank Warren's secretary.

5 November

Yesterday I drove to Zomba and Jeffrey and I visited the Chirunga site. The Library will be a very handsome building; the proportions of the rooms and the quality of the brickwork are particularly pleasing.

Returning from Zomba I came through a heavy thunderstorm, the heaviest I've been in for years. At 5:40 p.m. it was as black as midnight except for the glare of lightning. Flashes of lightning stabbed Ndirande, Michiru and Chiradzulu mountains. (44) Torrents of water swept across the road and as I sawed my way through them the wind threw waves of water, rising from the car wheels, across the windscreen. Twice, dazzled by nearby lightning, I stopped, but then came on again as it seemed no more hazardous to continue and possibly be struck by lightning than to risk being rammed from behind. Several cars were put out of action by flood water and the drivers of others gave up the effort and stopped, some without lights.

Today, after the rain, ants are pouring out of holes in the ground all over the garden. In a crevice beside the drive two *Braviceps* toads cling together like brown puffballs.

Tonight is the night of swarming termites, the first since the rains began. There is a chorus of frogs, cicadas, crickets and beetles.

I am tempering my period of 'malnutrition' with a spate of meals out - to Vera and George Dunn, Elizabeth and Frank Warren, June and John Leisten, Marion and Jeff at Zomba, and of course to Grace's. Last night at Grace's we sat in front of the fire and squelched through a delicious soup flavoured with parsley, then ate a dishful of tender young asparagus from her garden dipped in South African butter, then a platter of *chambo* from the Lake, followed by sweet pineapple slices and coffee topped with a gout of Mikolongwe cream.

I try to take the Old Lady whatever I can from the garden - beautiful onions golden skinned silver inside; young beans; the largest strawberries. In exchange she insists on giving me carrots, bananas from her trees, rhubarb, and pate de fois gras which I share with my visitors.

A letter from the Dinhams who have just been up at the Cottage says that the temperature on the veranda was 'only 100' but the temperature of the sand, across which they could only walk when properly shod, was 160 degrees Fahrenheit.

20 November

Gladys arrived from UK about 2:15 p.m. on 17 November.

The house alterations were not complete, nor are they now. But the roof of the two new bedrooms and a new kitchen and bathroom were on, the ceilings were in, and a new WC was in position although it could only be used for the first day by means of a superstructure placed over the top of it.

Some of the men worked over the week-end: the plumbers installed a wash basin and toilet, a painter appeared, four doors were hung and we may have glass in some of the windows by tonight.

Another of my begging letters has resulted in a grant from Witwatersrand Native Labour Association (WENELA) of K40,000 to assist in the development of the library at Bunda College of Agriculture.

26 November

Yesterday we bought a stainless steel sink and double draining board for the new kitchen at Blantyre - a sort of domestic lammergeyer with a wing span of nine feet. One of the workmen tiling the bathroom - who should perhaps be called a 'tegulator' - knows that the building project is running late and to save time he bites off the edges of tiles with his strong teeth. A septic tank for the servants' lavatory has been constructed and plastic piping, like entrails, is laid out in trenches in the vegetable garden. By nightfall, with luck, we may have water piped to the kitchen sink and also to the servants' lavatory and washroom.

Rain that has fallen in the past two nights has washed the cement dust off the flowers, vegetables and citrus trees and they all look new and fresh. Golden day lilies and Orange lilies contrast with blue agapanthus; the petreas have hundreds of blue spikes in flower; the golden granadilla has a flush of sweet scented flowers; and dahlias are growing four inches a day.

30 November

At Bunda College of Agriculture the American Principal, Ted Pinney, has been ordered to sack three Malawian staff members who were Jehovah's Witnesses. When he refused, the houses of the three Malawian staff were burned to the ground, two of the staff were killed and the third had his hands cut off. Children of the

College staff were made to look carefully at the corpses. Professor Pinney has been told to keep quiet and he is being peremptorily deported.

There is no doubt that Banda encourages his Young Pioneers and paid assassins to ill-treat their victims in any way they choose. Members of the League of Malawi Youth are as ruthless as the Young Pioneers. The Member of Parliament for Dowa has had his eyes scooped out. Other Witnesses have been smashed up, suffocated, or tortured to death; some have had their hair pulled out, others their genitals cut off.

* * * * * * * * * *

The volcano finally erupted on 2 December 1972.

I returned to work after four months' leave on Friday, 1 December. At 1:00 p.m. on 2 December a Police Land Rover came to our house and parked under the tree where there are sometimes loerie birds and in the shade of which our mongoose likes to forage with her tail bolt upright.

The Police Officer served me a pale green form No.7, 'Notice to Prohibited Immigrant', which stated that I was a 'PI' and ordered me to leave the country within three days of service of the notice. He had a sheaf of ten forms to deliver, another of which I noticed was addressed to Moira Woods.

From the refrigerator I gave him a cool drink, read the form I had taken from him and signed it.

'Can you tell me why I am being deported?' I asked him.

'Very sorry, Sir! They never tell me the reason. I just have to deliver this form No.7.'

After he had gone I remained standing for at least a minute, trying to think out what to do.

Gladys was not at home; she was in charge of a stall to raise money for the Save the Children Fund at the annual Christmas 'Fayre' of the Townswomen's Guild. I would have to inform her immediately. Then Rodrick. Then Grace. Then Vera and George Dunn. Then the Vice-Chancellor and the British High Commission.

In fact, it was Million I told first. I asked him too keep the news to himself while I went out to find Gladys. Smart was not in his quarters so he had to wait until later.

From behind her stall at the Christmas 'Fayre' G asked: 'What shall I do?'

'Probably the best thing is to remain here at your stall; we can decide what we're going to do when you come home at six o'clock. Before that I'll drive around and tell Grace, and Vera and George, and Rodrick. You can tell any friends who come here.'

Leaving the 'Fayre' I ran into Michael Blackwood our solicitor who is an MP - the only expatriate MP in Parliament. 'I will try to find out the reason,' he said. 'But normally, you know, they never state the reason for deportations.' (45)

I found Rodrick at his house along with his wife. He promised to notify library staff, including Dick who was about to go to Zambia on scholarship.

Vera and George were also at home. They offered any help they could give.

It was harder to tell Grace, of whom we had become very fond in the past two-and-a-half years and who, because of her age, I knew we should never see again. (46) In fact I lost my voice completely: my larynx emitted only a faint squeak and then seized up totally. I showed her the green form and we both wept, momentarily. She said she would come to the house later.

One thing I had to do was telephone my sister Eva in England and ask whether she could put us up until we could move into our own house in the next village.

An officer from the British High Commission came to obtain information and offer help. The Vice-Chancellor was away at Bunda where Ted Pinney, Principal of Bunda College of Agriculture, had also been peremptorily deported, On Saturday evening a stream of friends poured into the house to offer help; the telephone rang at intervals of ten minutes and other friends alternately offered help and cursed Dr Banda so vehemently that I had to remind them the telephone line might be 'tapped' and that, in their own interests, their language should not be so vituperative. Some of these people we scarcely knew.

On Sunday, prayers were said for us in the Baptist Church.

A great many matters had to dealt with speedily and thoroughly before we could leave: University forms, income tax, water, electricity, the telephone, insurance, servants, builders, arrangements about the Lake Cottage and the Blantyre house the extension of which was not yet finished. Frank Warren the Finance Officer and his wife Elizabeth were a great help to us. Frank dealt with the University documentation and agreed to help with the builders. I wrote references for Million and Smart and paid them their wages and gratuities. I sent money to Kandulu at the Lake for him to pass on to Henderson and the garden-boy; also Henderson's employment book and tax cards for them both. I informed the solicitors what arrangements I had made; and asked Harold Downs the auctioneers to sell the two houses and the Volvo.

Gladys and Elizabeth did the packing up of the Blantyre house, items we could bring away with us by air being sorted into one heap; everything else had to go into another heap to be packed ready for Glenn's Removal & Storage Company to collect and store pending despatch to us some time in the future as sea freight.

By a series of miracles we were ready to leave by Tuesday afternoon, 5 December. I asked all African staff to stay away from the airport for their own sakes. Rodrick insisted on driving me to Chileka. Gladys was claimed by Frank and Elizabeth. There was a great crowd of our friends and Moira's friends, and as we walked across the tarmac to the VC 10 the spectators' balcony of the airport was full of people clapping, crying, cheering and singing, 'For he's (and she's) a jolly good fellow', in angry defiance of Dr Banda and the Malawi government.

As for *why* I should be deported, there are at least nine possible, but sufficient, reasons:
1. Undoubtedly, as a result of personal spite on the part of two assistant librarians who reported me to the Malawi Congress Party in July 1972, claiming

that I had a 'negative attitude towards Africans'. This complaint was squashed at the time by the Vice-Chancellor but both of them made other attempts to discredit and defame me.

2.   Because I had signed an order for a copy of Philip Short's book, 'Banda', which was announced in 1972 but not published till 1974.

3.   Because Paul Theroux's book, 'Jungle lovers', which ridicules Banda, was shown to a member of staff of the Department of English who showed it to a student. The book had not been ordered for Chancellor College and I was unaware of its existence in our library. As librarian, however, I had to 'carry the can' for someone else's indiscretion.

4.   It is certain that I made incautious remarks in a family letter about the treatment of Jehovah's Witnesses. All outgoing mail was subject to scrutiny in the Post Office by the special branch of the police. I did not know this until too late.

5.   One of the assistant librarians who expected to become my successor knew I preferred someone else. By using his influence with a friend close to the Life President he could easily have me deported and the way left clear for his own appointment to my post.

6.   One of the disaffected assistant librarians may have been the would-be arsonist who attempted to cause a fire in the Chancellor College library on 28 March 1972. The Police did not bring a case against him because - I was told - he became a police informer. If that was so, he may have guessed I would hear of it, and it would be more convenient for him if I were sent out of the country.

7.   I was one of a few Europeans who knew that an attempt had been made to assassinate the President in September 1972. This was kept secret and I was told that the special branch of the police were anxious the news should not become public knowledge. If they knew that I knew I would be regarded as a 'security risk'.

8.   I was one of the few Europeans who knew that Banda encouraged people of the Lower Shire to believe he was a re-incarnation of Mbona, guardian spirit of the Mang'anja people.

9.   I was one of the few Europeans who knew that in 1959 children in certain Malawian schools were taught to sing a parody of the Lord's prayer:

> Our Kamuzu, who art in Blantyre,
> Hallowed be thy name,
> Thy Kingdom come;
> Thy will be done;
> Lead us not into the Federation
> But deliver us from the Imperialists,
> As in Ghana, for thine is the Country,
> The power and the glory
> For ever and ever... (50)

FRAGMENTS
OF UNIVERSITY OF MALAWI EARLY LIBRARY HISTORY
Taken from annual reports

Starting the Libraries
1965-1968

'Until 1 January 1967 the University had one library, that at Chancellor College; on 1 January 1967 the libraries at the Malawi Polytechnic, Soche Hill College and the Institute of Public Administration became university libraries; by the end of the period Bunda College of Agriculture had also started a library.

'The library at Chancellor College started under circumstances that, in retrospect, seem to have been unpropitious if not actually hazardous. The premises available - seven small rooms - can be described, without ambiguity, as inconvenient for university library purposes; the financial position was uncertain; adequate staff were not available. It was inevitable that difficulties would arise as a result of this situation.

'During its first two years the Library operated with approximately one-third the number of staff, senior and junior, regarded as normal in other universities; and for five weeks in 1966 and for nine weeks in 1967 the librarian had no other senior staff present. It seems prudent to make the point that the University cannot expect a normal library service unless it is able to provide a normal establishment of staff.

'During the years under review many of the staff, senior, junior and part-time, worked very hard and the Library could not have evolved, even as far as it has done, without their efforts.

'It was necessary to try to provide some professional education, as well as in-service training, for the library assistants so during 1967 a staff training programme, not confined to Chancellor College, was planned and implemented. The tutors were Miss PM Fiddes (Polytechnic library), Mr Visualingam Nadanasabapathy (Chancellor College), and Mr WJ Plumbe (university librarian). A course of 70 lessons (talks, tutorials, 'practicals', tests) each lasting approximately one and a half hours, was given. As a result there was a noticeable improvement in the routine work of the libraries and it is expected that seven assistants from Chancellor College, two from the Polytechnic, one from Soche Hill College and one from the British Council library will sit for the Entrance examination of the Library Association in November 1967. Besides the university libraries staff, one assistant from the British Council library and one from the library of the Malawi Broadcasting Corporation, participated in parts of the courses.

'Much of the administrative work of the librarian's office had to be done too hurriedly or at week-ends or not at all since the librarian had to take charge for long periods of the work of other sections, as well as participate in staff training. The

Library has gradually and spasmodically been organized, staff recruited, junior staff trained, personnel matters dealt with, equipment obtained, 600 files opened, essential mail written and answered, committee work done, details of a new main library building agreed with the architects, and a friendly working contact maintained with the librarians at the Polytechnic and Soche Hill College. In general, it has seemed more important to try to introduce normal university procedure and standards into the main library at Chancellor College rather than, at this stage, to create a more efficient office or pay more attention to cultivating good 'public relations.'

'During 1967-1968 the training scheme for library assistants resulted in eight out of ten candidates passing the Entrance examination of the Library Association in November 1967. The British government provided scholarships and the eight assistants concerned are now studying for professional qualifications in Britain.

'The stock of the libraries increased from 44,609 books to 63,723.

'Classification was completed at all libraries. Definitive cataloguing of 22,000 books at Chancellor College and nearly 15,000 at the Malawi Polytechnic was completed.

'Co-operation between the libraries and with libraries outside Malawi continued.

'At *Bunda College of Agriculture* it is expected to move to a new building with a floor area of 8,282 square feet on a very pleasant site, which should relieve many of the current difficulties. The present book stock is 3,150 volumes.

'At *Chancellor College* a shortage of funds, coupled with a precarious staffing situation, made progress slower than is customary in the third year of development. By the end of the year, however, the growing book stock and its better organization were leading towards a service of university standard, while success of the training scheme foreshadowed an end - three years hence - to the unsafe staffing situation.

'The staffing situation was precarious for two main reasons. A university library, to fulfil its function, must be professionally classified and catalogued, and at the end of September there had been a chief cataloguer on the library's staff for only eleven months of its three years' existence. Then, too, experienced library assistants are needed to keep the reading rooms in good order, answer enquiries, lend books, deal with periodicals, and carry out much work in the library's work rooms. Seven such assistants were trained but, in order to provide for the future, they had to be prepared for professional studies and released when the opportunity occurred for them to go overseas, leaving us to recruit new staff who had to carry on with their work without, initially, much training, and with no experience. Fortunately, we were able to recruit new assistants of potentially good calibre and users of the library were perhaps unaware how near the service was to a state of collapse at the end of the year and the beginning of the new session.

'The postal service to people engaged in study or research outside the University is appreciated. Book bags and parcels have gone to Chilema, Chilumba, Chintheche, Chisemphere, Chisenga, Chitipa, Dedza, Dowa, Kafukule, Kameme, Karonga, Kasungu, Kasupe, Likoma Island, Lilongwe, Luchenza, Mulanje,

Mponela, Mzuzu, Namadzi, Nchenachena, Nkhoma, Phalombe, Salima, Wimbe and Zomba; and so far there have been no losses.

'The library stock increased by 8,075 books to 29,242 and current serials increased by 309 to 1,407.

'At the *Institute of Public Administration* the book stock increased to 5,167 books.

'At the *Malawi Polytechnic* library the year saw the elimination of arrears of cataloguing but increasing difficulties in staffing which included almost 100% turnover of staff.

'The stock of books increased to 14,617 and 252 current periodicals were received.

'At *Soche Hill College* there was 100% turnover of junior staff in the year. The number of books in stock increased to 11,547.'

Developing the Libraries
1968-1969

'Overall growth of library stock was from 63,723 to 84,318 items, an increase of 20,595.

'One important policy decision was taken. After much discussion the university library committee agreed that the technical services of the library (i.e. classification, cataloguing, book ordering, bookbinding) should be centralized as soon as possible, and implementation of this policy began.

'The importance a university attaches to its library is reflected in the amount of money it spends on it which, in the early years when basic stock is being built up, often reaches 10% to 15% of total university expenditure. In 1968-1969 this University spent £57,755 of recurrent and special funds (gift funds excluded) on its libraries, which was approximately 5.9% of total university expenditure. Chancellor College, where the expenditure was in part for the University as a whole, reached a normal outlay of 10.06% of the college total spent on the library.

'At *Bunda College of Agriculture* the new library building, complete with garden and fish-pond, is an attractive place in which to work, remaining cool in the height of the hot season. The new library is open seventy seven and a half hours a week in term and is filled to capacity in the evenings. The total book stock is 5,100 volumes.

'At *Chancellor College* the stock of the library increased to 39,335 items. Important research materials were obtained. Besides orders placed for the library stock 5,697 books were ordered for re-sale to students; in addition 553 orders were placed for private individuals.

'More than 15,000 items were classified and given definitive cataloguing.

'At the *Institute of Public Administration* the introduction of an LLB programme placed heavy pressure on the library service. Two new extensions to the library were constructed, increasing seating capacity from 8 to 14. Law reports were acquired and the total book stock increased to 6,039.

'At the *Polytechnic* library there was a full staff establishment for six months, with the result that arrears of work were eliminated and re-cataloguing of stock went forward at an unprecedented rate. Mrs PM Larby, FLA, Librarian at the Polytechnic, resigned on 31.8.69 on appointment as deputy librarian, University College, Nairobi. Miss M Robinson, BA, DipLib, was appointed as sub-librarian. The junior staff situation became more satisfactory. The total stock increased to 18,110.

'At *Soche Hill College* the book stock increased to 16,495.

'The *Bindery* was established on 1 October 1968 when Mr J Stickley, bookbinding officer, commenced duty. (47)

'Owing to a shortage of suitable premises in the Blantyre/Limbe area, it was decided to start the bindery in Zomba where a building of adequate size was rented. The six trainee bookbinders have been given a course in theoretical and practical bookbinding which appears to be successful. It is likely that the annual output will be at least 3,000 bound volumes.

'A long-suffering tree which grows near the bindery door, and a block and tackle borrowed from the Ministry of Works, enabled heavy machines to be lifted still in packing cases from the lorry that delivered them straight into the bindery. The last of the machinery arrived in mid-April 1969.

'The power guillotine arrived at Chichiri on a Malawi Railways lorry at the time the library there was in the process of moving to new premises. It had to be diverted to Zomba where, the following day, Mr Stickley was able to offload it and coax it safely into the bindery, using much the same methods of haulage as were used in constructing the pyramids of Egypt 7,000 years ago.'

Years of Crisis
1969-1970

'In spite of having to face acute problems, the Library continued to develop and the academic year ended with the expectation that 1970 would see us out of our worst difficulties.

'The stock of the Library , taken as a whole, increased by 18,626 items to 102,944 volumes.

'Use of the collections was heavy and there can be no doubt that the libraries play a significant part in the lives of all university students and, to a lesser extent, in the facilitation of research.

'The staffing situation, although difficult and sometimes perilous, was no worse than in previous years.

'A Malawian graduate was appointed to specialize in African bibliography and seven members of staff continued their professional studies at the College of Librarianship Wales.

'The worst crisis was occasioned by the chief cataloguer, Mrs Yarr, who is responsible for cataloguing at three colleges, taking well-earned overseas leave.

'Changes in the technical, clerical and supporting ranks of the staff were so numerous that at times it was difficult to keep the libraries functioning, but fortunately 'key' staff remained with us.   Some concern must be shown, nevertheless, at the relatively high rate of loss of staff: at the Bindery it was 50%; at Chancellor College 40%; at the Institute of Public Administration 50%; at the Polytechnic 78%; at Soche Hill College 75%. Only at Bunda College of Agriculture was there stability.

'Expenditure was £ 58,332 which was 6% of total university expenditure. At Chancellor College, which accommodates the main library, it was 10% of total college expenditure.

At the *Bindery*, 3,125 books were bound for the University and 827 were repaired for Malawi National Library Service. Of the bookbinders who left during the year, one - Makaliaiinga - vanished without trace.

'At *Bunda College of Agriculture* the stock increased to 6,400 volumes. From January 1970 book orders were placed through the main library at Chancellor College. A total of 386 persons used the library; this included staff at Mitundu Day Secondary School, staff of the Department of Agriculture, staff engaged in the Lilongwe Land Development Scheme and former students of Bunda College. Mrs Margaret Ngwira, the librarian, resigned w.e.f. 15.9.70.

'At *Chancellor College* the library stock increased to 46,769 books, 390 microfilms, 110 gramophone records and 1,909 colour slides; 2,008 serials were received.

'A notable purchase was a collection of coloured slides depicting Nyau masks from the Mlolo-Nsanje and Makhwira-Chikwawa areas of southern Malawi. The masks were collected for the nation by Berlings Kaunda, curator of the Museum of Malawi, and photographed by Barbara Blackmun, a part-time lecturer in art appreciation. They are unique and exciting examples of a local branch of African art which, so far, has not been reported in any book or journal.

'In all, 12,864 books were classified and catalogued. Early in 1969 it was clear that the burden of work and the demands made on the cataloguers were too great and as a small ameliorative measure publication of the *Library Accessions List* was suspended, this being the step that would cause least permanent harm to the University.

'A new (and heavily used) microfilm reading room was constructed at one end of the reading room and also a 'Books on reserve' desk.

'At the *Institute of Public Administration* the book stock increased to 9,029. Capacity in the reading room was increased to 20 seats.

'At the *Polytechnic* library the book stock increased to 21,369.

'Mr Stephen Thompson, ALA, assistant librarian at the Polytechnic, operated the Leprosy Craft Shop to help raise funds for LEPRA on Saturday mornings.

'*Soche Hill College* library was in a dishevelled state for much of the year. Fortunately, it was possible to secure the services of Mrs Anna Wiens, BA, BLS, who agreed to serve as a temporary assistant librarian until a Malawian returned from Britain to take charge of the library. The stock at the end of September was 19,377 items.

'The attractive and handsome new building, provided with funds received from the British government, will accommodate 30,000 books and seat 60 readers. The architects were Norman & Dawbarn and the structure - except in some details - is a replica of that provided at Bunda College of Agriculture in 1968.'

The First Malawian Librarians
1970-1971

'The most significant event of the year was the return in December 1970 of seven Malawian members of staff who had been successful in passing the Part I and Part II examinations of the Library Association. As a result, the Library had enough qualified staff for the first seven months of 1971 to deal with current work although not enough in all the libraries to deal with arrears.

'Of the expatriate staff, Mr Hazeldine moved to a post in Indonesia, Mr and Mrs Yarr returned to Britain, and Mr Stickley, upon completion of his ODA assignment, was appointed to the staff of the University.

'The technical training of the library assistants, catalogue assistants and bookbinders was continued.

'Arrears of bookbinding were liquidated.

'Owing to rising prices of books, the stock of the Library increased more slowly than in other years - from 102,944 to 116,140. A Malawi collection was formed at Chancellor College.

'The catalogues were brought up-to-date at Bunda College of Agriculture, Chancellor College, the Institute of Public Administration and the Polytechnic, and reclassification of the stock was completed at Soche Hill College.

'Work commenced on erection of the new university library building at the Chirunga site.

'Expenditure was approximately K126,500, i.e. 6.17% of total university expenditure.

'The university librarian attended a Conference of the Standing Committee of African University Librarians (Eastern Area) held at Addis Ababa, 10-13 February 1971.

'At the *Bindery*, 1970-1971 was a year of consolidation, with the skill and efficiency of the bookbinders gradually increasing. A total of 4,084 books were bound: 3,180 for the University, 810 for the Malawi National Library Service and 94 for the National Archives. Messrs A. Mtuwa and E. Mkwate passed trade tests in October 1970 and were promoted to bookbinder grade I.

'At *Bunda College of Agriculture* it was also a year of consolidation. The book stock increased to 8,659 volumes. After the departure of Mrs M Ngwira in mid-September 1970 the library was managed on a part-time basis by Mrs J Moss until the arrival of Mr C R Namponya on 25 January 1971.

'At *Chancellor College* the stock increased to 54,404 volumes.

'About 200 local organizations were contacted and their publications requested; as a result the Malawi collection was greatly strengthened. Tourist literature was obtained from Botswana, Egypt, Ethiopia, Ghana, Kenya, Lesotho,

Malagasy, Malawi, Mauritius, Morocco, Mozambique, Rhodesia, Senegal, Sierra Leone, South Africa, Sudan, Tanzania and Zambia.

'At the *Institute of Public Administration* the year was one of the continued expansion with the usual problems of space and staffing. Mr John Banda II, a newly appointed library assistant, left for the USA where he is to study for a degree in librarianship.

'At the *Polytechnic* the library had a very stable year. The shortage of working space remained a handicap. The total stock at the end of the year was 23,721 books. (48)

'At *Soche Hill College* the whole of the old stock was reclassified by Mrs Yarr from the Dewey Decimal Classification to the Bliss Bibliographic Classification. The pocketing, labelling, book-carding, etc., was brought into line with practice at Chancellor College and the Institute of Public Administration in preparation for amalgamation of the three libraries in 1973. The main task that remains is definitive cataloguing of about 16,000 books. After unsuitable books had been pruned from stock, the stock figure at the end of the year was 19,531 books.'

Beginning of Normal Library Service (49)
1971-1972

'The new library building on the Chirunga site is expected to be ready for occupation in July 1973.

'The book stock increased from 116,640 to 136,582 volumes.

'The British government, through the Overseas Development Administration, granted the library £ 36,000 to be spent on British books.

'Expenditure on the Library was £48,480 or 4.34% of total university expenditure.

'In the *Bindery* 2,994 books were bound for the University, 670 for the Malawi National Library Service and 23 for the National Archives. In addition, 1,769 pamphlets were cased, 857 items were provided with wire stitched bindings and over 3,000 readers' tickets were manufactured.

'At *Bunda College of Agriculture* the stock increased to 10,748 volumes. A Nashua photocopying machine and a microfilm reader-printer were bought with funds provided by Thondwe Tobacco Company.

'At *Chancellor College* the book stock increased to 60,691 volumes.

Augustine Msiska, assistant librarian, was awarded a scholarship under the British Programme of Technical Assistance, utilizing funds from the Special Commonwealth African Assistance Plan. He will study at the College of Librarianship Wales for a post-graduate diploma in librarianship.

'At the *Institute of Public Administration* the library stock increased to 12,065 volumes. Another classroom was converted into library space.

'At the *Malawi Polytechnic* the book stock increased to 26,675. A demand for library facilities was noticeable from part-time students attending evening classes at the Polytechnic and from other persons studying technical subjects to whom the Polytechnic library is the only source of technical books.

'Beston G. Mphundi was appointed college librarian w.e.f. 1 December 1971.

'At *Soche Hill College* library the book stock increased to 22,132 books. Raphael Masanjika, formerly of the University of Zambia library, was appointed assistant librarian-in-charge w.e.f. 1 July 1972.'

Notes

1	But see also note 31 which refers to Mlawi Hill.
2	Pronounced 'Shee-ray'.
3	His original name was not Kamuzu but Kamunkhwala. His father was Mphonongo Banda and his mother Akupingana Phiri. He was brought up by his grandparents.
4	At the time of Independence (1964) there were fewer than 450 miles of tarred roads and less than 9,700 miles of unmetalled and earth roads.
5	A minor but real difficulty, unknown to most expatriates, was that after darkness fell each day some of the junior staff, including library assistants, were reluctant to travel on foot in the Chancellor College/Soche Hill area on account of *stukwanis* and *tokoloshes*. A *stukwani* was a fierce nocturnal creature visible only to a witch-doctor. A *tokoloshe*, according to Credo Mutwa, ('My People', London, Anthony Blond, 1969), was a 'great mysterious evil' created and trained by a wizard.
6	'Facts and policy', a circular of information, 13.12.65.
7	Nada is now University Librarian, Murdoch University, Western Australia.
8	Dunduza Chisiza and Masauko Henry Chipembere were arrested at the same time and placed in Gwelo Gaol. Dr Banda was released after thirteen months but he did not immediately seek the release of his two colleagues. Chisiza (who was said to be specially gifted) died in a car accident in 1963 at the age of 32. Chipembere became an exile in Tanzania and USA.
9	Margaret became acting College Librarian in August 1988 and now occupies a senior post in the University of Namibia.
10	Augustine subsequently returned to the University of Malawi as senior assistant librarian in charge of Malawiana and the library staff training. He obtained his FLA and is now College Librarian at Chancellor College.
11	Witch-doctors are occasionally encountered in the villages; nowadays they also exist in towns.
12	When Swanzie and Sir Fulque Agnew stayed there three years later, a hen entered their bedroom each day and laid an egg in their waste paper basket.
13	Besides David Susi and James Chuma, Livingstone had three other servants at the time of his death: Matthew Wellington, Majwara, and Tom Peter Sudi. Matthew Wellington's grave is in the Church Missionary

Society cemetery at Freretown, near Mombasa. There is a portrait of him in Emmanuel Church nearby.

14   'Southern Rhodesia' became 'Rhodesia' in 1965.

15   'The History of the Universities' Mission to Central Africa, 1859-1909,' by AEM Anderson-Morshead. 1909.

16   Kaziwiziwi became the centre of the coal-mining industry.

17   From 'A Handbook of Nyasaland', compiled by S.S. Murray, 1932.

18   In 1958 there were fears on the part of the European settlers and government officials that the Africans intended to massacre all whites and Indians. On 2 March 1959 a State of Emergency was declared by the Governor, Sir Robert Armitage, and in various clashes 41 Africans were killed. The most tragic incident was at Nkhata Bay where 20 Africans were killed and 28 wounded by so-called security forces. Their graves are here.

19   Ali, our previous cook, once alleged to me that he had witnessed Jeff Jeffrey quarrelling with, and beating his wife, Rubia in their garden. Ali commented: 'We Africans think it more proper to beat our wives in the house'.

20   Kamanja was killed in a car accident in 1988.

21   Mr Najira, sen., died on 12 April 1973.

22   'Usiku' is the Chichewa - and Swahili - word for 'night'.

23   Margaret Kalk, Professor of Zoology 1965-1975, is short, asthmatic, always in a hurry. At age 65 she retired to South Africa as Professor Emeritus and taught at the University of Witwatersrand in Johannesburg. At age 80 she was still putting the finishing touches to a monumental 'Natural History of Inhaca Island, Mozambique', embodying many years of painstaking research. (This book was eventually published by Witwatersrand University Press in 1995 when Margaret was 85).

Willie Kalk, husband of Margaret, ten years her senior, spare in build, was a life-long communist who spent three years studying in Russia. He knew several of the 'click' languages of southern Africa, was secretary of the Furniture Workers' Industrial Union and the Transvaal Leather & Allied Trades Industrial Union; in fact one of the pioneer socialists who helped to build a democratic labour movement in South Africa. He was imprisoned in 1960. Later, in Malawi, to which country he and Margaret moved in 1965, he worked as a supervisor at the Sawmills, Blantyre and after 1975, back in Johannesburg, he worked in a bank until he was 85. He died on 27 August 1989.

Blodwen Binns, Professor of Botany, approaching 70 in 1969 but still sprightly, was the author of several botanical books. In Malawi she compiled and in 1968 published 'A First Check List of the Herbaceous Flora of Malawi', of which I had the honour to be the proof-reader.

24   Richard Allen was the Principal of Domasi Teacher Training College. He and Joan were formerly staff members of Ahmadu Bello University, Zaria, Nigeria.

25   Besides the Malipenga, Nyau, Ndingala and Masikitiko, the best known traditional dances were the Beni, Ingoma, Chimtali, Chiponda, Chisukulumwe, Chiwoda, Gule Wamkulu, Likhuba, Likwata, Mganda and Vimbuza.

26   I include details in this book only to illustrate the kind of situation in which a librarian can find himself when there are no Statutes and no established procedures in a young university. (Adoption of Statutes was, of course, blocked by the President).

27   It was a good thing we rejected the graveyard as shortly afterwards, on the next kopje, Dr Banda built 'Sanjika' his Blantyre palace with its deep and spacious bunker which was said to be bomb-proof and have its own permanent and impregnable water and electricity supply, not to mention air-conditioning and enough food to outlast a siege. 'There's as   much construction deep underground as there is up on the surface,' technicians incautiously reported. Over the years Banda caused to be built thirteen state houses and palaces. 'Sanjika', his place in Blantyre, cost more than £2,000,000; the palace in Lilongwe at least £ 10,000,000. The British government was asked to fund part of this expenditure but refused.

28   Clemence Namponya became College Librarian at Bunda College of Agriculture. He was the first Malawian to gain FLA and a Master's degree. After 15 years at Bunda he moved to Botswana in January 1987 as Documentation/Information Office at the Southern Africa Centre for Co-operative Agricultural Research. Later he became deputy librarian in Cape Town University Library, Librarian of Fort Hare University, and deputy librarian in the Eastern Cape University in South Africa.

29   Walter Hyde Stansfield, was the owner of the Grand Beach Hotel, Salima. He died at Senga Bay 17 August 1991, 12 days before what would have been his 100th birthday.

30   Rita was the University Librarian of Haile Sellassie I University. Richard was Director of the Institute of Ethiopian Studies.

31   The Mang'anja were the first people known to live in the Shire river valley. Mbona is their guardian spirit. He came from Malawe in what is now the Agoni Highlands and was killed by his enemies in Ndione forest in the Ndindi marsh of the Lower Shire valley. According to SS Murray ('A Handbook of Nyasaland', 1932) Mbona had no successor but he lives in Mlawi Hill and his 'temple' (a thatched hut) is in 'a clump of forest known as Kuluvi, almost at the foot of Mlawi', where his descendants make sacrifices to him every year. He is believed to intercede directly with Mulungu the supreme god to call the rain and so control the food supply of the tribe. It is claimed that in the 1960s President Banda, in order to strengthen the loyalty of the Mang'anja, encouraged them to believe *he* was the re-incarnation of Mbona.

32   Apart from the University Library, the Malawi National Library Service, established under the National Library Service Act, 1967, was the only large library to develop in the country. Its first director, with whom I

had worked in Malaya, was AF Johnson, a well-known librarian and educator; he and his wife Irene became our close friends. The second director was Geoffrey P. Rye of Weston-super-Mare. When he retired in 1978 Rodrick Samson Mabomba succeeded him and was later designated 'National Librarian'. By 1989 the Malawi National Library Service had an annual government subvention of K726,000, it had accumulated a book stock of 172,751 volumes, it issued 372,801 books in 1988/1989 plus many thousands more through its Rural Services and School Services, and its total staff of 85 included 13 qualified librarians.

33   Night adder, *Causus rhombeatus*, normally more interested in toads than in humans.

Renamo, the military group operated by white South Africa to destabilize Mozambique and cut Malawi's communications with the coast, established its base at Gorongosa. This was overrun and captured by Zimbabwean troops in 1985.

34   He became Sir Walter Robert Haydon, KCMG, CMG.

35   Jeanette was co-author of a text-book on District Nursing and, written in retirement, a small book of Shropshire reminiscences entitled 'The Rock' (1979). Dolly was author of 'A Merry Family Omnibus', privately published in 1974.

36   The Malawi Censorship Board was established in 1968. In the next eight years it banned more than 840 books, 100 periodicals and 16 films.

37   There is a Nyungwe Forest in SW Rwanda. Is it possible that a prehistoric people migrating south down the Rift Valley can have brought the name to Malawi? 'Batwa' is another name shared with Rwanda.

38   Albert Andrew Muwalo Nqumayo became Secretary General of the Malawi Congress Party and Minister of State in the President's Office. In 1977 he was convicted of treason, on the evidence of tapped and recorded telephone calls, and he was hanged in Zomba Central Prison.

39   After the release of detainees from 1994 onwards Dzeleka detention camp became a refugee camp accommodating 1,000 refugees from Somalia, Rwanda, Burundi, Zaire, Nigeria, Tanzania and the Republic of Cameroon.

40   Livingstone wrote of the fish eagle: 'It seems as if he were calling to someone in the other world.' That is still true but to many country people the cry of the eagle became a shriek of pain from family and friends being persecuted and killed in this world. The bird is the national symbol of Malawi; its powerful flight in wild and unspoiled places represents the freedom wrenched from colonialism. But to many its passionate and unearthly cry was a reminder that freedom had yet to be achieved.

41   Perhaps 1873, the year Livingstone died.

42   According to Kandulu Chintambo the *Chongwe* is a 'big black snake with a comb on its head like that on a cockerel'. Might it, alternatively, be a monitor lizard from Namilenji Island or a 'monster' of some kind? Apparently no one has actually seen it. If the 'Akafula' (Abatwa?)

migrated from Lake Bangweulu it is possible they brought with them a folk memory of the *Chipekwe*, a monster alleged to inhabit Lake Bangweulu. Could the *Chongwe* be a successor to the *Chipekwe*? ('*Chipenkwe*' to some people.) Kenneth Bradley in 'The Diary of a District Officer' mentions the existence of a 'crowing snake' that lived on top of a conical peak near Chief Kapatamoyo's villages on the Nyasaland border of Northern   Rhodesia. It was evidently an old cobra which had a throaty hiss - hence, perhaps, the 'crowing snake.' During World War II people on the Lakeshore claim that a 'monster' swam up and down Lake Malawi.

Some of the earliest remains of extinct reptiles have been found in northern Malawi. Can such reptiles have survived in Lake Malawi? Is there any connection between them and the *Chongwe*?

43 The assailant, one of the elite corps of the Young Pioneers in his personal bodyguard, was instantly shot. On this occasion officers present steered him back into the safe rooms of his presidential residence at the foot of Zomba mountain. There he personally burned the black hat with its bullet holes. And at night he ceased to sleep in his own bedroom although his bed sheets - a different colour for each day of the week - continued to be changed daily. The Young Pioneers were 'turned on' to Jehovah's Witnesses, killing, torturing, mutilating and raping them so that thousands of them fled to Zambia.

All persons in employment were ordered by radio to acquire Malawi Congress Party cards and I gave Million and Smart money so that they and Esnath, Jane, Christopher and Aswan could all have cards.

Miss Cecilia Tamanda Kadzamira, niece of J.Z.U. Tembo, formerly a trained nurse at Banda's medical practice and later his official private secretary and hostess at State House, Zomba, is credited with keeping Banda in good health and spirits. She is a colourful lady who is known on one occasion when she was younger and Dr Banda out of the country, to have taken a taxi from Zomba to the premises of a white photographer [later deported] forty miles away in Blantyre and had herself photographed in full colour in each of her beautiful dresses in turn, apparently so that she would have pictures to send to her Presbyterian relations. Before her association with Dr Banda she had been engaged to Augustine Mnthambala a school teacher who worked at the Henry Henderson Institute, Blantyre, and later at St. Patrick's secondary school, Mzedi. When Mnthambala claimed publicly that President Banda had stolen his woman he was placed in detention to keep him out of the way, and in fact he was in and out of prison several times during the next thirty years. In 1994 he became vice-president of one of the new political parties. Cecilia, meanwhile, gained greatly in several respects: she became head of the League of Malawi Women and later of another women's organization, the Chitukuko Cha Amai M'Malawi (CCAM); she accompanied Dr Banda to Buckingham Palace and was received by the Queen of England; she became friendly with the first ladies of Zambia, Zimbabwe and Kenya; she received many presents - including allegedly, a tea estate from Dr Banda - and become very rich; at one time the Malawi Army VIP jet was used to fly her fortnightly or monthly to South Africa on her shopping trips; as 'Mama Cecilia, Mother of the Nation' - and in alliance with Tembo - she became almost a national monument with incomparable influence and political and personal power; she was arrested and house imprisoned in 1995 but was later released after being acquitted of a conspiracy - a charge that arose from her closeness to Banda - to murder the 'Mwanza Incident' cabinet ministers in 1983.

44   Heights 5,304', 5,000', 5,500' respectively.

45   Michael Blackwood was MP for Blantyre. He had been leader of the European United Federal Party. He was later appointed chairman of the Malawi Development Corporation and had a seat on the board of Directors of the Reserve Bank of Malawi. Of great interest to future historians, a record of current land conveyances in Malawi was compiled and circulated to subscribers from his office. This brief record cost subscribers £28 a month.

46   Grace Snowden died in Newlands Home for Elderly Europeans on 27 July 1980, aged 94.

47   Jeffrey had been bookbinding officer at Ahmadu Bello University in Nigeria.

48   Space remained a problem until February 1987 when a new building, provided by USAID. and costing K2.7 million, was opened. It had a capacity of 100,000 volumes and could seat almost 500 readers.

49   During the next fifteen years the university had six university librarians; the library staff increased in number to 112; and the book stock increased to 315,957 volumes.

50   Democratic government was experienced in Malawi only after the General Election in May 1994 when votes cast for the three main parties were:

    UDF: United Democratic Front (Bakili Muluzi) 1,404,754
    MCP: Malawi Congress Party (Kamuzu Banda) 996,553
    AFORD: Alliance for the Restoration of Democracy
                        (Chakufwa Chihana) 585,689
    The fourth presidential candidate, Kamlepo Kalua of the Malawi Democratic Party, received 15,624 votes.

INDEX of Places mentioned in the text.